*Rescuing Science from Politics* debuts chapters by the nation's leading academics in law, science, and philosophy, who explore the ways that special interests can abuse the law to intrude on the way that scientists conduct research. The high stakes and adversarial features of regulation create the worst possible climate for the production and use of honest science, especially by those who will ultimately bear the cost of the resulting regulatory standards. Yet the academic or popular literature has paid scant attention to efforts by dominant interest groups to distort the available science in support of their positions. The book begins by establishing what should be noncontroversial principles of good scientific practice. These principles serve as the benchmark against which each chapter's author explains how science is misused in specific regulatory settings and isolates problems in the integration of science by the regulatory process.

Wendy Wagner is the Joe A. Worsham Centennial Professor at the University of Texas School of Law in Austin, Texas. She received a master's degree in environmental studies from the Yale School of Forestry and Environmental Studies and a law degree from Yale Law School. Wagner teaches courses in torts, environmental law, and regulation. Her research focuses on the law–science interface in environmental law, and her articles have appeared in numerous journals, including the law reviews of Columbia, Cornell, Duke, Illinois, Texas, Wisconsin, and Yale.

Rena Steinzor is the Jacob A. France Research Professor of Law at the University of Maryland School of Law and has a secondary appointment at the University of Maryland Medical School Department of Epidemiology and Preventive Medicine. She received her B.A. from the University of Wisconsin and her J.D. from Columbia Law School. Steinzor teaches environmental and administrative law, critical issues in law and science, and negotiation. She has written extensively on environmental federalism, alternative designs of regulatory systems, and law and science, publishing in the *Minnesota Law Review, Harvard Environmental Law Review, Duke Journal of Law and Policy, Yale Journal on Regulation, Environmental Forum,* and *Environmental Law Review.*

# Rescuing Science from Politics

## REGULATION AND THE DISTORTION OF SCIENTIFIC RESEARCH

Edited by

**Wendy Wagner**

University of Texas School of Law

**Rena Steinzor**

University of Maryland School of Law

**CAMBRIDGE**
UNIVERSITY PRESS
OCM 65203232

CAMBRIDGE UNIVERSITY PRESS
Cambridge, New York, Melbourne, Madrid, Cape Town, Singapore, São Paulo

Cambridge University Press
32 Avenue of the Americas, New York, NY 10013-2473, USA

www.cambridge.org
Information on this title: www.cambridge.org/9780521855204

First published 2006

Printed in the United States of America

A catalog record for this publication is available from the British Library.

Library of Congress Cataloging in Publication Data

ISBN-13   978-0-521-85520-4 hardback
ISBN-10   0-521-85520-9 hardback

ISBN-13   978-0-521-54009-4 paperback
ISBN-10   0-521-54009-7 paperback

# Contents

# About the Contributors

**David E. Adelman** is an associate professor at the University of Arizona's James E. Rogers College of Law. His work focuses on the interfaces between law and science, with a particular emphasis on evaluating environmental and regulatory issues relating to new or controversial technologies. He has been a member of the U.S. Department of Energy's (DOE) Environmental Management Advisory Board and was recently appointed to two National Academy of Sciences committees. From 1998 to 2001, he was a senior attorney with the Natural Resources Defense Council's (NRDC) Nuclear and Public Health programs in Washington, D.C., where he monitored and litigated issues pertaining to the environmental cleanup of the nuclear weapons complex and developed proposals for appropriate regulatory mechanisms for agricultural biotechnology. Prior to joining NRDC, he was an associate at the law firm of Covington and Burling in Washington, D.C., where he litigated patent disputes and provided counsel on environmental regulatory matters. He received a B.A. in chemistry and physics from Reed College in 1988, a Ph.D. in chemical physics from Stanford University in 1993, and a J.D. from Stanford Law School in 1996. He is a scholar with the Center for Progressive Reform.

**John S. Applegate** is the associate dean and Walter W. Foskett Professor of Law at the Indiana University School of Law–Bloomington. Before he joined the Indiana faculty in 1998, he was the James B. Helmer, Jr., Professor of Law at the University of Cincinnati College of Law and a visiting professor of law at Vanderbilt University. Professor Applegate has written extensively on environmental law topics, including risk assessment, the Superfund program, public participation in environmental decision making, and the precautionary principle. He is a coauthor of a casebook, Applegate, Laitos, and Campbell-Mohn, *The Regulation of Toxic Substances and Hazardous Wastes* (Foundation Press 2000), and the editor of the two-volume collection of articles, *Environmental Risk* (Ashgate 2004). From 1993 to 1998, Applegate chaired the Fernald Citizens Advisory Board, which developed the blueprint for the environmental cleanup of the U.S. Department of Energy's nuclear weapons production facility at Fernald, Ohio. He has also been a member of the Department of Energy's National Environmental Management Advisory Board and has served as a member, presenter, or reviewer for National Research Council committees on radioactive waste management. Before entering teaching in 1987, Applegate practiced law with the Washington, D.C., law firm of Covington and Burling, and he clerked for the Honorable Edward S. Smith of the U.S. Court of Appeals for the Federal Circuit. He received his J.D. from Harvard Law School and his B.A. from Haverford College. Professor Applegate is a scholar with the Center for Progressive Reform.

**Carl F. Cranor** is a professor of philosophy at the University of California, Riverside. He did his undergraduate work at the University of Colorado with a major in mathematics and a minor in physics (1966) and received his Ph.D. in philosophy from UCLA (1971). He received a post-doctoral master of studies in law from Yale Law School in 1981. Specializing in legal and moral philosophy, his recent work has been on philosophical issues that arise in the legal and scientific adjudication of risks from toxic substances and from the new genetic technologies. The National Science Foundation and the University of California supported his research on theoretical issues in risk assessment and on philosophical issues concerning the use of science in regulatory and tort law. He has published numerous articles in these fields as well as authoring *Regulating Toxic Substances: A Philosophy of Science and the Law* (Oxford University Press, 1993, paperback 1997), editing *Are Genes Us? The Social Consequences of the New Genetics* (Rutgers University Press, 1994), and coauthoring the U.S. Congress' Office of Technology Assessment report, *Identifying and Regulating Carcinogens* (1987). His articles have appeared in such diverse journals as the *American Philosophical Quarterly*; *Environmental Toxicology and Pharmacology*; *Ethics, Law and Philosophy*; *European Journal of Oncology Library*; *Industrial Relations Law Journal*; *Jurimetrics*; *Law and Contemporary Problems*; *Plant*

*Physiology; Risk; Risk Analysis; Virginia Environmental Law Journal;* and *Yale Law Journal.* He has served on the State of California's Proposition 65 Science Advisory Panel (1989–92), a National Academy of Sciences Panel to Czechoslovakian Academy of Sciences (1990), several NSF peer review panels, and California's Science Advisory Panel on Electric and Magnetic Fields (1999–2002). In 1998 he was elected a Fellow of the American Association for the Advancement of Science and in 2003 he was elected a Fellow of the Collegium Ramazinni. Professor Cranor is a member scholar with the Center for Progressive Reform.

**Holly Doremus** is Professor of Law and Chancellor's Fellow at the University of California, Davis. She received her B.S. in biology from Trinity College (Hartford, Connecticut), Ph.D. in plant physiology from Cornell University, and J.D. from the University of California, Berkeley (Boalt Hall). Before joining the faculty at UC Davis, she clerked for Judge Diarmuid O'Scannlain of the United States Court of Appeals for the Ninth Circuit and practiced municipal and land-use law in Corvallis, Oregon. Her research interests include environmental policy generally, endangered species and biodiversity protection, management of public lands, and the role of science in environmental policy decisions. Her articles have been published in numerous journals, including the *Stanford Environmental Law Journal, UC Davis Law Review,* and the *Washington University Law Quarterly.* Professor Doremus is a member scholar with the Center for Progressive Reform.

**Paul M. Fischer** is a doctor of family practice in Evans, Georgia. Before joining private practice, Dr. Fischer was a full professor at the Medical College of Georgia and published widely, including a series of articles on his research on Joe Camel in the *Journal of the American Medical Association*

**Donald T. Hornstein** is the Aubrey L. Brooks Distinguished Professor in Law at the University of North Carolina School of Law, where he was also Associate Dean for Faculty between 1993 and 1995. Professor Hornstein was a Fulbright Scholar posted to Eritrea, Africa, in 1996–7, where he taught environmental and natural resources courses, and he currently serves on the university-wide Faculty Advisory Board of the interdisciplinary Carolina

Environmental Program. At North Carolina, he teaches environmental law, natural resources law, administrative law, and insurance law. He has won the law school's McCall Award for Teaching Excellence five times and, in 1999, he won the university-wide prize for Distinguished Teaching in Post-Baccalaureate Instruction. Among his many articles and publications, his article "Accounting for Science: The Independence of Public Research in the New Subterranean Administrative Law" was recently published in *Law and Contemporary Problems*. Professor Hornstein received his B.A. from UCLA and his J.D. from the University of Oregon School of Law, where he was editor-in-chief of the law review. After graduation, he clerked for Judge Abner Mikva of the United States Court of Appeals for the District of Columbia Circuit and worked as an honors attorney in the Environment and Natural Resources Division of the U.S. Department of Justice. He is a scholar with the Center for Progressive Reform.

**Donald Kennedy** is the Bing Professor of Environmental Science and President emeritus at Stanford University. He received A.B. and Ph.D. degrees in biology from Harvard. His research interests were originally in animal behavior and neurobiology – in particular, the mechanisms by which animals generate and control patterned motor output. In 1977, Dr. Kennedy took a two-and-a-half-year leave to serve as commissioner of the U.S. Food and Drug Administration (FDA). This followed an increasing academic interest in regulatory policy regarding health and the environment, which included the chairmanship of a National Academy of Sciences study on alternatives to pesticide use and membership on the committee to study world food and nutrition. Following his return to Stanford in 1979, Dr. Kennedy served for a year as provost and for twelve years as president, a time marked by renewed attention to undergraduate education and student commitment to public service, and successful completion of the largest capital campaign in the history of higher education. During that time, Kennedy continued to work on health and environmental policy issues, as a member of the Board of Directors of the Health Effects Institute (a non-profit organization devoted to mobile source emissions), Clean Sites, Inc. (a similar organization devoted to toxic waste cleanup), and the California Nature Conservancy. His present research program, conducted partially through the Institute for International Studies, consists of interdisciplinary studies on the development of policies regarding such transboundary environmental problems as: major land-use changes; economically driven alterations in agricultural practice; global climate change; and the development of regulatory policies. He codirects the Environmental Studies Program in the Institute for International Studies and oversaw the introduction of the environmental policy quarter at Stanford's center in Washington, D.C., in 1993. Dr. Kennedy is a member of the National Academy of Sciences, the American Academy of Arts and Sciences, and the American Philosophical Society. He holds honorary doctorates from several colleges and universities. He served on the National Commission for Public Service and the Carnegie Commission on Science, Technology and Government.

**Sheldon Krimsky** is Professor of Urban and Environmental Policy and Planning at Tufts University. He received his bachelor's and master's degrees in physics from Brooklyn College, CUNY, and Purdue University respectively, and a master's and doctorate in philosophy at Boston University. Professor Krimsky's research has focused on the linkages among science/technology, ethics/values, and public policy. He is the author of eight books, including *Genetic Alchemy: The Social History of the Recombinant DNA Controversy* (MIT Press, 1982); *Biotechnics and Society: The Rise of Industrial Genetics* (Praeger, 1991), and *Hormonal Chaos: The Scientific and Social Origins of the Environmental Endocrine Hypothesis* (Johns Hopkins University Press, 2000). He is coauthor of *Environmental Hazards: Communicating Risks as a Social Process* (Auburn House, 1988) and *Agricultural Biotechnology and the Environment: Science, Policy and Social Values* (University of Illinois Press, 1996) and coeditor of a collection of papers titled *Social Theories of Risk* (Praeger, 1992) and *Rights and Liberties in the Biotech Age* (Rowman and Littlefield, 2005). Professor Krimsky has published more than 150 essays and reviews that have appeared in many books and journals. His most recent book, *Science in the Private Interest: Has the Lure of Profits Corrupted Biomedical Research?* (Rowman and Littlefield, 2003), explores conflicts of interest in biomedical research. Professor Krimsky served on the National Institutes of Health's Recombinant DNA Advisory Committee from 1978 to 1981. He was a consultant to the Presidential Commission for the Study of Ethical Problems in Medicine and Biomedical and Behavioral Research and to the Congressional Office of Technology Assessment. He participated on a special study panel for the American Civil Liberties Union that formulated a policy on civil liberties and scientific research. Professor Krimsky was chair of the Committee on Scientific Freedom and Responsibility for the American Association for the Advancement of Science for 1988–92. He serves on the Board of Directors for the Council for Responsible Genetics and as a Fellow of the Hastings Center on Bioethics. Professor Krimsky currently holds the following editorial and advisory board positions: Associate Editor of *Accountability in Research*; member of the Editorial Advisory Board of *Science, Technology and Human Values*; member of the Life Sciences Advisory Board of the *Journal of BioLaw and Business*; member of the Advisory Board of *Human Gene Therapy*; member of the International Editorial Board of *New Genetics and Society*; member of the Editorial Board of *Expert Opinion on Pharmacotherapy*; member of the Editorial Board of *Gene Watch: Bulletin of the Committee for Responsible Genetics*; and member of the Editorial Board of the *International Journal of Environmental Technology and Management*. Professor Krimsky has been elected a Fellow of the American Association for the Advancement of Science for "seminal scholarship exploring the normative dimensions and moral implications of science in its social context."

**Thomas O. McGarity** holds the W. James Kronzer Chair in Trial and Appellate Advocacy at the University of Texas School of Law. He has taught environmental law, administrative law, and torts at the University of Texas School of Law since 1980. Prior to that, he taught at the University of Kansas School of Law. After clerking for Judge William E. Doyle of the Federal Court of Appeals for the Tenth Circuit in Denver, Colorado, Professor McGarity served as an attorney-advisor in the Office of General Counsel of the Environmental Protection Agency in Washington, D.C. Professor McGarity has written widely in the areas of environmental law and administrative law. He has written two books on federal regulation. *Reinventing Rationality* (Cambridge University Press, 1991) describes and critiques the implementation of regulatory analysis and regulatory review requirements that were put into place during the Carter and Reagan administrations. *Workers at Risk* (Praeger, 1993) (coauthored with Sidney Shapiro of the Wake Forest School of Law) describes and critiques the implementation of the Occupational Safety and Health Act (OSHA) during its first twenty years. Professor McGarity is president of the Center for Progressive Reform, a nonprofit organization consisting of scholars committed to developing and sharing knowledge and information, with the ultimate aim of preserving the fundamental value of the life and health of human beings and the natural environment.

**David Michaels** is Professor and Associate Chair of the Department of Occupational and Environmental Health at the George Washington University School of Public Health and Health Services. Trained as an epidemiologist, Dr. Michaels served as the U.S. Department of Energy (DOE) Assistant Secretary for Environment, Safety and Health from 1998 through January 2001. In that position, he had primary responsibility for protecting the health and safety of workers, the neighboring communities, and the environment surrounding the nation's nuclear weapons complex. He is the chief architect of the Energy Employees Occupational Illness Compensation Program, a historic initiative to compensate workers in the nuclear weapons complex who developed cancer or lung disease as a result of exposure to radiation, beryllium, and other hazards. He also oversaw promulgation of the DOE's Chronic Beryllium Disease Prevention rule. In the early 1990s, Dr. Michaels developed a widely cited mathematical model estimating the number of children and adolescents orphaned by the HIV/AIDS epidemic. He also was a Robert Wood Johnson Health Policy Fellow with the Committee on Education and Labor of the U.S. House of Representatives in 1993–4, the year Congress considered national health reform legislation.

**Sidney A. Shapiro** is University Distinguished Chair in Law at the Wake Forest School of Law. Previously, he was the John M. Rounds Professor of Law and Associate Dean for Research at the University of Kansas School of Law. Professor Shapiro is a scholar and board member of the Center for Progressive Reform. His most recent book is *Risk Regulation at Risk: Restoring a Pragmatic Approach* (Stanford University Press, 2003), coauthored with Robert Glicksman of the University of Kansas School of Law. He is the coauthor of two law school textbooks: one on regulatory law and practice and administrative law, the other a one-volume administrative law treatise. Professor Shapiro has written widely on regulatory policy and process topics, including a book on occupational safety and health law and policy. He has been a consultant to the Occupational Safety and Health Administration (OSHA) and the Administrative Conference of the United

States (ACUS), and he has testified in Congress on regulatory policy and process issues. He recently published an article on the Office of Management and Budget's (OMB) peer-review proposal in the *Environmental Law Reporter*.

**Katherine S. Squibb** is an associate professor in the Department of Epidemiology and Preventive Medicine at the University of Maryland at Baltimore and director of the University of Maryland System-Wide Graduate Program in Toxicology. Dr. Squibb received her Ph.D. in biochemistry from Rutgers, the State University of New Jersey, in 1977, and completed a postdoctoral fellowship at the National Institute of Environmental Health Sciences (NIEHS) in Research Triangle Park, North Carolina, in 1982. She has a basic research interest in cellular mechanisms of metal ion toxicity and carcinogenicity, and she has studied the health effects of air particles and the renal toxicity of heavy metals. Since 1994, Dr. Squibb has worked with the University of Maryland Law School Environmental Law Clinic in the risk assessment and public health field, providing technical support to citizen groups involved in the evaluation of health effects and remediation of hazardous waste sites in their communities. Professor Squibb is a Center for Progressive Reform member scholar.

**Rena Steinzor** is the Jacob A. France Research Professor of Law at the University of Maryland School of Law. She has a secondary appointment at the University of Maryland Medical School, in the Department of Epidemiology and Preventive Medicine. Steinzor teaches courses in environmental law and regulation, law and science, and administrative law. She received her B.A. from the University of Wisconsin and her J.D. from Columbia University. She is a founder and board member with the Center for Progressive Reform. Professor Steinzor served as the reporter for EPA's Title VI Committee, established under the Federal Advisory Committee Act, which convened a broad range of stakeholders to discuss environmental justice in permitting decisions. She also served as senior staff to the only municipal official serving on the National Commission on Superfund. Professor Steinzor joined the law school faculty in 1994 from the Washington, D.C., law firm of Spiegel and McDiarmid, where she was the partner in charge of the firm's environmental practice. Prior to joining the firm, from 1983 to 1987, she was staff counsel to the U.S. House of Representatives' Energy and

Commerce Committee's subcommittee with primary jurisdiction over the nation's laws regulating hazardous substances. From 1976 to 1983, Professor Steinzor was an attorney at the Federal Trade Commission (FTC), serving in a variety of consumer protection positions, including attorney-advisor to Commissioner Patricia P. Bailey. She has written extensively on law and science, unfunded mandates, environmental federalism, and efforts to reinvent the EPA in preparation for the twenty-first century. She also teaches courses on risk assessment and critical issues in law and science.

**Wendy Wagner** is the Joe A. Worsham Centennial Professor at the University of Texas School of Law in Austin, Texas. Before joining the Texas faculty, Wagner was a professor at Case Western Reserve University School of Law and a visiting professor at Columbia Law School and the Vanderbilt School of Law. Wagner received a master's degree in environmental studies from the Yale School of Forestry and Environmental Studies and a law degree from Yale Law School, and she clerked for the Honorable Judge Albert Engel, Chief Judge of the U.S. Court of Appeals for the Sixth Circuit. Before entering academia, Wagner served as an honors attorney with the Environmental Enforcement section of the Environment and Natural Resources Division of the U.S. Department of Justice in Washington, D.C., and as the pollution control coordinator in the Office of General Counsel of the U.S. Department of Agriculture. Wagner teaches courses in torts, environmental law, and regulation and seminars on law and science and on complex problem solving. Her research focuses on the law–science interface in environmental law, and her articles have appeared in numerous journals, including the law reviews of Columbia, Cornell, Duke, Illinois, Texas, Wisconsin, and Yale. Wagner serves on the National Research Council's Committee on the Selection and Use of Models in the Regulatory Decision Process, on the Council of the Administrative and Regulatory Law Section of the American Bar Association and on the Council of the Society for Risk Analysis. She is also a member scholar of the Center for Progressive Reform.

**Vern R. Walker** is Professor of Law at Hofstra University School of Law, where he teaches scientific evidence, torts, products liability, administrative law, European Union law, and comparative law on product regulation and liability. He received his Ph.D. in philosophy from the University of

Notre Dame and his J.D. from Yale University. His doctoral and postdoctoral studies in philosophy centered on knowledge theory – epistemology, logic, the conceptual foundations and methodologies of the sciences, and artificial intelligence. Before joining the Hofstra faculty, he was a partner in the Washington, D.C., law firm of Swidler and Berlin, where his practice included representation before federal and state administrative agencies and courts on matters dealing with health, safety, and the environment. Professor Walker has published extensively on the logic and design of governmental fact-finding processes, in particular on the use of scientific evidence in risk assessment and risk management. He has been a consultant on such issues to both private and governmental institutions. Coauthor of the book *Product Risk Reduction in the Chemical Industry* (Island Press, 1985), Walker is on the editorial board of the journal *Law, Probability and Risk*, and he is past president of the Risk Assessment and Policy Association.

# Acknowledgments

As the editors of a volume that was such a collaborative and interactive effort, it is difficult to acknowledge the many people, organizations, and institutions who contributed to it.

Nevertheless, it is fair to attribute the book's existence in large part to the active support of the Center for Progressive Reform (CPR), a virtual think tank comprised of forty-one colleagues, all of whom are working academics in the fields of law, economics, philosophy, and science. Eight of the authors contributing chapters to this book (Professors Adelman, Applegate, Cranor, Doremus, Hornstein, McGarity, Shapiro, and Squibb), as well as ourselves, are CPR member scholars.

We conceived of the principles that are at the heart of this book, and developed many of the ideas that are presented to explain them, at meetings organized and sponsored by CPR and the Project on Scientific Knowledge and Public Policy (SKAPP). We are especially grateful to CPR funders – the Beldon Fund and the Deer Creek Foundation – for providing the financial resources that made many of the key sessions possible. We also thank the University of Maryland and University of Texas Schools of Law for supporting our scholarship through summer grants and fall sabbaticals, and the Maryland Law School and the George Washington University Medical School for providing meeting facilities. A crucial session at the Maryland School of Law was supported by the Ward Kershaw Environmental Symposium Fund.

Professor Alyson Flournoy, a CPR board member and Director of the Environmental and Land Use Program at the University of Florida Levin College of Law, and Katherine Baer, a CPR senior policy analyst, provided invaluable insights and suggestions as peer reviewers of an early draft of this book. Andrea Curatola provided superb research assistance, and Dottie Lee and Laura Mrozek provided excellent administrative support. We also thank Leslie Boden, Richard Clapp, Lynn Goldman, Linda Greer, Molly Jacobs, Celeste Monforton, Anita Nager, Erik Olson, and Jennifer Sass for their contributions to the conversations that helped shape the substance of the book. Joanna Goger and Polly Hoppin were particularly helpful in initiating the project and keeping the momentum going, and we are grateful for their energy and inspiration. Members of the SKAPP project, chaired by professors David Michaels and David Ozonoff, also provided much appreciated scientific insight. Dean Karen Rothenberg and Associate Dean Diane Hoffmann have been extremely generous in their efforts to assist the development of this dialogue regarding law and science, which has also enriched the University of Maryland Environmental Law and Science Program.

John Berger at Cambridge University Press was enthusiastic about this project from its inception, and Andy Saff provided a painstakingly careful edit of the book, front to back. We are most grateful to both of them for helping to make the book become a reality.

Last but not least, we thank our wonderful families for putting up with us as we saw this project through to conclusion: Mike, Will, Becky, Daniel, and Hannah – you are all the best!

# Prologue

## Donald Kennedy*

These are difficult times for science in the zone where it converges with public policy. Of course it should not be expected that peer-reviewed science, even carefully done, will be a commanding presence in policy discussions, even where scientific issues are prominent. Other matters, like the relationship between costs and benefits of a project or distributive justice implications, may be more decisive, for perfectly good reasons. But science has been playing a critically important role in several areas that have become important exercises of government responsibility, including, but not limited to, environmental quality regulations, litigation over damages associated with the external costs of private activity ("toxic torts"), and the legal responsibility of manufacturers for product harms. What has happened, in this more political contemporary environment, to science and the people who practice it? That is the subject of this book. In this prologue, I hope to provide a quick overview of some features of the new terrain. In later chapters, others will deliver a much closer and more scholarly look at them.

In the mid-1970s – a few years after the first volley of laws protecting environmental quality – there was little public skepticism about, and only limited political pressure against, the role of science in regulation under these statutes, or its influence in legal proceedings about product harms. When I became commissioner of the Food and Drug Administration early in 1977, the Medical Devices Amendments were only a year old, and we were just trying to figure out how to implement them. Our only model was the approval process for new drugs – a much older part of the law, and

* Editor-in-chief, *Science*

one about which there were chronic complaints from both left and right. Was it too fast, exposing Americans to unsuspected hazards, or too slow, robbing them of potentially useful therapies? That debate is alive and well and scheduled for a long run. After all, there is no normative standard by which we may judge whether the cost of foregone innovation is perfectly balanced against the cost of iatrogenic illness. Points of optimum social utility are notoriously hard to identify. But the science used by the agency, and the role of science in the other contexts I have mentioned, generally enjoyed respect in those years.

My impression is that things are quite different now, and the difficulties analyzed in the succeeding chapters afford a rich sketch of the current environment. I suggest that the change is the result of a major policy shift – one that began before the Bush Administration took office but was extended and made more forceful by policies advocated during both of the last two presidential election campaigns and made explicit by legislative and administrative actions since. The overarching theme has been that government is too large and complex and that the effect of its combination of size and regulatory mission unnecessarily disrupts the efficient operation of a market economy. President George W. Bush in his election campaigns repeatedly called attention to the size of the federal bureaucracy. He has not set specific goals for its reduction in force, and indeed has achieved none. But the call is still heard from more colorful Republican Party conservatives such as Grover Norquist, who says that he hopes for a government that he can "take into his bathroom and drown in the tub."

Thus, to the extent that science still plays an important role in most regulatory decisions, its role has become more suspect by those who find regulations burdensome or of questionable legitimacy. The challenges to science do not all come from the right; members of consumer organizations and others have often charged science establishments with paying too little attention to legitimate representatives of the public – "stakeholders" in the current patois. But the strongest current challenge comes from a quite different quarter. It probably evolved from the Republican congressional sweep in 1994, when Representative Newt Gingrich and his newly elected allies promised a radical deconstruction of environmental regulation. They discovered that the American public actually liked the environmental rules, and that campaign largely failed. But it left behind a Republican majority and antiregulatory embers that could be fanned into flames by the interest of

President Bush and his cabinet in redistributing power in the agencies and in the courts. A particular objective was the challenge to scientific findings as dispositive, or even influential, in determinations about regulation or product harm.

One early theme fits under the heading of "tort reform." Administration spokespersons regularly point to the health care costs associated with medical malpractice litigation, taking advantage of public skepticism about lawyers. They have also emphasized the charge that plaintiffs' attorneys regularly introduce "junk science" in support of malpractice or product liability claims. Of course, there is some truth here: Some expert witnesses have offered questionable scientific conclusions in support of plaintiffs, and that has led to the series of three Supreme Court decisions regarding the admissibility of expert testimony in jury trials. The so-called "*Daubert* trilogy" (*Daubert, Kumho Tire,* and *Joiner,* all discussed in much greater detail in Chapters 1 and 6) has had a lingering effect on product liability litigation. In the view of most observers, the "*Daubert* criteria" for permitting expert testimony have made it more difficult for scientists to present evidence, adding up to some degree of bias in favor of defendants.

The *Daubert* principle, however, has invaded other provinces of the law only to a very limited extent. In criminal courts, it has almost never been applied to challenge the "expert" testimony of police or other government experts (medical examiners, fingerprint experts, and the like) despite a general sense among scientists that forensic data are very open to question. Nor have *Daubert* challenges been characteristic of administrative law procedures in the regulatory arena. But this is not a time for confidence that the latter, in particular, may be just over the horizon.

Developments in the legislative arena have also broadened the zone for attacks on science. In fulfilling its responsibility under the Clean Air Act to use scientific data in establishing National Ambient Air Quality Standards, the Environmental Protection Agency cited a study done by researchers at the Harvard School of Public Health on the effect of small (PM 2.5) particles in the air-sheds of several cities. It was cited in the proposed regulation, but a late-night Senate amendment opened the primary data in the study to examination by other interested parties. The "Shelby Amendment," more formally called the Data Access Act, made federally supported research project data eligible for public access through the Freedom of Information Act. In issuing governing regulations under the statute as required, the

Office of Management and Budget limited the scope to scientific findings used in regulatory actions that had significant policy or economic impacts.

But the amendment widened a zone that industry had already opened through discovery proceedings in litigation. For example, well before the Shelby Amendment, Professor Herbert Needleman's studies on the effect of lead toxicity on intellectual development in children had been made the subject of a lawsuit by the lead industry. In the course of discovery, "expert witnesses" for the industry had obtained Needleman's research records. They developed a basis for a charge of research misconduct, which went to the Office of Research Integrity at the National Institutes of Health (NIH), the funder of Needleman's work. Needleman's campus at the time was the University of Pittsburgh, perhaps not an ideal venue for someone contesting with the heavy metals industry. When the university was asked to investigate, the process was prolonged until a faculty body arranged for a session in which Needleman and his attorneys were able to confront the claimants and cross-examine them. The charge was found baseless, but the matter died, leaving some damaged confidence behind it.

That incident and others have made many scientists worry that more recent actions will open their work to reinterpretation and to whatever revision critics want to make in the findings. The worry has been exacerbated by recent regulatory developments, as well as by new events in an area where the science has become especially political. The Shelby Amendment was followed by another statutory initiative, the Data Quality Act – sometimes referred to as "son of Shelby." Regulations under this statute permit petitioners to challenge the quality of science proffered by the government to educate consumers or to support other actions. This new zone of challenge has produced challenges to agencies and to the science on which they have based advice to the public – for example, on salt consumption. But there have also been challenges to the scientists themselves, including demands for underlying data.

Perhaps the most recent and most alarming development has come from congressional friends of those with particular economic and political interests. A well-organized opposition to the scientific consensus on global climate change has produced little original science of its own, but it has campaigned successfully to obtain primary data from scientists whose findings have supported global warming. As a journal editor, I sometimes get reasonable requests from a scientist-reader for reagents, materials, or data in a paper we have published. That's a strong scientific tradition, and it is our policy to support it. Recently, however, the requests for data from climate scientists have taken on a pattern that borders on harassment. Worse still, Representative Joe Barton (R-TX), chair of the House Committee on Energy and Commerce, sent a series of demand letters to prominent climate scientists, asking for detailed accounts of methodology and data analysis. These inquiries came only to scientists whose work supported the involvement of greenhouse gas emissions in recent global warming. The chair of the House Science Committee, Representative Sherwood Boehlert (R-NY), objected to this harassment on jurisdictional grounds, but Barton has not given it up.

How does all this add up? You will have to draw your own conclusions after exploring what follows. But I know what many of my fellow scientists are saying to one another, because *Science* has a news page that receives a lot of submissions from researchers, and my colleagues and I talk to them often. Many are wary of work that may find use in some regulatory proceeding. They wonder whether the data underlying their findings may be subject to examination and reinterpretation, perhaps with some "spin" supplied by the revisionists. They know that charges of research misconduct could arise from hostile access to their scientific work. They know they are vulnerable to personal attack from those whose interests may be adversely affected by the product of their research.

In some ways, there has never been a better time for science. It is exciting, and the fact that it is subject to political attention means that it matters – more than ever. But though it is a good time for science, it is a perilous time for scientists.

# Introduction

Wendy Wagner, J.D., and Rena Steinzor, J.D.

## Scientists under Attack

To the casual observer, scientists might appear to be the most influential group in the United States with respect to public health and environmental policy. Exhortations that we must use "sound science" to make decisions about whether to prevent potential risks are ubiquitous. No less an authority than a Supreme Court justice, as well as a wide range of other decision makers in the legislative, regulatory, and judicial arenas, have urged that scientists be elevated to the pinnacle of power, entrusted by the rest of us with the authority to resolve our most important and complex problems.[1] Deference to scientists as the ultimate arbitrators of policy resonates every time Congress debates such controversies, suggesting that lawmakers and those who work to affect their decisions have nothing but respect for the sanctity and wisdom of the scientific process and its results, wherever they may lead us.

Why, then, do many scientists deployed at the front lines of the most heated disputes – over global warming, mercury in the human food chain, or the safety of antidepressants for adolescents – feel not like anointed and omniscient saviors, but instead like hunted prey? For all the lip service paid to the naïve but convenient notion that science has all the answers, the moment that researchers announce a discovery that has significant economic implications for industry or some other affected group, scientists in the spotlight quickly learn to run for cover.

---

[1] Stephen G. Breyer, *Breaking the Vicious Circle: Toward Effective Risk Regulation* (Cambridge, MA: Harvard University Press, 1993); Daniel R. Sarewitz, *Frontiers of Illusion: Science, Technology, and the Politics of Progress* (Philadelphia, PA: Temple University Press, 1996).

Beset by scientific misconduct allegations or threatened with breach-of-contract lawsuits if research is published over a private sponsor's objections, more and more scientists are finding themselves struggling to maintain their credibility in a climate designed to deconstruct the smallest details of their research. Studies are not criticized in an effort to advance research to the next stage of the search for truth, but rather are dissected in an effort to discredit both their results and their authors. Some experts are concerned that the severity of these problems could deter the best and the brightest young scientists from entering the very disciplines that have the greatest potential to inform public affairs.[2]

These events are disconcerting not just because they frustrate the goal of using reliable science to formulate policy, but because they could undermine scientific integrity, independence, and transparency to the point that we are deprived of the progress that objective science could offer on a wide range of pressing social problems. When scientists cannot control their own research agendas because they are preoccupied with responding to subpoenas and data requests, when private funding comes only with long strings attached, and when scientists are sanctioned for communicating results that do not serve the economic interests of their sponsors, the core values that define science are threatened.

## An Overdue Debate

*Rescuing Science* collects perspectives from academics specializing in science, law, and philosophy on these worrisome developments. In their individual chapters, the authors describe important clashes between science and law with more precision and identify promising pathways toward reform. Since the focus of the book is on identifying problems and suggesting solutions, the authors consciously set out to find examples of how science has been distorted by special interests using legal tools. While subsequent researchers or commentators may ultimately debate the overall significance of these problems, the well-supported accounts provided in

---

[2] National Research Council, *Access to Research Data in the 21st Century: An Ongoing Dialogue among Interested Parties* (Washington, DC: National Academy Press, 2002), 14 (quoting Dr. Bruce Alberts' concern that "there is a danger that the [Data Access A]mendment could be used to harass scientists whose work is found objectionable by anyone, for any reason").

this book leave little doubt that the problems exist and that a variety of regulatory and legal pressures are causing unwarranted intrusions on science.

The book's collection of individual essays are organized around a set of neutral principles that were crafted in discussions with a wide range of experts on the use of science in policymaking. These principles should be non-controversial throughout the scientific and legal community. If the principles were followed, the threats to scientific integrity and objectivity posed by misuse of legal tools would diminish substantially.

This effort to document the adverse impacts of the law on science is long overdue. Others, including contributors to this book, have written eloquently and at length about mounting threats to scientific integrity in the area of food and drug safety and efficacy. But scholars have not yet focused on the broader problems that arise from the law's insensitivity to the basic principles of science, with particular attention to the protection of public health and natural resources. Nor has anyone endeavored to identify reforms that would forestall such interference. This book meets those challenges.

## The Pressure on Science

Scientists unfamiliar with the legal system generally assume that the path of their research from the laboratory to policy makers is a straight and uncomplicated one. Research is published in a peer-reviewed journal so that it can be judged on the merits by knowledgeable colleagues. Well designed studies with original discoveries can then play a significant role in formulating social policy, while studies with evidence of bias or unclear methodology are discounted. Scientists might also expect that when policy makers are confronted with important questions regarding scientific evidence, they will utilize a "weight of the evidence" approach, viewing available data as a composite and reaching conclusions only after considering the strengths and weaknesses of all of the individual pieces of research. After all, judicial, legislative, and regulatory institutions have the same objectives as scientific institutions: improving social welfare. Thus, scientists reason, rational use of research by policy makers is one of the most promising ways to make sure that this overriding objective is achieved.

Scientists who have been reluctantly drawn out of their laboratories into political or courtroom battles over the last few decades have learned that legal processes are quite different from this idealized view. Rather than incorporating science into policy dispassionately and using research to further a quest for truth, the legal system makes most decisions through an adversarial process driven by affected parties who interpret and re-interpret the science to prove that they should "win." This method of making decisions is largely alien to scientific practice and counterproductive to the production of reliable research. Over the last three decades, as science has become increasingly influential in the regulation of industry, these adversarial processes have increased and now pose a substantial threat to scientists who work in controversial areas such as climate change, pesticide registration, toxic chemical risk assessments, and the protection of endangered species.[3]

Three concurrent developments, in particular, have placed science under intense pressure. The first is the dramatic expansion of the regulatory system, characterized by a growing body of statutory and administrative law, as well as multiple agencies that regulate products, manufacturing processes, and waste disposal activities through thousands of separate requirements. The multiplication of legal requirements reaches nearly every firm in the manufacturing sector, as well as large portions of the service sector. At the same time, regulators look to science for guidance when they make difficult decisions regarding the stringency of public health and environmental protection. The more emphasis that regulators place on science, the greater the affected parties' incentives to do what they can to control its content and production.

The second source of pressure is the expansion of liability for damages caused by defective products, including toxic chemicals. The American judiciary has led the world in developing liability principles for products and activities that cause unreasonable or significant harm to society, provoking great concern from the manufacturing sector. It is not uncommon for liability judgments to be in the millions of dollars for a single victim, and the science supporting plaintiffs' alleged injuries is critical in determining whether they win or lose.

The third development is the continuing failure of the U.S. government to provide meaningful financial support to public research on health and the environment. Rather than increasing funding as environmental and

---

[3] Feature Issue: Corporate Corruption of Science, *International Journal of Occupational and Environmental Health* 2, no. 4 (2005).

health sciences grow in importance, public investment in badly needed research has been relatively flat for the past several decades.[4] This dearth of research support may be based, at least in part, on the hope that private parties will pick up the slack.[5] Yet that expectation overlooks the intrinsic differences in incentives between companies that conduct research to develop new technologies and companies expected to conduct research on the adverse effects of their pollution and products. Pharmaceutical companies, for example, invest heavily in research in the hope of inventing a new miracle drug that will help humanity and earn large returns for investors, but research regarding the effects of industrial activities on public health and natural resources presents quite the opposite equation for most private companies. If the research suggests unexpected harms and other adverse effects, it leads directly to the expenditure – as opposed to the making – of money. In fact, manufacturers understand the significance of science to liability and regulation so well that they may actually resist conducting basic tests on their products or auditing the potential harms caused by their activities. As long as scientific information can be incriminating and lead to costly liability and regulatory requirements, ignorance is bliss.

While each of the three factors has a powerful effect on science, their synergism can be overwhelming. The Information Age intensifies these effects in ways not imaginable a decade ago. With the invention of the worldwide web, adverse information about a product circulating in commerce travels rapidly, prompting rapid fluctuations in markets and expanding liability for mistakes in amazingly short order.

Scientific discoveries were the foundation for crushing liability on industries engaged in the manufacture of asbestos, tobacco, beryllium, and a number of pharmaceuticals and medical devices.[6] The mere specter of liability leads virtually every industry to scrutinize research that suggests their

---

[4] National Research Council, *Trends in Federal Support of Research and Graduate Education* (Washington, DC: National Academy Press, 2001), 122–3.

[5] National Research Council, *Toxicity Testing: Strategies to Determine Needs and Priorities* (Washington, DC: National Academy Press, 1984), 48, 84–5.

[6] Paul Brodeur, *Outrageous Misconduct: The Asbestos Industry on Trial* (New York: Pantheon, 1985); Stanton A. Glantz et al., eds., *The Cigarette Papers* (Berkeley, CA: University of California Press, 1996); Gerald Markowitz and David Rosner, *Deceit and Denial: The Deadly Politics of Industrial Pollution* (Berkeley, CA: University of California Press, 2002); Morton Mintz, *At Any Cost: Corporate Greed, Women, and the Dalkon Shield* (New York: Pantheon, 1985); Christian Warren, *Brush with Death: A Social History of Lead Poisoning* (Baltimore, MD: Johns Hopkins University Press, 2000).

activities are more hazardous than generally supposed. Because scientific data appear to have gained the legal power of ending businesses and entire manufacturing sectors, isolated pieces of research can attract scrutiny more fierce than most researchers should be expected to withstand.

Science has also distinguished itself as one of the main drivers of regulatory requirements. Learning of unexpected hazards or the possibility for adverse effects often leads to public demands for changes in regulations that will prevent or mitigate such threats. In the past three decades, certain pesticides, asbestos, polychlorinated biphenyls (PCBs), lead, and other common chemicals have been banned in whole or in part in the United States as a result of research that revealed the significant harm they could cause.

These trends and their complex interactions have multiplied the opportunities for destructive collisions between the worlds of law and science. Science is used and occasionally misused in making regulatory, legislative, and judicial decisions. Scientists, with little or no preparation and often without their consent, are drawn into combat between warring advocates within the legal system. Too often, these scientists become lightning rods in battles involving clashes between powerful institutions, both public and private.

## Clashing Cultures

Underlying these conflicts between science and law are the two very different approaches that each discipline uses to assess the reliability of empirical evidence and establish the "facts." In contrast to the overriding principles of disinterestedness and collaboration that dominate scientific inquiry, the legal system is founded on the premise that the clash between equally represented disparate interests metes out justice. Lawyers who represent affected parties place a significantly lower value on objectivity than do scientists, and they are focused on winning immediate results rather than engaging in a lengthy quest to discover the true answer.

Science demands that, to the maximum extent possible, scientists have no stake in the outcome of the research. The law, by contrast, must solicit input from precisely the opposite types of participants – those who *are* sorely affected, aggrieved, and stand to lose or win from the outcome. Although documented facts and empirical knowledge are generally welcome, the law can proceed on negotiated truths and tentative assumptions as long as the affected parties are all participating vigorously in the process. The primary criterion for evaluating the reliability of the science in court is whether the testimony of the expert survives challenge by the other interested parties in a highly stylized format (for example, cross-examination) before an audience comprised largely of lay people. In the legislative, regulatory, and judicial contexts, if the credibility of participating scientists is abused or impaired along the way, that injury is just another unavoidable byproduct of a vigorous adversarial system. Science is geared to a fundamentally different approach: maintaining colleagiality so that hypotheses can be vetted and new discoveries advanced.

While it is relatively easy for anyone familiar with both professional disciplines to see and accept these differences, problems arise when scientists are drawn into legal disputes in a way that invades their independence to conduct research. For example, affected parties in legislative, regulatory, and judicial disputes have on occasion commissioned research specifically to produce an outcome that will help them win their fight. Too often, researchers are asked, and even required, to sign contracts that compel them to suppress any findings contrary to the private sponsor's overall goals. Experts are also hired to engage in the "deconstruction" and "corpuscularization" of adverse research, casting doubt on every aspect of a study's methodology and findings. Such deconstruction is intended to discredit the research even though many of the methodological choices targeted by the attack may be perfectly acceptable to the broader scientific community.[7]

The tobacco industry is the most notorious intruder on the integrity of independent research, but it is by no means alone.[8] Virtually every category of stakeholder that participates in vigorous policy contests over public health and environmental protection has engaged in at least one of the underhanded assaults on science detailed in this book. Industry lawyers and trade associations, plaintiffs' attorneys, public interest groups, and grassroots citizen groups, as well as the scientists they hire to represent them, have distorted science, harassed researchers, or manufactured results.[9] Because public interest groups have fewer resources, however, the most accessible and well-documented cases tend to involve industry.

---

[7] Sheila Jasanoff, "Research Subpoenas and the Sociology of Knowledge," *Law and Contemporary Problems* 59, no. 3 (1996): 95, 98–100.

[8] Glantz et al., 171–200.

[9] Marcia Angell, *Science on Trial: The Clash of Medical Evidence and the Law in the Breast Implant Case* (New York: W.W. Norton, 1996).

## Restoring Scientific Integrity

The increased number of attacks on science and the influence of private sponsorship on research have generated alarm within the scientific community. In their struggle to fend off such intrusions, a number of scientific organizations have developed positions and tools to preserve the independence of science. Biomedical journal editors, for example, now require the disclosure of possible conflicts of interest before allowing scientists to publish scientific findings or serve as peer reviewers in order to ensure that colleagues are alerted to their potential financial biases.[10] The Union of Concerned Scientists collected signatures from hundreds of scientists, including dozens of Nobel Prize winners, in protest of the politicized use of science by the Executive Branch.[11] Even large, apolitical societies such as the American Association for the Advancement of Science have passed resolutions and filed comments on the increasing problems of biased research and literature reviews that damage scientific credibility.[12]

This book reinforces these efforts. As mentioned earlier, we have organized the twelve chapters, this introduction, and the conclusion around a set of fundamental principles of scientific practice. These principles are grounded in the values long assumed to be the bedrock of scientific independence, disinterestedness, and transparency. They help to identify how far the legal system has strayed in its use of science, threatening scientific integrity at its core. We begin and end with these fundamental principles in order to propose a more productive and honest process for incorporating science into policies that protect public health and the environment:

- *Independence:* Scientists must be able to conduct research without unjustified restrictions, including undue influence by research sponsors.
- *Transparency:* The data and results of research must be communicated honestly and expeditiously to the research community and broader

---

[10] International Committee of Medical Journal Editors, "Uniform Requirements for Manuscripts Submitted to Biomedical Journals" (Oct. 2004) (available at http://www.icmje.org/index.html).

[11] Union of Concerned Scientists, "Restoring Scientific Integrity in Policymaking" (Feb. 18, 2004) (available at http://www.ucsusa.org/global_environment/rsi/page.cfm?pageID=1320).

[12] Peg Brickley, "Attack on Panel Politics," *Scientist* (March 12, 2003) (available at http://www.biomedcentral.com/news/20030312/01/).

public. Researchers and those using their research must be careful to represent the findings accurately, including the limitations of that research.

- A *Public Infrastructure for Science*: Government support of independent research is essential to produce discoveries that benefit the public good. In appropriate circumstances, peer review may serve an important role in assisting the government's decision making regarding the use and funding of science, but peer review must never be used to censor research.

These principles, which are specified in more detail in the "Principles of Good Regulatory Science" beginning on the following page, were drafted after extensive discussions among a community of scientists, lawyers, and philosophers, many of whom are authors of the chapters in this book. Yet the general consensus supporting these principles is evident throughout the scientific literature. As we discuss in more detail, sociologists of science and reports produced by scientific communities, especially the National Academy of Sciences and the American Association for the Advancement of Science, confirm that these principles of objectivity, independence, and transparency are cornerstones of high-quality science. Scientists appear committed to these principles not only in their own research, but also in their review of others' research. They value and nurture honest and open communication about the limitations of research and the underlying data. And they acknowledge the need for public support of important areas of research.

## Independence and Freedom

The first principle underscores the widespread view that objectivity and independence are central to the development of high-quality science. The central value of disinterested inquiry runs through all phases of science, from initial funding to final publication decisions.[13] Indeed, the very productivity of the scientific enterprise depends, in large part, on the commitment of each researcher to perform studies in a disinterested way. While studies must be replicable, and typically are, precious research resources

---

[13] Robert K. Merton, "The Normative Structure of Science," in *Sociology of Science*, ed. Jerry Gaston (San Francisco: Jossey-Bass, 1973), 267, 275.

# Principles for Good Regulatory Science

**Scientists must be able to conduct research without unjustified restrictions, including undue influence by research sponsors.**

- Sponsors must never place restrictions or otherwise influence the design or conduct of a study in an attempt to obtain results favorable to their interests.

- Research must never be suppressed because it produces results that are adverse to a sponsor or other interested party.

- No publication or summary of research should be influenced – in tone or content – by the sponsoring entity. Scientists must be able to conduct research without unjustified restrictions.

- If vested interests use the legal system to harass scientists whose research or expert testimony calls into question the safety of their practices or products, the harassers must be held accountable with sanctions and must compensate injured scientists for the resulting interference with their research and damage to their reputations.

**Researchers and those using their research must be careful to represent their findings accurately, including the limitations of that research. The data and methods of research that inform regulatory decisions must be communicated honestly and expeditiously to the research community and broader public.**

- Researchers and those using their data must be honest about the limits of the research and remaining uncertainties. If others misrepresent research to suggest an outcome not supported by the study, researchers must correct these misstatements as soon they become aware of them.

- Research must never be dismissed or excluded because it does not provide a complete answer to a larger policy or science question. Research, by its nature, is incomplete, and to dismiss research because it does not provide a definitive answer could result in the exclusion of valuable science from regulatory decision making.

- The data underlying a published study, as well as a comprehensive description of the methods, must be available to other scientists and the public at large upon publication of the study or submission of the results to a federal agency, in compliance with prevailing rules for preserving the privacy of human research subjects. Regulatory agencies should rigorously review and challenge exaggerated claims, however, that underlying data must be kept confidential for business and other reasons.

Government support of independent research is essential to produce discoveries that benefit the public good. In appropriate circumstances, peer review may play an important role in assisting the government's decision making regarding the use and funding of science, but peer review must never be used to censor research.

- Legitimate scientific peer review does not encompass processes that enable outside stakeholders to pressure scientists to change their views in light of an anticipated policy outcome.

- Peer review should be done by a balanced group of peer reviewers who have no present or past conflicts of interest likely to affect their review and who specialize in the area. Peer reviewers should disclose the limits of their expertise in assessing the research.

- Entities that select peer reviewers should disclose any financial conflicts of interest and affiliations or perspectives that may influence their choice of reviewers. The selection of reviewers must never be politicized.

- Much research that benefits the public good does not generate private compensation for its production. Generous public funding of research is essential for advancements in scientific knowledge, especially in areas where there are no private benefits to be gained from the discoveries.

- All research produced or used by the government should be subject to basic quality assurance/quality control checks, especially if that research is not published or disseminated widely within the scientific community.

- Public research monies should be allocated in ways that are disinterested and do not reflect a stake in the outcome of the research.

are best used when scientists can build on the objective work of their peers to advance the scientific enterprise rather than dedicate time and energy to replicating suspect results. Individual scientists can be so wedded to this disinterested norm that they refrain from political activity, at least regarding their research, to ensure that their findings are not tainted by the appearance of bias.[14] The scientific community embraces the need for objectivity so uniformly that departures from that core value can produce a loss of professional credibility on the part of the researchers who are

[14] V.L. Melnick et al., "Participation of Biologists in the Formulation of National Science Policy," *Federation Proceedings* 35, no. 9 (1976): 1957.

associated with producing research under significant conflicts of interest. Ultimately, such lapses undermine the scientists' overall reputation and jeopardize promotions or other career opportunities.

Requirements that scientists disclose potential conflicts of interest before publishing scientific findings or serving as peer reviewers are the remedy of choice used by the world's best biomedical journals to combat hidden bias. Forceful commentaries in both the *New England Journal of Medicine* and the *Journal of the American Medical Association* underscore the importance of researcher compliance with these disclosure requirements.[15]

The significance of this norm is also underscored by the considerable angst generated within the scientific community when the objectivity of individual researchers or an entire area of scientific practice is called into question. Researchers facing scientific misconduct charges alleging research bias suffer damage to their reputations even if they are later exonerated.[16]

This insistence on disinterested scientific practice also extends to less visible issues. For example, research on the peer-review process has suggested that matters as seemingly insignificant as the affiliation or fame of the researcher can affect the outcome of a peer review.[17] Even these relatively minor deviations from the requirement that scientists remain objective have triggered calls for reform by leaders within the scientific community.

Largely because of this unfaltering commitment to objectivity, the growing role of private funding of academic research has provoked a near-crisis at the nation's most respected universities. When the plant biology department at the University of California at Berkeley accepted a five-year

---

[15] David Blumenthal et al., "Withholding Research Results in Academic Life Science: Evidence from a National Survey of Faculty," *Journal of the American Medical Association* 277, no. 15 (1997): 1224–8; Catherine D. DeAngelis et al., "Reporting Financial Conflicts of Interest and Relationships between Investigators and Research Sponsors," *Journal of the American Medical Association* 286, no. 1 (2001): 89–91; Jeffrey M. Drazen and Gregory D. Curfman, "Financial Associations of Authors," *New England Journal of Medicine* 346, no. 24 (2002): 1901–2; Drummond Rennie, "Thyroid Storm," *Journal of the American Medical Association* 277, no. 15 (1997): 1238–43; Steven A. Rosenberg, "Secrecy in Medical Research," *New England Journal of Medicine* 334, no. 6 (1996): 392–3.

[16] Glenn H. Reynolds, "'Thank God for the Lawyers': Some Thoughts on the (Mis)regulation of Scientific Misconduct," *Tennessee Law Review* 66, no. 3 (1999): 814.

[17] Sheila Jasanoff, *The Fifth Branch: Science Advisers as Policymakers* (Cambridge, MA: Harvard University Press, 1990), 69–71.

$25 million "basic research" grant from Novartis, a drug and pesticide company, the faculty was thrown into turmoil that persists to this day, provoking a stinging article in the *Atlantic Monthly* entitled "The Kept University."[18] The controversy was so intense that Berkeley ultimately hired a team of ten sociologists from Michigan State University to study the arrangement over the course of two years.[19] The investigators were blunt in their final recommendations, urging that the university "avoid industry agreements that involve complete academic units or large groups of researchers"; "be attentive to the formulation of new goals when motivated by a disruption of patronage or by self-interest"; and "work to identify and prevent the masking of intended applications [or] negative consequences of commercialization with the privileges implied by academic freedom."[20]

Despite growing efforts by scientists to address such conflicts, legal processes continue to play a major role in provoking and facilitating the loss of scientific objectivity, transparency, and – ultimately – credibility. In Part I of this book, four essayists discuss the importance of preserving scientific independence of research and the various ways that the law serves to violate this commitment to disinterested research. Professor Thomas McGarity introduces Part I by providing an overview of the ways that legal processes intrude on scientific independence. Relying in part on case studies, he identifies a series of legal tools that affected parties and sponsors use to discredit research, all of which impinge in significant ways on scientists' commitment to objective inquiry. Professor McGarity also proposes specific changes to the legal rules that would correct these abuses.

Dr. Katherine Squibb's chapter addresses specific violations of the scientific value of independence in the field of toxicology. After discussing the centrality of this principle in toxicology research, Dr. Squibb identifies ways that the law permits sponsors to impose contractual restrictions on researchers or otherwise influence the design or conduct of toxicology studies. She explains some troubling cases where private sector

---

[18] Eyal Press and Jennifer Washburn, "The Kept University," *Atlantic Monthly* 285, no. 3 (2000): 38–54.

[19] Lawrence Busch et al., *External Review of the Collaborative Research Agreement between Novartis Agricultural Discovery Institute, Inc. and The Regents of the University of California* (East Lansing, MI: Institute for Food and Agricultural Standards, Michigan State University, 2004) (available at http://evcp.chance.berkeley.edu/documents/Reports/documents/NovartisBerkeleyFinalReport071204.pdf).

[20] Ibid., 13–14.

sponsors were able to use legally enforceable contracts to suppress adverse results they did not like, even though the research warranted disclosure because of its implications for the protection of public health and the environment.

In Chapter 3, Dr. Sheldon Krimsky details the significant adverse consequences that flow to both science and policy from allowing sponsor control over biomedical research. Pulling from the empirical, scientific, and social science literature, Dr. Krimsky identifies three types of impairments that afflict biomedical research produced under conditions that violate the scientific principle of disinterestedness: (1) control and withholding of data by the private sponsor; (2) private funding of research that is structured in ways that disproportionately favor the sponsor's interests; and (3) the so-called funding effect that identifies a correlation between favorable outcomes and private funding. He explains the empirical research and statistical analyses documenting how privately funded studies produce results more favorable to their sponsors than independently funded studies. Professor McGarity, Dr. Squibb, and Dr. Krimsky close their chapters with more specific recommendations on how the law could either prohibit or discourage sponsor control over research.

The final chapter in Part I provides a cautionary tale about the destructiveness of the legal system once a researcher is caught in the cross-hairs of a legal controversy. Dr. Paul Fischer explains how his research on the use of R.J. Reynolds Joe Camel logo in marketing tobacco products to children led to a firestorm of legal proceedings against him. Most of these manuveurs appeared designed primarily to harass Fischer and discredit his research, as opposed to generating information of legitimate use to the company. They included seeking the release of confidential information regarding the children who participated in his study, the filing of meritless scientific misconduct charges, and burdensome subpoenas seeking the release of all information associated with by past and ongoing research, including lab notebooks.

## Transparency and Honesty

The second principle, designed to ensure that science used in policymaking remains transparent, underscores the need for researchers and others to be honest about the limitations of their findings and to share underlying data and models when the research is submitted to inform regulation or court adjudications. These tenets, like objectivity, are considered vital to scientific progress. Openness in science allows scientists not only to replicate, and thereby validate, their colleagues' work, but to build on prior research and make new discoveries. Sociologists of science[21] and scientific committees[22] underscore the importance of these values to the success of science, even though in practice there are far more violations than scientists might otherwise care to admit.

Regardless of their different approaches to the disinterestedness principle, law and science appear to embrace a commitment to openness with equal enthusiasm. In theory, equitable legal processes require that parties have access to all relevant information, with only limited exceptions for especially important privileges such as attorney-client communications. At least superficially, the law honors and supports scientists' need for access to data and methods and the larger concept of open records. Despite this outward appearance of harmony, however, in practice the legal system provides strong incentives for both private actors and public decision makers to be quite nontransparent, and even secretive, when it comes to disclosing data.

In the regulatory context, decision makers have often found that the best way to avoid attack is to be coy about the underlying trade-offs made in reaching a regulation: Science provides a perfect foil for obfuscating the underlying policy choices. For example, rather than be candid about the numerous policy judgments used to arrive at a toxic standard, a regulator can portray the standard to be the result of sophisticated modeling, technical assumptions, and research studies.[23] By looking to science for answers and representing the results as if they were preordained by science or are the only credible outcomes of a technical analysis, decision makers hope to avoid attack by angry interest groups.[24]

---

[21] Robert K. Merton, *The Sociology of Science: Theoretical and Empirical Investigations*, ed. Norman Storer (Chicago: University of Chicago Press, 1973), 273–5.

[22] National Research Council, *Risk Assessment in the Federal Government: Managing the Process* (Washington, DC: National Academy Press, 1983), 7–8; National Research Council, *Science and Judgment in Risk Assessment* (Washington, DC: National Academy Press, 1994), 81; National Research Council, *Sharing Publication-Related Data* (Washington, DC: National Academy Press, 2003), 4–11, 51–60.

[23] Howard Latin, "Good Science, Bad Regulation, and Toxic Risk Assessment," *Yale Journal on Regulation* 5, no. 1 (1988): 89.

[24] Mark E. Rushefsky, *Making Cancer Policy* (Albany, NY: State University of New York Press, 1986), 6.

The legal system provides even more disincentives for private actors to be honest about the limits of research when those limits cut against their interests. As discussed, the adversarial system produces a climate for debate and discussion where each party presents its "best" case and lay judges or regulators are expected to arrive at a result based on these extreme portraits. The adversarial process not only allows, but encourages opposing parties to conceal the research that undercuts their positions and, conversely, to exaggerate the limitations and weaknesses of studies submitted by their adversaries. These adversaries thus have few incentives to share their data or be honest about their methodological choices. Even if a party demands full disclosure of the research in its opponent's possession, the owners of the data may be able to rely on a number of generous, legally sanctioned rights to conceal it, including intellectual property protections and privilege claims.[25]

Part II of the book surveys a number of legal settings that reward both public and private entities for concealing or confusing the limitations of research and underlying data. Professor Donald Hornstein opens Part II by highlighting how several new U.S. laws provide private parties with adversarial mechanisms to distort the shortcomings of publicly funded research that is adverse to their interests while insulating from similar scrutiny the limitations and data underlying their own, privately-commissioned research. Hornstein advocates abandonment of such laws and outlines new structural mechanisms for public policy that better match open and honest scientific principles.

The analysis then shifts to the courts and identifies ways that the judiciary discourages honesty about the limits of research in some settings. In Chapter 6, Dr. Carl Cranor discusses an evidentiary screening rule used by federal courts that amplifies the opportunities for adversaries to conceal limits of their research while attacking their opponents' science with few restraints. Because this screening rule is ostensibly designed to sort "real" (or replicable) science from "junk" science, it is particularly effective in encouraging counterproductive deconstruction of valid research. Dr. Cranor discusses cases in which judges have capitulated to this deconstruction and excluded testimony based on types of research, such as

---

[25] Wendy E. Wagner, "Commons Ignorance: The Failure of Environmental Law to Produce Needed Information on Health and the Environment," *Duke Law Journal* 53, no. 6 (2004): 1619, 1699–1711.

animal studies, that are widely accepted within the scientific community as probative of causal connections.

In Chapter 7, Dr. Holly Doremus details how agencies and stakeholders in natural resource disputes often use science to obscure underlying policy and value conflicts. A constellation of forces, not the least of which is the unwelcome spectre of being held accountable to the public and incurring the resulting political costs, make such a strategy rational from the perspective of agency officials. Unfortunately, this form of scientific obfuscation can deter the public and other interested parties from participating in important decisions. Dr. Doremus provides not only general evidence of this science "charade" in natural resources law, but discusses it in the context of a specific dispute – the Klamath Basin water conflict. She closes her chapter with the recommendation that the legal system define the boundary between science and policy more clearly.

Dr. Vern Walker then considers this same problem – the tendency of formal legal rules to discourage honesty about the limits of research and underlying data – from a different vantage point, utilizing examples from international trade. He argues that the law demands logical and rigorous supporting evidence, but does not allow for this evidence to be placed in a broader context that explicates remaining uncertainties. This contradiction leaves decision makers with an incomplete understanding of the relevant science and accompanying uncertainties and conflicts with the more open-ended and dynamic traditions of transparency within the scientific community. The Japan-Apples case, arising from a trade conflict within the World Trade Organization, illustrates this mismatch between transparency in science and legal fact-finding, producing outcomes that serve neither the goals of good science nor good policy. Dr. Walker concludes with suggestions for how this science–law conflict can be redressed by providing more frank dislosures of uncertainties in a manner that is consistent with the scientific community's approach to discussing the limitations of their research.

Dr. David Adelman closes Part II by examining the implications for transparency produced by the two statistical methodologies used to validate research results – the Bayes Theorem and frequentism. He explains from a scientific perspective how these sophisticated and apparently objective methodologies in fact mask important value judgments that affect outcomes, sometimes in drastic ways. Because a choice between the two methods has become so important in the development of scientific findings across a wide range of disciplines, Adelman argues that making these value judgments more explicit is the only way to ensure that science remains transparent, both within the scientific community and when it enters the legal system.

## A Public Infrastructure for Science

The third principle originates less directly from the practice of science and instead recognizes the practical realities of producing reliable and comprehensive research – the dearth of public funding of environmental and public health research. Statements of the National Academy of Sciences (NAS) underscore the very real limitations of relying exclusively on the private sector for research relevant to public needs.[26] They also stress the importance of including balanced peer-review bodies to allocate and oversee the utilization of that research by the government.[27] As a NAS committee observed in a 1997 report:

> Recognizing that private sector interests do not always coincide with the full range of national interests, EPA should concentrate its own research and grants programs in areas where the private sector has little incentive to conduct research or develop better solutions to environmental problems. . . . No one company, industry, or municipality has a unique stake in these issues, making risk reduction research and evaluation of control options hard to justify to management or investors. These are areas of "public good" for which a national agency like EPA should have lead responsibility and undertake the relevant research.[28]

Legal and political processes again tend to work at cross purposes with these objectives of coherent and balanced public research. One of the most visible sources of criticism concern the peer-review practices used by federal agencies. To ensure fair processes for research allocations and scientific review, agencies have created "advisory" or "peer-review" boards to protect the quality of research and funding decisions. Yet since agency administrators control appointments to these expert bodies, acting with only limited oversight, there are countervailing incentives for administrators to advance

---

[26] National Research Council, "Toxicity Testing."
[27] National Research Council, *Building a Foundation for Sound Environmental Decisions* (Washington, DC: National Academy Press, 1997), 15, 53–4.
[28] Ibid., 53–4.

the political agenda of the Executive Branch instead of objective science. "Stacking" of these scientific boards continues to be a serious concern.[29]

The use of peer-review panels appears to be even more irregular when science advisory boards are used to "advise" agencies on how to use available research. It is the latter use of peer review that is discussed by Dr. David Michaels and Professor Sidney Shapiro in Chapters 10 and 11, respectively. These two authors explore – first from a scientific perspective and then from a legal perspective – how mandatory peer review employed in the regulatory process can conflict with standard principles for peer review adopted by scientists. Such disparities include excluding or censoring research and failing to require that peer review panels remain balanced. Both Dr. Michaels and Professor Shapiro recommend reforms for regulatory peer review that would insulate panels from such inappropriate bias and pressure.

A more subtle but equally serious problem is that the threat of liability or regulation serves as a powerful disincentive for private sector research. These implications mean that even when companies undertake research, they are extremely reluctant to share potentially incriminating information voluntarily. These strong legal disincentives, which are rarely offset by affirmative testing requirements, underscore the importance of public funding to support badly needed research. In his closing chapter, Professor John Applegate proposes criteria for distinguishing between situations when privately funded research can be expected to make a major contribution to science and situations when publicly funded research is preferable.

## The Future

Restoring the balance between scientific independence and integrity, on the one hand, and, on the other, the rough handling that science receives by policy makers in the real world will require the establishment of "safety zones" between scientists and those who run legal institutions. Given the fundamental differences in the prevailing norms of the two cultures, however, we should not harbor illusions regarding the difficulty of reforming legal rules to better take into account their adverse effects on science.

The conclusion to the book outlines immediate and long-term strategies for reform. Individual chapters offer much of the information that supports

---

[29] Donald Kennedy, "Science in the U.S. Government: Interim Report," *Science* 296, no. 5570 (2002): 981; David Michaels et al., "Advice without Dissent," *Science.* 298, no. 5594 (2002): 703.

and defines these proposals, which are intended to mitigate or eliminate some of the worst violations of the principles that form the core of this book. The conclusion weaves these individual proposals into a broader tapestry that identifies the most significant intrusions of law into science and then identifies the most promising paths for reform.

Throughout this discussion, the principles serve as the outline for a "safety zone" in which scientists can do their work with minimal interference from the law. Scientists who conduct research with relevance to public affairs must be prepared to defend their results, their methodology, and even their integrity. But there is a world of difference between expecting science to stand up to scrutiny and expecting individual researchers to withstand unlimited deconstruction and harassment without support from the law. As a result, the law and the legal system must be reformed to:

- establish more stringent penalties and disincentives for unjustified intrusions to science and its researchers;
- discourage sponsor control of research and the adversarial use of research without restrictions or sanctions;
- establish standard requirements for the communication of research that will force more honesty about the limitations of research and provide access to underlying data, regardless of whether the researcher is private or publicly funded; and
- allocate research responsibilities in a more balanced and coherent matter, and prevent the hijacking of expert panels to serve political ends.

Such proposals for reform are ambitious, but they are justified by the law's misuse of science, which is becoming a severe and potentially irreversible social problem. Some scientists are recognizing these threats, just as policy makers are gradually recognizing the long-term erosion of wise policy making that arises from the misappropriation of science and experts for economic and political ends. This book alerts a broader audience to these forces and suggests ways that counterproductive rules can be fixed to stave off the worst attacks on science. We hope that future authors can build on our work to devise more permanent structures by which law and science can peacefully coexist, and even support, one another.

# FREEDOM AND INDEPENDENCE

This book opens with four chapters that explain how interested parties have abused the legal system to threaten scientific independence, undermine the objectivity and therefore the integrity of research, and, in some cases, threaten the careers of individual scientists. These abuses violate several basic, noncontroversial principles of scientific independence:

- Scientists must be able to conduct research without unjustified restrictions, including undue influence by research sponsors.
- Sponsors must never place restrictions or otherwise influence the design or conduct of a study in an attempt to obtain results favorable to their interests.
- Research must never be suppressed because it produces results that are adverse to a sponsor or other interested party.
- No publication or summary of research should be influenced – in tone or content – by the sponsoring entity.
- If vested interests use the legal system to harass scientists whose research or expert testimony calls into question the safety of their practices or products, the harassers must be held accountable with sanctions and must compensate injured scientists for the resulting interference with their research and potential damage to their reputations.

Part I begins with a survey by Professor McGarity of the various tools special interests have used to attack research in scientifically illegitimate ways when the research threatens their economic interests. McGarity explains how such attacks on individual research projects can also cause the "corpuscularization" of science. By systematically attacking each of the individual studies supporting an environmental regulation and arguing that each study should be excluded from consideration because of some specific flaw, rather than including all relevant research as part of a larger scientific record, special interests attempt to undercut the scientific support for protective regulation. The legal system tolerates and even invites this corpuscularization of science through legislation such as the Information Quality Act, which allows affected parties to challenge and even censor individual research projects disseminated or used by the government. McGarity contrasts the legal system's tolerance of this corpuscularization with the traditional "weight of the evidence" approach used by scientists. Weight of the evidence means considering all available research and weighing its relevance and reliability in an integrated manner. McGarity concludes with a series of recommendations designed to realign science-based regulation with processes used by scientists.

In the second chapter of Part I, Dr. Squibb takes a closer look at unjustified intrusions on scientific research in the field of toxicology, with an emphasis on the chilling effect that these intrusions have on young scientists who are considering research in particularly controversial areas. Using specific examples of the emerging toxicological research on atrazine (a common pesticide) and perchlorate (a toxic component of rocket fuel), she describes how private sector sponsors have interfered with study designs and attempted to suppress research results. Squibb urges government intervention to restore scientific independence. She suggests that we diminish the influence of private sector funding by strengthening the infrastructure for public funding of science, especially support of "mechanistic" research that explores how exposure to a toxic chemical causes harm within the body.

Dr. Krimsky considers these same types of intrusions on scientific freedom in the pharmaceutical arena, where violations of the principles of scientific independence have been particularly well documented. Krimsky provides several case studies of drug sponsors attempting to suppress, through contract, the dissemination of adverse research findings. He also discusses various infringements of the principle that scientists must remain disinterested in conducting their work, including evidence of a "funding effect" in biomedical research that reveals a positive correlation between private sector sponsorship and results favorable to that sponsor. Krimsky concludes his chapter with several provocative proposals for counteracting violations of scientific independence, particularly with respect to sponsor control over research on drug safety and efficacy.

Part I closes with a disturbing autobiographical account of the impact that these violations of scientific freedom can have on the researchers themselves. In this chapter, Dr. Fischer describes the illegitimate attacks that he and his colleague sustained from the tobacco industry against their research on the effects of cigarette advertising on children. The legal system facilitated, rather than penalized, some of these attacks. Indeed, in Fischer's case, the judicial system showed remarkable tolerance for the tobacco industry's illicit efforts to access all of Fischer's research records and require their public release, threatening the privacy of his individual research subjects. Fischer's story underscores the extent to which special interests can intrude not only on the principles of scientific independence in general, but on the research projects and careers of individual scientists in particular.

# 1

# Defending Clean Science from Dirty Attacks by Special Interests

Thomas O. McGarity, J.D.

## Deconstruction Writ Large

When a new scientific study suggests that an industry's products or activities may be causing unanticipated adverse effects on health or the environment, a typical reaction by that industry or other affected stakeholders is to attack the messenger. This chapter details the strategies that risk-producing industries have employed to deconstruct scientific studies and to create the impression among regulatory agencies and the general public that such studies are no more than "junk science." These strategies depend on a number of legal processes and tools that not only legitimate partisan, biased attacks on research, but also provide a broad array of mechanisms to facilitate these attacks.

Scientific studies documenting risk pose a serious threat to an industry's economic well-being, motivating companies and industry trade associations to mount aggressive efforts to belittle that threat by demanding the underlying data, reanalyzing those data, finding flaws with the study's conception and execution, hiring scientists to publish letters to the editors of scientific journals, withdrawing support from the academic institutions that employ the authors of the study, and challenging the integrity of the scientists in available forums. The scientists who produce such studies are rarely prepared to ward off such attacks on their work and even on their personal integrity. Unlike the industries that launch the attacks, they cannot afford to pay other scientists to respond to the attacks, hire expensive lawyers to defend their studies in court, and retain public relations firms to defend their reputations in academia and the public at large. Conscientious scientists can spend years of their own time responding to the letters to the editor, overly broad demands for data and other information, and attacks in the press. As a result, their research agendas suffer, and they may come to regret having undertaken scientific studies in policy-relevant areas. Worse, as word gets out that policy-relevant research is likely to precipitate vicious attacks from economically interested industries, academic scientists may shy away from such research, preferring instead to labor in less controversial vineyards. This problem is dsucssed further by Dr. Katherine Squibb in Chapter 2 of this book.

The first step in determining the proper public response to attempts by risk-producing industries to deconstruct policy-relevant scientific research is to understand the techniques that those industries employ. One special interest strategy, characterized here as "attack science," consists of various techniques for casting sufficient doubt upon individual scientific studies so that the threatened company or trade association can plausibly portray them as "fatally flawed" in subsequent litigation or regulatory contexts. A second strategy, referred to here as the "corpuscular approach," focuses on the legal settings in which scientific studies are used and consists of attempts to dissuade courts and agencies from relying upon "fatally flawed" studies for any purpose and thereby to prevent them from adopting the "weight of the evidence" approach that scientists typically take toward evaluating all relevant scientific information.

Robust debates about the quality of the data underlying scientific reports and about the inferences that may properly be drawn from those data are beneficial to the scientific enterprise when they reflect genuine differences in analytical techniques and exercises of scientific judgment. Disputes that economically interested industries manufacture for the purpose of avoiding accountability and responsibility for risk-producing products and activities, however, are unlikely to contribute to genuine efforts to use scientific information in the policy-making process. More importantly, well-financed and widely publicized attacks on scientific research and the integrity of the scientists undertaking that research ultimately threaten the viability of all scientific research as public respect for the scientific community fades and public support for science dwindles.

The chapter concludes by suggesting reforms that both the legal community and the scientific community should consider for addressing attempts by risk-producing industries to deconstruct policy-relevant scientific research. In cases of outright harassment, appropriate sanctions (both legal and moral) must be available to hold the harassers accountable, and legal vehicles must be available to require the harassers to compensate injured scientists for the interference with their research and damage to their reputations. Legal vehicles must also be available for obtaining and publicizing documents underlying industry-sponsored attacks on scientific studies so that policy makers and the public can become aware of industry-manufactured scientific disputes. Scientific publications must implement conflict-of-interest policies requiring authors of letters to the editor to disclose any financial incentives for writing such letters, and governmental data access procedures should require data requesters to disclose who is paying for the disclosure requests.

## Attack Science

Risk-producing industries have developed an arsenal of science-based strategies for avoiding and challenging agency use of science in health, safety, and environmental regulation. In regulatory contexts in which the regulated industries are required to produce scientific support for the continued use of their products in the marketplace (such as regulatory programs for pesticides, drugs, and food additives), the companies producing that information obviously have a great deal of influence over how the studies are conducted. Indeed, recent controversies over unpublished drug studies have focused public attention on the fact that companies frequently control whether adverse studies ever see the light of day.[1] The following discussion, however, will focus upon the techniques that risk-producing industries employ in attacking scientific studies that have not been produced under their control or supervision but that may threaten adverse regulatory consequences for their products or activities.

Professor Joseph Sanders has observed that "[m]uch of what goes on in trials involving claims for damages allegedly attributable to exposure to toxic substances is a process of deconstructing science."[2] Much the same

---

[1] *Christian Science Monitor*, "Veil of Secrecy to Lift on Drug Tests," p. 11, Sept. 13, 2004; *Los Angeles Times*, "Drug Firms Say Secrecy Fostered Credibility 'Crisis,'" part A, Sept. 10, 2004.

[2] Joseph Sanders, "Scientific Validity, Admissibility, and Mass Torts after *Daubert*," *Minnesota Law Review* 78, no. 6 (1994): 1437.

is true of the regulatory process.[3] In fact, the process of deconstructing scientific studies with potential regulatory implications begins long before the relevant regulatory agency takes any sort of public action, such as issuing a notice of proposed rule making. The planned obfuscation begins when the first scientific studies and reports begin to appear at scientific meetings and in scientific journals, and it continues well beyond the point at which most reasonable members of the scientific community have drawn scientific conclusions based upon the weight of the available evidence.

## Prepublication Attacks

Companies and trade associations often get wind of a study that has been submitted to a journal for publication long before it appears in the journal. Sometimes the scientist reveals the results of some or all of the study at scientific conferences to which industry scientists, industry consultants, or scientists sympathetic to the industry's position are also invited. Scientific journals frequently ask industry scientists and consultants who have expertise in relevant subject areas to provide peer review of papers submitted to scientific journals. This affords the industry an opportunity to keep the study's conclusions out of the public eye altogether by providing negative peer reviews or by otherwise urging the journal not to publish the "fatally flawed" study.[4]

For example, on December 14, 1982, a tobacco industry consultant, Francis J. C. Roe, wrote to Philip Morris scientist Manuel Bourlas "in strictest confidence" to provide a photocopy of a paper submitted for publication to the prestigious *British Medical Journal* that discussed mutagen levels in the urine of nonsmokers.[5] Dr. Roe recommended that the paper not be published.[6] Although the paper was ultimately published, the peer-review process is supposed to be confidential. Industry scientists

---

[3] Sheila Jasanoff, *The Fifth Branch: Science Advisers as Policymakers* (Cambridge, MA: Harvard University Press, 1990), 37.

[4] Dan Fagin and Marianne Lavelle, *Toxic Deception: How the Chemical Industry Manipulates Science, Bends the Law, and Endangers Your Health* (Monroe, ME: Common Courage Press, 1999), 61.

[5] Letter from Francis J. C. Roe, Tobacco Industry Consultant, to Manuel Bourlas, Scientist, Philip Morris (Dec. 14, 1982).

[6] Comments on Paper 6286 (undated). Bates No. 2501324330.

and consultants who are asked to review manuscripts for scientific journals should not be permitted to leak the drafts to affected companies and
thereby permit them to begin preparations for deconstructing the studies
as soon as they are published.

## Postpublication Demands for Correction or Retraction

Most scientific periodicals provide a formal opportunity for scientific give-
and-take through exchanges in the "letters" section of the journal. Letters
from scientists can be quite lengthy and detailed, replete with charts and
tables containing reanalyses and reinterpretations of the data that were
presented in the original published study. The authors of the studies are
typically given an opportunity to respond, and the exchanges can go on
through several iterations. Risk-producing industries frequently hire scientists to find flaws in adverse studies, reanalyze and reinterpret the data,
and provide general critiques to be submitted in letters to the journals. For
example, the tobacco industry paid thirteen scientists a total of $156,000
to write letters to scientific journals criticizing early papers on the health
effects of environmental tobacco smoke.[7] In addition to creating uncertainty about the validity of a study's conclusions, such letters allow the
companies to make the case in subsequent regulatory proceedings that the
study was "highly controversial." One scientist referred to such tactics as
"a systematic effort to pollute the scientific literature."[8]

Soon after a team of experts from the World Health Organization, the
Environmental Protection Agency (EPA), Harvard University, and the
World Resources Institute submitted a global assessment of the adverse
health effects of burning fossil fuels to *The Lancet* for publication, one of
the authors received an urgent fax from the journal relating "what appeared
to be a very serious set of charges about our paper, claiming that our data
were flawed and our analysis was wrong."[9] The author discovered that
the fax had come from a scientist at the industry-sponsored Citizens for a
Sound Economy Foundation who had not published a single peer-reviewed

---

[7]  Sheldon Rampton and John Stauber, *Trust Us, We're Experts: How Industry Manipulates
     Science and Gambles with Your Future* (East Rutherford, NJ: Penguin Putnam, 2001), 199.
[8]  Ibid., 199.
[9]  Devra Lee Davis, *When Smoke Ran Like Water: Tales of Environmental Deception and the
     Battle against Pollution* (Philadelphia: Basic Books, 2002), 261

article in the field of environmental health and whose most recent work "consisted primarily of letters to the editor and other attacks" on groups that had estimated public-health impacts of air pollution.[10] The author then spent more time persuading the journal that this was not a serious scientific critique than the team had spent in responding to the original peer reviewers' substantive comments.[11]

## Hand-Picked Expert Panels

A very common industry response to the publication of a study with adverse economic implications is to appoint a "blue ribbon panel" of carefully chosen experts to re-evaluate the study. The purpose of these excursions is to "manufacture uncertainty" about the validity of their conclusions.[12] The industry-assembled experts invariably conclude that one or more aspects of the study could be improved, thus permitting the sponsoring industry to take the position in public forums that the study was "fatally flawed." For example, when an article by two North Dakota doctors published in the *New England Journal of Medicine* (NEJM) concluded that the diet drug Fen-Phen caused a very serious heart valve disease, a prominent public relations firm advised the manufacturer to "[e]nlist individual third parties to rebut allegations in . . . NEJM and provide balance to media coverage."[13] The company created an expert panel that included cardiologists from Harvard and Georgetown universities to evaluate the cases that were the subject of the publication.[14] The experts traveled to the city where the data were gathered, met with the researchers, examined their files, and, not surprisingly, reached a much different conclusion.[15] Sometimes the relevant industry will even send such panels on "road tours" to highlight the flaws at scientific meetings or other important venues.[16]

---

[10] Ibid.

[11] Ibid.

[12] Wendy E. Wagner, "Commons Ignorance: The Failure of Environmental Law to Produce Needed Information on Health and the Environment," *Duke Law Journal* 53, no. 6 (2004): 1653.

[13] Alicia Mundy, *Dispensing with the Truth: The Victims, the Drug Companies, and the Dramatic Story Behind the Battle Over Fen-Phen* (New York: St. Martin's Press, 2001), 105.

[14] Ibid., 109.

[15] Ibid., 109–10.

[16] Rampton and Stauber, 147.

## Harassing Scientists

Scientists who uncover important new discoveries are usually rewarded in the academic coin of peer recognition, and they sometimes receive prestigious monetary prizes. New scientific discoveries are not always greeted so warmly, however, by organized interests whose power and economic well-being depend upon status quo understandings of the natural world. Discoveries suggesting that certain products or activities pose environmental or health risks are likely to engender condemnation from scientists employed by companies whose products or activities might be adversely affected by the new research. Subtle industry-generated harassment of scientists impertinent enough to publish such adverse studies can take many forms, including complaints to the scientist's superiors, threats of lawsuits against the scientist and his institution, and scientific misconduct complaints addressed to funding agencies.

## Complaining to Superiors

Perhaps the easiest way to threaten a scientist is to complain to the scientist's superiors that the scientist is biased or otherwise incompetent in the hope that pressure from above will cause the scientist to modify or even retract his or her conclusions. For example, soon after Dr. Takeshi Hirayama published the first epidemiological study demonstrating that environmental tobacco smoke (ETS) caused an increased incidence of lung cancer in nonsmokers in the *British Medical Journal*, the Tobacco Institute wrote a letter to Dr. Hirayama's superior containing a stinging critique of Dr. Hirayama's ETS study.[17] Representatives of the U.S. tobacco industry then met privately with Dr. Hirayama's boss, Dr. T. Sugimura, in Japan to voice the industry's complaints more directly.[18] Sugimara was "remarkably frank" about Hirayama's work on ETS, suggesting that he had been "over ready to jump into publication without adequate scientific discussion first."[19] He later told the Tobacco Institute's public relations director that

[17] Thomas O. McGarity, "On the Prospect of 'Daubertizing' Judicial Review of Risk Assessment," *Law and Contemporary Problems* 66, no. 4 (2003): 190.
[18] Ibid., 185.
[19] Ibid., 185 (citing P. N. Lee, Notes on Visit to Japan: April 24th to May 1st [April 5, 1981] [Bates No. 504798208]).

he "was skeptical of the conclusion of the study, right from the start."[20] Although Hirayama remained at the institution, he had been severely undercut by his own boss.

## Threatening Lawsuits or Legal Process

A much more viable threat to the settled life of an academic scientist and a potentially devastating prospect for a small testing company is the threat of a major lawsuit. In 1986, Carlos Santos-Burgoa, an M.D. who was also a candidate for a Ph.D., conducted an epidemiological study concluding that workers exposed to high levels of butadiene were more than six times more likely to contract cancer than other similarly situated workers. The rubber industry, which had exposed its workers and neighbors to butadiene emissions, threatened to sue the university if it allowed Santos-Burgoa to use these data in his doctoral dissertation.[21] Similarly, when Randolph Byers, a pediatrician at the Boston Children's Hospital, discovered that children who had been successfully treated for lead poisoning were still experiencing profound learning problems, the lead industry threatened to file a million dollar lawsuit.[22] As Dr. Paul Fischer explains in Chapter 4 of this book, enmeshing scientists in the legal process through subpoenas and depositions has equally devastating effects. Although none of these scientists yielded to the threats, the more important but unanswered question is how many scientific studies have never seen the light of day because of such borderline extortion.

## Scientific Misconduct Complaints

Many years ago, Congress established the Office of Scientific Integrity (OSI) to investigate allegations that federally funded researchers have engaged in "scientific misconduct," including fabrication, falsification, plagiarism, and similar abuses of the scientific method.[23] Scientists in the employ of adversely affected industries have in the past attempted to use

---

[20] Ibid., 194 (citing Memorandum from William Kloepfer, to Wilson Wyatt et al. [June 17, 1981] [Bates No. TI0427–2866]).

[21] Davis, 140.

[22] Rampton and Stauber, 94.

[23] Scientific Misconduct Regulations, 42 C.F.R. §§ 50.102–3 (2004).

these formal disciplinary procedures to destroy the reputations of scientists who persist in publishing studies suggesting that their products and activities are potentially harmful.

For example, after Herbert Needleman published a study in the *New England Journal of Medicine* concluding that very low exposures in children to lead caused impaired mental development, a lead industry consultant filed a formal complaint against Needleman with EPA. After Needleman persuaded EPA that his report was correct, the consultant filed a formal scientific misconduct complaint with the National Institutes of Health alleging that Needleman had failed to cooperate with her and another industry consultant in their attempts to discredit his studies. Needleman's university then convened two separate inquiries after which it concluded although Needleman's research methods were "substandard," there was no evidence of scientific misconduct. The matter was then referred to OSI for still another hearing, after which OSI cleared Needleman of all of the scientific misconduct charges. The lead industry, however, continued to publicize the accusations.[24] Professor Needleman paid a terrible price for his temerity in taking on a wealthy and powerful industry. One chronicler of his saga notes that he "spent more than ten years and thousands of dollars facing repeated challenges, including demands for all his original data, legal subpoenas to reproduce his files, and efforts to discredit him personally." [25]

The Needleman case is by no means an isolated incidence of grotesque misuse of the scientific misconduct complaint process by anonymous accusers to cast doubt on science that threatens the economic well-being of an industry.[26] Scientists in the employ of risk-producing industries can easily enough claim that interpretations and analyses with which they disagree constitutes scientific misconduct, and it is very difficult and time-consuming for accused scientists to answer such charges.[27] Because scientific misconduct claims can be devastating to an academic career, enormous damage can be done even if the charges ultimately prove to

---

[24]  Davis, 127–9; Rampton and Stauber, 96–7.

[25]  Davis, 129.

[26]  Glenn Harlan Reynolds, "Thank God for the Lawyers: Some Thoughts on the (Mis)Regulation of Scientific Misconduct," *Tennessee Law Review* 66, no. 3 (1999): 808.

[27]  Paul M. Fischer, "Science and Subpoenas: When Do the Courts Become Instruments of Manipulation?" *Law and Contemporary Problems* 59, no. 3 (1996): 159, 166; Herbert L. Needleman, "Salem Comes to the National Institutes of Health: Notes from Inside the Crucible of Scientific Integrity," *Pediatrics* 90, no. 6 (1992): 977.

be groundless. On the other hand, there is no penalty for attacking a scientist's integrity with exaggerated or even wholly specious charges of scientific misconduct. Scientists contemplating research that might adversely affect the economic interests of risk-producing industries will no doubt think twice before they head down that road.

## Sponsoring Counter Research

The easiest, though perhaps not least expensive, way to "manufacture uncertainty" about a study is to sponsor additional studies on the same topic under conditions that are carefully controlled by the sponsoring company. This strategy is entirely consistent with the scientific norm of reproducibility, and it frequently has the added advantage of buying time while the additional study or studies are being completed. For example, the tobacco industry created the Center for Indoor Air Quality Research (CIAR) primarily to support scientific studies casting doubt on the conclusion that secondhand smoke caused adverse health effects in nonsmokers.[28] A study of publications covering CIAR-funded research concluded that those CIAR projects resulting from "special reviews" by industry officials, as opposed to reviews by scientific peers, were generally of poor quality and were more likely to support the tobacco industry's position.[29] Since the scientific data relevant to assessing health and environmental risks are nearly always subject to many interpretations, it is obviously useful to have some control over the interpretative exercise.

## Deconstruction through Reanalysis

When academic or government-sponsored research suggests that a company's products or activities pose unacceptable health and environmental risks, the company does not have immediate control over the relevant information. If the company can obtain the underlying data from the

---

[28] Monique Muggli et al., "The Smoke You Don't See: Uncovering Tobacco Industry Scientific Strategies Aimed against Environmental Tobacco Smoke Policies," *American Journal of Public Health* 91, no. 9 (2001): 1419; Elisa Ong and Stanton Glantz, "Tobacco Industry Efforts Subverting International Agency for Research on Cancer's Second-Hand Smoke Study," *Lancet* 355, no. 9211 (2000): 1253.

[29] Deborah E. Barnes and Lisa A. Bero, "Industry-Funded Research and Conflict of Interest: An Analysis of Research Sponsored by the Tobacco Industry through the Center for Indoor Air Research," *Journal of Health Politics, Policy and Law* 21, no. 3 (1996): 526.

relevant studies, however, it can hire its own scientific experts to "rean-alyze" the data in the expectation that the reanalysis will yield a different result. For example, when the Food and Drug Administration (FDA) pro-posed to regulate certain ephedra-based dietary supplements as drugs on the basis of the agency's own analysis of adverse event reports, an indus-try group in 2000 contracted with so-called "independent" toxicologists to conduct their own reviews of FDA's adverse event reports. The industry consultants concluded that any adverse effects were associated with misuse of ephedra and that it was safe when used correctly.[30] In light of this infor-mation and general pressure from the dietary supplement industry, FDA delayed regulating ephedra for four more years.[31]

It has not always been possible, however, for the industry to gain access to the underlying data. For example, when EPA in the late 1990s was revising the National Ambient Air Quality Standards for particulate matter, it relied heavily upon a large epidemiology study of mortality in six U.S. cities. The American Petroleum Institute, the electric utility industry, and the diesel trucking industry launched a major effort, assisted by Citizens for a Sound Economy and the Center for Regulatory Effectiveness, to characterize EPA's epidemiological work as "junk science."[32] As part of that effort, they demanded access to the underlying data to permit industry consultants to reanalyze the data, and they even dressed actors in lab coats and paid them to picket Harvard's School of Public Health with signs demanding that the researchers "Give us your data."[33]

As explained in greater detail by Professor Donald Hornstein in Chapter 5 of this book, the result of these shenanigans and similar tactics by the tobacco industry was congressional passage of a single-sentence rider, now referred to as the Data Access Act (DAA) to the four-thousand-page 1999 Appropriations Act.[34] The Act requires the Office of Management and

---

[30] Marion Nestle, *Food Politics: How the Food Industry Influences Nutrition and Health* (Berkeley, CA: University of California Press, 2002), 284.

[31] Final Rule Declaring Dietary Supplements Containing Ephedrine Alkaloids Adulterated Because They Present an Unreasonable Risk, 69 Fed. Reg. 6788 (Feb. 11, 2004) (to be cod-ified at 21 C.F.R. § 119).

[32] Davis, 151–2.

[33] Ibid., 154.

[34] Donald T. Hornstein, "Accounting for Science: The Independence of Public Research in the New Subterranean Administrative Law," *Law and Contemporary Problems* 66, no. 4 (2003): 230–8.

Budget (OMB) to amend its "Circular A-110," which governs discretionary federal grants, to "require Federal awarding agencies to ensure that all data produced under an award will be made available to the public through the procedures established under the Freedom of Information Act."[35] Since its enactment, the Act has survived at least two attempts at repeal.[36] The extent to which risk-producing industries are employing this new tool is unclear, because there is no central repository of data access requests under the Act. OMB may have discouraged abusive demands for data to some extent in its 1999 DAA compliance guidelines by limiting the scope of data requests to "published" studies and by allowing researchers to demand that data requesters pay the reasonable cost of responding to the requests.[37] The tool nevertheless remains available to industries set on challenging government studies, and no equivalent tool is available to public interest groups to demand the data underlying industry-funded studies that belittle health and environmental risks.

## The Corpuscular Approach

When a regulatory agency decides to take action to protect health or the environment from a risk-producing product or activity, it must be prepared to support that action with reasons and analysis. If it does not provide adequate support in the record for conclusions concerning the potential adverse effects of the regulated products or activities, adversely affected companies may challenge the agency action in court. If the reviewing court finds the action to be "arbitrary and capricious" in some regulatory contexts or unsupported by "substantial evidence" in others, the court must "set aside" the action, and the agency must start over again or just give up.[38]

---

[35] Omnibus Consolidated and Emergency Supplemental Appropriations Act of 1999, Pub. L. No. 105–277, 112 Stat. 2681 (1998); Richard Shelby, "Accountability and Transparency: Public Access to Federally Funded Research Data," *Harvard Journal on Legislation* 37, no. 2 (2000): 378–9.

[36] Hornstein, 231.

[37] Uniform Administrative Requirements for Grants and Agreements with Institutions of Higher Education, Hospitals, and Other Non-Profit Organizations, 64 Fed. Reg. 54,926, 54,930 (Oct. 8, 1999); Wendy E. Wagner, "The 'Bad Science' Fiction: Reclaiming the Debate over the Role of Science in Public Health and Environmental Regulation," *Law and Contemporary Problems* 66, no. 4 (2003): 70.

[38] Richard J. Pierce, Sidney A. Shapiro, and Paul R. Verkuil, *Administrative Law and Process* (St. Paul, MN: West, 2004).

Drawing upon a litigation strategy that has proven spectacularly successful in toxic tort litigation, risk-producing industries have recently adopted a "corpuscular" approach to challenging agency use of scientific information to support regulatory action.


## The Corpuscular Approach in Tort Litigation

In the seminal case of *Daubert v. Merrell Dow Pharmaceuticals, Inc.*, the Supreme Court of the United States held that federal district courts must perform a "gatekeeper" role in cases involving expert testimony.[39] Trial judges must determine whether expert testimony represents a sufficiently sound application of the relevant scientific principles to a sufficiently robust set of scientific data to justify the expert's scientific conclusions. At the same time, the trial judge must determine whether the "fit" between the scientific testimony and the issues raised by the parties is sufficiently tight to render that testimony legally relevant.[40] In a subsequent case, *General Electric Co. v. Joiner*, the Court suggested that the trial court had an obligation to evaluate the scientific validity of an expert's conclusions as well as the basis for those conclusions.[41] The Federal Rules of Evidence, which are applicable in all civil cases tried in federal courts, were then amended to incorporate the *Daubert/Joiner* approach to judicial assessment of expert testimony.[42]

As explored by Professor Carl Cranor in Chapter 6 of this book, most federal courts have reacted to these developments by adopting a corpuscular approach to determining the admissibility of expert testimony in toxic tort cases.[43] Under this approach, the party offering scientific expert testimony must establish the relevance and reliability under the *Daubert/Joiner* criteria of each individual study upon which the expert relies as well as the relevance and reliability of the expert's overall conclusions. If the plaintiff fails to establish the relevance and reliability of a sufficient number of the individual studies, the trial judge must exclude the expert's testimony.

---

[39]   *Daubert v. Merrell Dow Pharmaceuticals, Inc.*, 509 U.S. 579 (1993).
[40]   509 U.S. at 591, 593–5.
[41]   *General Electric Co. v. Joiner*, 522 U.S. 136 (1997).
[42]   FED. R. EVID. 702.
[43]   Erica Beecher-Monas, "A Ray of Light for Judges Blinded by Science: Triers of Science and Intellectual Due Process," *Georgia Law Review* 33, no. 4 (1999): 1067; McGarity, 155.

As a practical matter, under the corpuscular approach, the plaintiff must bear the burden of validating each of the studies relied upon by the plaintiff's experts as well as the burden of establishing the scientific reliability of their overall conclusions. This reality invites defendants to focus upon flaws in the corpuscles of data underlying the testimony rather than upon the scientific reliability of the expert's overall conclusions.

One of the best examples of the corpuscular approach in action is the Supreme Court's opinion in *General Electric v. Joiner*.[44] In that case, a man who had been exposed to PCBs offered the testimony of two experts to prove that the PCBs had probably caused his small cell lung cancer. Their testimony depended primarily upon on a laboratory animal study and four epidemiological studies. The Court found that animal study could not validly support a conclusion that PCBs were capable of causing cancer in humans because the animals were young (not middle-aged like the plaintiff), the route of administration was different (direct injection of single doses into the stomach as opposed to continuous dermal and inhalation exposure), the doses the animals received were much larger than the plaintiff's exposure, and the mice developed a different form of cancer.[45]

The four epidemiological studies upon which the plaintiff's experts relied were, according to the Court, likewise scientifically invalid for the purpose of demonstrating that PCB exposure could cause lung cancer in humans. In a study of lung cancer deaths in workers exposed to PCBs in an Italian capacitor factory, the authors of the study found "no grounds for associating lung cancer deaths (although increased above expectations) and exposure in the plant."[46] The plaintiff's experts could therefore not rely upon that study in any way, no matter what additional supporting scientific information it might contain. The same was true of a second study of workers exposed to PCBs at the Monsanto Corporation's Sauget, Illinois, PCB manufacturing facility. That study found the incidence of lung cancer among PCB-exposed workers to be "somewhat higher" than would ordinarily be expected," but not "statistically significant" in the authors'

---

[44] *General Electric Co. v. Joiner*, 522 U.S. 136 (1997).

[45] Ibid., 144–5.

[46] Ibid., 145 (quoting Pier Alberto Bertazzi et al., "Cancer Mortality of Capacitor Manufacturing Workers," *American Journal of Industrial Medicine* 11, no. 2 (1987): 165, 172. Neither the trial court nor the Supreme Court inquired into what might have motivated the authors to conclude that the PCB exposures were not associated with the lung cancers.

judgment.[47] The plaintiffs' experts were not permitted to disagree with the Monsanto scientists as to the level of statistical significance required to support a cause-effect conclusion.

Although the third study of Norwegian employees exposed to mineral oil in a cable manufacturing plant did report a statistically significant increase in lung cancer, the plaintiff's experts could not rely on it because it made no mention of PCBs.[48] The plaintiff's experts apparently believed that the mineral oil contained PCBs, as did much of the mineral oil produced at that time, but because the published study made no mention of PCBs, it was, in the Court's view, irrelevant. The fourth study detected a statistically significant increase in lung cancer deaths in a PCB-exposed human cohort in Japan. The Court nevertheless rejected that study, because the "subjects of this study . . . had been exposed to numerous potential carcinogens, including toxic rice oil that they had ingested."[49] Apparently, the Court concluded that the study's authors had not adequately accounted for this confounding factor, which is likely to be present in any Japanese cohort. The study was therefore invalid and could not support an overall conclusion that PCBs cause lung cancer in humans.

As the *Joiner* opinion demonstrates, the corpuscular approach effectively prevents the expert in toxic torts cases from applying the weight of the evidence approach that scientists typically employ in assessing the risks that toxic substances pose to human beings.[50] Under the weight of the evidence approach, the scientist considers all of the proffered studies and determines the weight to be afforded to each study on the basis of the identified strengths and weaknesses of that study. Some studies are so poorly conducted that they are entitled to no weight at all, but many studies that are otherwise flawed in one or more regards may be appropriately considered to the extent that they add to or detract from conclusions based upon studies in which the agency is inclined to place more confidence.[51]

---

[47] Ibid., 145. Again, neither the trial court nor the Supreme Court inquired into what might have motivated the authors (who no doubt undertook the study at the behest of the Monsanto Corporation) to conclude that the increase in lung cancer was not "statistically significant."

[48] Ibid., 145–6.

[49] Ibid., 146.

[50] Beecher-Monas, 1067; Lucinda M. Finley, "Guarding the Gate to the Courthouse: How Trial Judges Are Using Their Evidentiary Screening Role to Remake Tort Causation Rules," *Depaul Law Review* 49, no. 2 (1999): 336; McGarity, 165–7.

[51] Sanders, 1390.

The weight of the evidence approach focuses upon the totality of the scientific information and asks whether a cause-effect conclusion seems warranted. Given the inevitability of flaws in individual studies and the fact that some of the studies were not undertaken with the litigative or regulatory process in mind, this necessarily involves the exercise of scientific judgment grounded in scientific expertise. The corpuscular approach focuses upon the inevitable flaws in individual studies and asks whether a sufficient number of unflawed studies that are sufficiently relevant to the causation issue remain to support a conclusion that is in itself relevant and reliable. Under the corpuscular approach, a study is either valid or invalid, and it is either relevant or irrelevant. A conclusion based upon invalid or irrelevant studies cannot be relevant and reliable and must therefore be rejected.

## The Corpuscular Approach under the Data Quality Act

Like the Data Access Act, the Data Quality Act (DQA) (also known as the Information Quality Act) was an obscure rider to the Treasury and General Government Appropriations Bill for fiscal year 2001.[52] (Professor Donald Hornstein presents a more detailed discussion of this law and its implications in Chapter 5 of this book.) The rider required OMB to promulgate "policy and procedural guidance to Federal agencies for ensuring and maximizing the quality, objectivity, utility, and integrity of information . . . disseminated by Federal agencies." The agencies were in turn required to promulgate their own guidelines and establish procedures under which affected persons could "seek and obtain correction of information . . . that does not comply with the guidelines."[53]

As interpreted in OMB's 2002 Information Quality Guidelines,[54] the DQA appears to be an ideal vehicle for corpuscular attacks on the science underlying health and environmental regulatory decision making.

---

[52] Consolidated Appropriations Act of 2001, Pub. L. No. 106–554 § 515, 114 Stat. 2763, 2763A-153-154 (2000); Hornstein, 232; Sidney A. Shapiro, "The Information Quality Act and Environmental Protection: The Perils of Reform by Appropriations Rider," *William and Mary Environmental Law and Policy Review* 28, no. 2 (2004): 339.

[53] Information Quality Act, Pub. L. No. 106–554 § 515, 114 Stat. 2763A-153-154 (2000).

[54] Guidelines for Ensuring and Maximizing the Quality, Objectivity, Utility, and Integrity of Information Disseminated by Federal Agencies, Republication, 67 Fed. Reg. 8452 (Feb. 22, 2002).

Professor Wendy Wagner observes that DQA petitioners "can allege, through a formal process, that a study should be excluded from regulatory decisionmaking because it is too unreliable to be useful, an allegation taken more seriously if the study plays an 'influential' role in a policy decision."[55] This is, of course, precisely the objective of litigants employing the corpuscular approach under *Daubert/Joiner*. Professor Sidney Shapiro has noted "the potential that administrative appeals will become part of the litigation strategy of regulated entities to slow, or even stop, the government from disseminating information that is legally or politically inconvenient for them."[56] Not only is there a potential for such abuse, the opportunity to dismantle health and environmental regulation through corpuscular DQA challenges may be precisely what the lobbyists for the risk-producing industries who secured the appropriations rider had in mind. Although it is too soon to tell whether the strategy will ultimately be successful, many of the challenges that have been filed so far are, at the very least, troubling.

In early 2003, the Competitive Enterprise Institute, a think tank that has historically opposed national and international efforts to abate greenhouse gases, filed an DQA challenge in three agencies demanding that they "withdraw" the National Assessment on Climate Change (NACC), an interagency report on the role that greenhouse gases play in global warming.[57] Although the report had received extensive peer review and public vetting,[58] CEI nevertheless launched a classic corpuscular attack on various aspects of the report that were not, in CEI's view, based on "sound science."[59] After the White House Office of Science and Technology Policy (OSTP) denied CEI's petition, CEI sued President George W. Bush and the director of OSTP seeking a judicial ruling on the merits of its DQA challenge. The case subsequently settled when the federal government agreed to place a disclaimer on the NACC advising that it had not been prepared in accordance with the requirements of the DQA.[60] More recently, the Salt Institute and the Chamber of Commerce filed a lawsuit demanding

---

[55] Wagner, "The 'Bad Science' Fiction," 69.

[56] Shapiro, 358.

[57] Ibid., 359.

[58] National Research Council, *Climate Change Science: An Analysis of Some Key Questions* (Washington, DC: National Academy Press, 2001).

[59] Letter from Christopher C. Horner, Competitive Enterprise Institute, to Director of the Office of Science and Technology Policy (Feb. 20, 2003) (available at http://www.cei.org/pdf/3360.pdf).

[60] Shapiro, 360. *Salt Inst. v. Thompson*, 345 F. Supp. 2d 589 (E.D. Va. 2004).

that the court "invalidate" the action of the National Heart, Lung, and Blood Institute in "disseminating" two published articles concluding that reduced salt intake reduces blood pressure in humans. A panel of judges on the Fourth Circuit Court of Appeals dismissed the lawsuit on the basis that the Act does not create a "legal right" to correct information and that, therefore, plaintiffs lacked standing to challenge such action.[61]

Some corporate lawyers and academics have urged the courts to employ so-called *Daubert* principles in reviewing agency action.[62] Although no court has held that rejected Data Quality Act claims are independently subject to judicial review, the possibility that the courts will begin to apply so-called *Daubert* principles in reviewing agency risk assessments and regulations is a very real one. This would represent the final triumph of attack science, and it would no doubt portend a steady decline in the regulatory protections that federal agencies are able to provide to the potential victims of risky products and activities.

## Pushing Back: Strategies for Defending Science in Regulation

So far the risk-producing industries and their allies in academia and conservative think tanks have enjoyed an unbroken string of successes in their efforts to stymie the implementation of protective statutes by attacking the science underlying regulatory interventions. By contrast, the federal government has established very few formal defenses for scientists whose work is subjected to withering attacks from the lawyers and scientific consultants for risk-producing industries. Moreover, federal agencies themselves have adopted very few protections against corpuscular attacks on the science that they rely upon in regulating risky products and activities. Risk-producing industries have every incentive to "manufacture uncertainty" by challenging the science that agencies must rely on, and they have few incentives to

---

[61]  *Salt Institute v. Leavitt*, 4th Cir., CA-04-359-1 (March 6, 2006).
[62]  Paul S. Miller and Bert W. Rein, "'Gatekeeping' Agency Reliance on Scientific and Technical Materials after Daubert: Ensuring Relevance and Reliability in the Administrative Process," *Touro Law Review* 17, no. 1 (2000): 297; Alan Charles Raul and Julie Zampa Dwyer, "Regulatory Daubert: A Proposal to Enhance Judicial Review of Agency Science by Incorporating Daubert Principles into Administrative Law," *Law and Contemporary Problems* 66, no. 4 (2003): 7; D. Hiep Truong, "Daubert and Judicial Review: How Does an Administrative Agency Distinguish Valid Science from Junk Science?" *Akron Law Review* 33, no. 3 (2000): 365; Charles D. Weller and David B. Graham, "New Approaches to Environmental Law and Agency Regulation: The *Daubert* Litigation Approach," *Environmental Law Reporter* 30, no. 7 (2000): 10,557.

refrain from frivolous and even unconscionable attacks on scientific studies, the scientists who produce them, and the agencies that rely upon them. It is time for proponents of effective health and environmental regulation to begin pushing back against these abusive practices. The remainder of this chapter will suggest possible reforms for reducing the influence of attack science on health and environmental regulation.

## Disclose Sources of Attacks

A scientist engaged in such "attack science" strategies for pay should disclose his or her benefactor. Thus, scientists who are paid to write letters to the editor, demand underlying data from other scientists under the Data Access Act (DAA), publish or publicize reanalyses of data gathered by other scientists, or file scientific misconduct complaints against other scientists should disclose the identity of every entity that has retained them and in whose interest the scientist is acting. Similarly, scientists who prepare comments or participate in scientific advisory committee meetings, either as members of the committee or as commentators, should likewise disclose who is paying for their time. When scientists practice their trade for pay, rather than for the intellectual advancement of the enterprise, their peers should be aware of that fact.

## Repeal the Data Quality Act

In the two years since Data Quality Act (DQA) petitions began to stream into federal agencies, industry and trade organizations have expansively interpreted the rider, attacking any scientific information that they believe to be of insufficient quality. Indeed, industry groups appear to use the new procedures in a strategic manner to slow, or even stop, the release of information that might damage their economic interests.[63] Worst of all, the

---

[63] Letter from William G. Kelly, Center for Regulatory Effectiveness, to EPA Water Docket (Feb. 27, 2003) (available at http://www.thecre.com/pdf/20030310_biosolids.pdf); Request for Correction of "Guidance for Preventing Asbestos Disease among Auto Mechanics from Morgan Lewis and Bockius, to EPA Information Quality Guidelines Staff (Aug. 19, 2003) (available at http://www.epa.gov/quality/informationguidelines/documents/12467.pdf); Request for Correction of Information Contained in the Atrazine Environmental Risk Assessment from Kansas Corn Growers Association, the Triazine Network, and the Center for Regulatory Effectiveness, to EPA Information Quality Guidelines Staff 2 (Nov. 25, 2002) (available

DQA has become a vehicle for circumventing the substantive mandates of the nation's health and environmental laws. The statute's suspicious origins, the lack of any demonstrated need for its requirements, and numerous examples of its misuse all justify its repeal.

## Discourage Abuse of Data Quality Act Challenges

If Congress declines to repeal the DQA, OMB and the other agencies subject to that statute should establish procedures designed to discourage abuse of that ill-conceived process. At the very least, both the agencies and the general public should be fully aware of the real source of any DQA requests. In addition, entities demanding correction of data disseminated by regulatory agencies should have to bear the reasonable cost of complying with such demands.[64] Finally, Professor Wendy Wagner has suggested that one "straightforward" reform would be to "impose hefty sanctions for abuse" of the Act.[65]

## Discourage Abusive Data Access Requests

The OMB amendments to Circular A-110 attempt to protect the privacy of research subjects by exempting from the Data Access Act's disclosure requirements "medical information and similar information the disclosure of which would constitute a clearly unwarranted invasion of personal privacy."[66] The Circular also allows agencies to demand that data requesters pay the reasonable cost of responding to the requests.[67] Professor Wagner has suggested that Congress provide a cause of action on behalf of researchers on the receiving end of unfounded Data Access Act requests against the persons who filed such complaints. Researchers would be able to claim

---

at http://www.thecre.com/pdf/petition-atrazine2B.pdf); Request for Correction of "Technical Review of Diisononyl Phthalate" from the Center for Regulatory Effectiveness, to EPA Information Quality Guidelines Staff (Oct. 16, 2003) (available at http://www.epa.gov/quality/informationguidelines/documents/13166rfc.pdf).

[64] Wagner, "Commons Ignorance," 1735.

[65] Ibid.

[66] Uniform Administrative Requirements for Grants and Agreements with Institutions of Higher Education, Hospitals, and Other Non-Profit Organizations, 64 Fed. Reg. 54,926, 54,930 (Oct. 8, 1999).

[67] Ibid. Wagner, "The 'Bad Science' Fiction," 70.

"not only damages for their time and expense, but also a punitive award for any delays or adverse impacts on the progress of their research and reasonable attorney fees."[68] Congress should also consider adding a private cause of action against any companies or trade associations on whose behalf a consultant or "public interest" group files a claim.[69]

## Penalize Unfounded Scientific Misconduct Charges

Scientists who launch such attacks against fellow scientists as hired mercenaries should be required to disclose the identities of and the financial arrangements with the entities that have hired them. Even if scientists are not currently accepting compensation from a particular industry, they should reveal any past arrangements with entities that might be adversely affected by the studies produced by the scientist under attack and any expectation of future compensation. Finally, the scientists on the receiving end of such attacks should have a common law cause of action against scientists who file unfounded complaints of scientific misconduct and against the commercial entities in whose interests such complaints were lodged. Punitive damages should be available against the financial backers of unfounded charges of scientific misconduct.

## Enact Data Access Requirements for Corporate-Controlled Information

The Data Access Act is limited to federally funded studies that are used by regulatory agencies. The logical next step in the evolution of this statue is to extend its range to the private sector. Congress should amend the Data Access Act to provide access to the data underlying any scientific studies submitted by private entities to agencies in connection with regulatory agency proceedings insofar as those data are reasonably available to the entities that submit them. At the very least, the data underlying any studies paid for by a company on whose behalf the study is submitted to a regulatory agency should be made available to any participant in the regulatory proceedings. Finally, Congress should empower agencies to subpoena such

---

[68] Wagner, "Commons Ignorance," 1636.
[69] Ibid.

underlying data when companies refuse to submit them and allow other private entities to petition the agencies to issue such subpoenas.

## Oppose Regulatory *Daubert*

Whatever the merits of *Daubert* in the common law context, applying *Daubert*-like judicial review in the administrative law context is wholly unwarranted. Unlike judges, agencies have experience in evaluating the weight of the scientific evidence, and agencies are generally more adept at identifying unwarranted and abusive attacks on scientific studies and the scientists who produce them. Under the regulatory *Daubert* approach, corpuscular attacks stand a good chance of producing the desired result – a regulatory process malfunction. Courts should therefore resist the attempts of lawyers to challenge agency rule to invoke *Daubert*-like principles for judicial review, and Congress should reject attempts to impose regulatory *Daubert* on agencies by statute.

## Conclusion

Appeals to science are more persuasive in the political arena than appeals to economics because they are not so clearly made to advance the narrow interests of the companies that are making them. High-minded appeals to "sound science" are less easily construed as attempts to avoid accountability and shirk responsibility than appeals to economic self-interest. It is always possible that sound scientific information will point in the direction of increased liability or more stringent regulation. Advocates of "sound science" can rest assured, however, that in most of the litigative and regulatory battles, the rules of engagement are structured in such a way that appeals for more or better science will work to their advantage. Failing that, they have over the years developed a wide range of techniques for attacking scientific information that does not correspond to their economic needs. Left unchecked, this strategy will leave a legacy of regulatory neglect for future generations.

## 2

## Basic Science at Risk: Protecting the Independence of Research

Katherine S. Squibb, Ph.D.

There are in fact two things, science and opinion; the former begets knowledge, the latter ignorance.

– Hippocrates (460 – 377 B.C.)

### Independence as a Cornerstone of Science

When the National Research Council of the National Academy of Sciences outlined its recommendations for managing health risks and set up the risk assessment process in 1983, scientific knowledge of the effects of hazardous chemicals on biological systems was established as the cornerstone upon which risk assessment and risk management decisions would be made.[1] The purpose underlying this decision was to ensure that risk management decisions would be based on objective and honest assessments of the true health hazard of chemicals in our environments.

The wisdom of this decision is clear. Independent scientific research provides an unbiased assessment of a problem – in this case, a chemical's ability to cause adverse human and ecological health effects. As the National Research Council recognized, an objective determination of risk is critical to policy-based discussions regarding how much risk society is willing to accept and the subsequent need for regulations and cleanup activities.

Unfortunately, the independence that is at the core of good scientific research is being threatened by current day funding mechanisms for basic

---

[1] National Research Council, *Risk Assessment in the Federal Government: Managing the Process* (Washington, DC: National Academy Press, 1983), 191.

46

toxicology and environmental health research and the regulations that allow companies with financial interests in chemicals to be responsible for generating the scientific data needed for health risk assessments. Thus, an increasing number of sponsors of scientific research have a vested interested in the outcome of the research they fund, and research is often restricted to standardized testing protocols. This situation leads to a loss of flexibility, objectivity, and independence in a number of key areas, including study design, interpretation of results, and the sharing of results through publications and public presentations that allows the constructive exchange of ideas leading to new insights and investigations. These constraints are severely limiting advancements in our knowledge of the toxicity of chemicals and our ability to make accurate determinations of risk. In other words, science is being controlled by private interests to advance their own agendas rather than to arrive at basic truths that will ensure our protection.

Good science requires the absence of bias in the interpretation of results and the formulation of further studies. Unrestricted scientific research leads to discovery of truth and enhances our knowledge. Whether it is physics, chemistry, or biology, our current understanding of why things happen the way they do comes from centuries of scientific research in which scientists were "willing to abandon preferred hypotheses in the face of geological evidence."[2] The scientific method developed by Francis Bacon in the early 1600s is a method of induction that involves observation, hypothesis, and experimentation. Advancement of knowledge comes when results of experimentation are examined with an open mind to determine whether they are consistent with the hypothesis that was tested, or whether a different explanation – a new hypothesis – is needed. The key to making progress in science is the willingness and the ability to continue the research that leads one closer to the truth. Scientists must be independent in their judgment and make decisions free from outside pressure.

This chapter addresses the importance of independent research, or the protection of a scientist's ability to conduct research without unjustified restrictions. Neither research sponsors nor lack of funding for critical research needs should impose undue restrictions on study design, data interpretation, conclusions, and public release of results. The chapter

---

[2] Stephen J. Gould, "Creationism: Genesis vs. Geology," in *The Flood Myth*, ed. A. Dundes (Berkeley, CA: University of California Press, 1988), 434.

explains how the regulatory process has captured the science supporting chemical risk assessment and provides suggestions for remedying this unacceptable state of affairs. It begins with an introduction to risk assessment, the framework that dominates the scientific investigation of the threats to public health caused by toxic pollution. It then considers how sponsor-imposed restrictions on the design of basic studies and the reporting of their results can distort the information we gain from research efforts. The chapter suggests the steps we can take to ensure more independent research by preventing contractual arrangements that carry restrictions. It explores the importance of independent, public funding for basic research that can enhance our understanding of how chemicals move in the environment, threaten fragile ecosystems, and cause human health problems. Only under these circumstances will scientific investigations provide the depth and breadth of knowledge needed to support risk assessment and the protection of public health and natural resources adequately.

## Science-Based Risk Assessments

Risk assessments determine the level of risk associated with exposure to chemicals using a four-step process: exposure assessment, hazard identification, dose-response assessment, and risk characterization.[3] Exposure assessment gathers information on the pathways by which humans or animals are likely to be exposed to a chemical of concern in a given scenario and provides a quantitative determination of potential exposure doses. Hazard identification and dose-response assessment involve gathering available information on the toxicity of chemicals and characterizing the doses at which health effects occur. Risk characterization combines the information on expected exposure doses and dose-response relationships for each potential health effect to establish the risks associated with the release of chemicals into the environment under the defined conditions.[4]

Basic research strengthens each component of the risk assessment process. Prediction of the movement of chemicals released into the

[3] National Research Council, *Risk Assessment in the Federal Government, and Science and Judgment in Risk Assessment* (Washington, DC: National Academy Press, 1994).
[4] Joseph V. Rodericks, *Calculated Risks: Understanding the Toxicity of Chemicals in Our Environment* (New York: Cambridge University Press, 1992).

environment is based on our knowledge of fundamental physical, chemical, and biological processes that take place in the air, soil, and water. Research in atmospheric chemistry, for example, has greatly strengthened our ability to model the dispersion, formation, degradation, and fate of air pollutants, allowing better determinations of exposure doses. Accurate hazard identification is also highly dependent on the scientific research that determines how a chemical interferes with normal biological processes to alter cell metabolism and replication, with subsequent effects on organ system functions. Interactions between damaging chemicals and protective and repair mechanisms within cells determine the ultimate effects that occur from chemical exposures. Attempts to curtail or control scientific studies designed to provide knowledge of what effects occur at specific doses damage the risk assessment process at its core.

## Science, Policy, and Uncertainty

Once health risks are quantified based on science, risk managers and policy makers are responsible for determining how best to handle these risks. Management decisions are based on such factors as how much risk individuals and society are willing to accept, what benefits are gained by accepting these risks, and what monetary costs are associated with controlling the risks. In an ideal situation, calculations of risk and management of risks are independent processes. The line between science and policy in the present day, however, is often blurred, and scientists are pulled into the process to help make these "trans-science" decisions.[5] This is particularly true in discussions of how to handle uncertainties involved in risk calculations.

Uncertainties in risk determinations arise for a number of reasons. The precision with which health risks can be predicted for different chemicals varies depending on the extent to which they have been studied and our basic level of understanding of the mechanisms by which they cause their effects. Some of these uncertainties are due to statistical variations in experimental results and can be handled mathematically. Others arise from gaps in knowledge that exist because needed experiments have not

[5] Wendy E. Wagner, "The Science Charade in Toxic Risk Regulation," *Columbia Law Review* 95, no. 7 (1995): 1613.

been conducted. Ideally, recognition of these data gaps should help prior-
itize research needs and guide funding; however, the availability of funds,
both private and public, often restricts further research. Thus, scientists are
being asked to make judgments based on inadequate knowledge, and regulations become more policy-based and less science-based. As described
by Professor Wendy Wagner,[6] this "science charade" does science an injustice, because when the regulation does not hold up under scrutiny, it is
science – and scientists – that "take the rap." Throughout my career as
an academic scientist, I have seen fear of this outcome deter several capable scientists from becoming involved in chemical regulation issues; these
concerns even steer them away from conducting research in areas where
their expertise is needed most.

## Restrictions on Publication and Public Discussion of Results

If I have seen further, it is by standing on the shoulders of giants.
                                              – Issac Newton (1642–1727)

As explained by Professor Sheldon Krimsky in Chapter 3 of this book, the
most well-known constraint on research that limits the advancement of our
knowledge of chemical toxicity is restrictions on publication and public discussion of research findings imposed through contract stipulations by drug
companies sponsoring clinical trials. Large clinical trials most often take
place at multiple sites, including academic institutions as well as private
testing companies. While it makes sense to keep data confidential until
results from all the sites have been fully analyzed in order to prevent incorrect statements from being prematurely released, it is certainly not in the
public's best interest to keep the data confidential indefinitely. The impact
of this confidentiality can be that only results showing positive effects of
a drug (efficacy with the absence of toxicity or side effects) are published,
while research that is negative with respect to efficacy or that shows evidence of adverse effects is never released. Thus, the scientific community
does not have access to full data sets and, in fact, the results available for
review are biased with respect to the safety of the drug. It is only when dangerous side effects become apparent that investigations begin in an effort to

[6]  Ibid.

understand why these effects are occurring and whether they should have been recognized and prevented.

For example, in a recent case involving the use of antidepressants in children and adolescents, evidence began to emerge that the use of drugs such as Paxil, Zoloft, and Prozac was associated with an increased risk of suicide in young children.[7] When the scientists who had conducted clinical trials involving these drugs gathered to help determine whether data from the trials should have alerted the Food and Drug Administration (FDA) to this risk, drug companies resisted releasing all the data, insisting that the trials constituted confidential business information. These claims made it very difficult to continue the investigation.

Even if research findings are not needed to investigate the safety of a specific drug, the results of drug trials can be very valuable in general for understanding why some people react differently to drugs compared to the general population. If results of studies sponsored by drug companies were publicly available, subpopulations of people at greater risk of adverse side effects would more likely be identified early and problems with reactions to existing drugs could be prevented.

Restrictions on publishing and sharing results are not limited to the pharmaceutical industry. Chemical companies, including pesticide manufacturers and marketers, have also used such techniques. All pesticides sold in the United States must be registered for use by the Environmental Protection Agency (EPA). As part of the registration process, a company is required to provide EPA with information about the ecological and human health effects of the pesticide. Dose-response assessments that quantitatively relate exposure to potential health effects are a very important part of the risk determination that EPA conducts as part of the registration process.

As with clinical drug trials, most of the research conducted by pesticide companies to determine the toxicity of their products is contracted to either toxicology testing laboratories or research laboratories within universities. In cases where specific EPA requirements and protocols do not constrain these tests, manufacturers sometimes enjoy considerable freedom to control the resulting research.

---

[7] Barry Meier, "Contracts Keep Drug Research Out of Reach," *New York Times*, Nov. 29, 2004, sec. A.

A recent example of a clash between a researcher wishing to publish results that he felt would help the scientific community in its understanding of the toxicity of endocrine disruptors and company control of the publication of "its" data occurred in a developmental biology laboratory at the University California, Berkeley. In a series of studies conducted to determine the safety of the commonly used herbicide atrazine in support of its re-registration by EPA, Dr. Tyrone Hayes obtained results that suggested that effects of this chemical on sexual development in frogs occurred at much lower doses than expected.[8] Dr. Hayes was prevented from publishing these findings due to wording in his contracts from Syngenta, the company marketing atrazine, and EcoRisk, a consulting company that hired him on behalf of Syngenta to conduct the atrazine studies. Only after Dr. Hayes repeated his studies with research funds from other sources was he able to publish his findings.[9]

## Public Disclosure of Research Results

Why do universities and academic scientists sign nondisclosure contracts that limit the freedom of their faculty to publish when publishing is so important to the advancement of science? The fact that a substantial portion of funds available for research these days lies in the private sector is the primary driving force. Many academic institutions are becoming more and more dependent on industry money for research support, and competition among research laboratories is high.

Universities could work cooperatively to develop a standard contract that would be used for all corporate-funded studies to preserve their right to publish research results without sponsor approval. However, private sector funders have resisted this approach.[10] Since changes are not likely to occur through voluntary means, Congress should consider legislation to prohibit

---

[8]  Goldie Blumenstyk, "The Story of Syngenta abd Tyrone Hayes at UC Berkeley: The Price of Research," *Chronicle of Higher Education* 50, no. 10 (2003): A26.

[9]  Tyrone B. Hayes et al., "Atrazine-Induced Hermaphroditism at 0.1 ppb in American Frogs (*Rana pipiens*): Laboratory and Field Evidence," *Environmental Health Perspectives* 111, no. 4 (2003): 568; Tyrone B. Hayes et al., "Hermaphroditic, Demasculinized Frogs after Exposure to the Herbicide Atrazine at Low Ecologically Relevant Doses," *Proceedings of the National Academy of Sciences* 99, no. 8 (2002): 5476–80.

[10]  Meier.

study sponsors from placing contractual restrictions on the release of studies when they do not like the results.

A report issued by the Carnegie Commission on Science, Technology, and Government in the early 1990s highlighted the need for making chemical toxicity data publicly available if human health and our environment are to be adequately protected.[11] One of the major recommendations for improving regulatory decision making was the creation of a shared database of health effects data. However, the Commission noted that legal protections of confidential business information pose a substantial impediment to data sharing and analysis. The Commission recommended that Congress and regulatory agencies modify provisions and practices to curtail the protection of confidential business information as much as possible.

One straightforward approach to these issues would be to require that all studies used to support EPA or FDA approvals or other regulatory decisions must be published in the open literature. This requirement would ensure that the experimental design, results, and conclusions of the studies generating the data are peer-reviewed, and they would be available to help guide other scientists in their toxicology research.

Since clinical trial studies are conducted at multiple sites, researchers would have to decide whether each site would publish separately or whether a publication combining results from all the sites involved in the study would be required. Scientists would also have to overcome resistance to publishing negative data because the absence of an effect in toxicity testing is just as important a finding as a positive effect for risk assessment purposes. Toxicology and environmental health journals would have to recognize this phenomenon and encourage publication of such studies.

Although publishing is an important step toward full disclosure, a requirement to publish would not assure access to the full data sets, but only a summary of the results. Thus, support for the development of a public database continues to grow. In response to pressure to release their data, some drug companies have volunteered to post their data on their own websites or on a site created by the Pharmaceutical Research and Manufacturers Association, although many companies have not yet fulfilled these

---

[11] Carnegie Commission on Science, Technology, and Government, *Risk and the Environment: Improving Regulatory Decision Making*, (New York: Carnegie Commission on Science, Technology, and Government, 1993), 150.

promises. Medical associations such as the American Medical Association and the Association of American Medical Colleges are also supporting the mandatory reporting of clinical trial results in a public database operated by the federal government.[12]


## Restrictions on Study Design

The important thing in science is not so much to obtain new facts as it is to discover new ways of thinking about them.

— Sir William Bragg (1892–1942)

Restrictions placed on the design of studies conducted to determine the toxicity of chemicals are probably the most damaging to the scientific community's attempts to characterize accurately the risk associated with exposure to hazardous chemicals. Unfortunately, this larger problem is actually being driven, in part, by the risk assessment process itself. Because one of the most critical parts of a risk assessment is the determination of the lowest dose at which health effects occur, a substantial amount of money and energy is expended on conducting and interpreting dose-response studies for specific chemicals; in contrast, relatively few resources are focused on mechanistic studies that tell us how chemicals cause damage to living systems.

The golden rule in classical toxicology is that dose-response curves are linear; thus studies with decreasing doses should be able to establish the lowest dose that causes adverse effects (known as the lowest observed adverse effect level, or LOAEL) and the dose at which no adverse effects occur (the no observed effect level, or NOEL). State and federal regulatory agencies then use these values to develop standards and guideline values.

When data from experiments do not conform to this expectation – that is, they do not show a classical dose-response curve – a rational reaction of individuals with a financial interest in the results is to discount the validity of the study, especially when the low doses in the tests indicate greater effects than the higher doses. If research were allowed to proceed as it should, investigations would continue to determine whether the unexpected effects at low doses are due to problems with the experiment or whether they

---

[12] Meier.

are an indication that the action of the chemical at low doses is not well understood. In science, data from one experiment should guide the design of future studies that will test whether the currently accepted hypothesis about the way a chemical is acting is indeed true.

Unfortunately, researchers funded by corporations to provide data for EPA review most often cannot independently design their next experiment due to contract limitations. The design of their research studies is determined by the corporation or possibly a working group formed to investigate the toxicity of the chemical. If the financial stakes are high, the results of the study showing effects at low concentrations may be discounted pending reanalysis. Studies are repeated in different ways to prove or disprove the original results. Such reanalysis often takes more time and money than basic research studies designed to identify the mechanism of action of the chemical at the lower doses. This mechanistic research could help determine whether the results of the original study were artifactual or real more quickly, in addition to advancing our knowledge about different ways chemicals can act to alter biological systems. Yet, unless there is a clear financial benefit to be gained from conducting mechanistic research – for example, the opportunity to rebut the protective presumption that the safe dose to a carcinogen is zero – the private sector is unlikely to bear the financial burden for doing this basic research. Some are fearful of opening up a new "can of worms" for their product if unknown mechanisms of toxicity are identified at low dose exposures. Yet the importance and utility of such research is well recognized in the scientific community.

## Two Case Studies

Two case studies provide examples of the need for independent, mechanistic research on chemicals that act as endocrine disruptors, that is, chemicals that alter normal physiological processes by either acting as hormones themselves or by inhibiting normal hormone activity. Because hormones function by binding to receptor molecules in cells or within cell membranes, very low concentrations of a hormone are required for activity. Also, the synthesis and release of most hormones are highly regulated by intricate feedback mechanisms, which allow fine control over hormone-dependent functions. Thus, chemicals able to bind to hormone receptors or alter hormonal regulation can do so at very low concentrations.

## Atrazine

Consider once again the recent controversy over the herbicide atrazine. Disputes over the effects of atrazine at low exposure doses revolves around its ability to increase the synthesis of the enzyme aromatase, which converts the male sex hormone, testosterone, to the endogenous estrogen, 17β-estradiol.[13] As mentioned earlier, results reported by Tyrone Hayes and coworkers from his laboratory at the University of California, Berkeley, showed that atrazine exposure resulted in retarded gonadal development and testicular oogenesis (hemaphroditism) in frogs exposed during larval development at 0.1 ppb, a concentration that is thirty times lower than levels currently allowed by EPA.

Multiple studies have since been conducted to determine whether these results at the low 0.1 ppb dose can be repeated. Some showed similar effects, while others failed to reproduce the results reported by Hayes' research group.[14] At the heart of this controversy, though it is seldom mentioned in this debate, is *how* atrazine regulates the synthesis of aromatase, and whether this change is indeed the mechanism by which atrazine disrupts gonadal development. The regulation of protein synthesis involves receptor binding and a cascade of intracellular events that eventually lead to increased gene expression. Multiple factors can regulate the synthesis of proteins, working in concert or antagonistically to each other.

The mixed results that have been obtained from low-dose atrazine exposure studies most likely reflect differences in experimental conditions that alter the response to the herbicide in ways that are currently unknown. Mechanistic studies that teach us more about the induction of aromatase and the control of estrogen synthesis by aromatase during larval development in amphibians would answer many of our questions about why it

[13] D. Andrew Crain et al., "Alterations in Steroidogenesis in Alligators (*Alligator mississipiensis*) Exposed Naturally and Experimentally to Environmental Contaminants," *Environmental Health Perspectives* 105, no. 5 (1997): 528–33; J. Thomas Sanderson et al., "Effects of Chloro-s-triazine Herbicides and Metabolites on Aromatase Activity in Various Human Cell Lines and on Vitellogenin Production in Male Carp Hepatocytes," *Environmental Health Perspectives* 109, no. 10 (2001): 1027–31.

[14] Environmental Protection Agency, "The Interagency Steering Committee (IPSC)," (http://www.epa.gov/safewater/ccl/perchlorate/ipsc.html); Marcus Hecker, "Plasma Sex Steroid Concentrations and Gonadal Aromatase Activities in African Clawed Frogs (*Xenopus laevis*) from South Africa," *Environmental Toxicology and Chemistry* 23, no. 8 (2004): 1996; Rebecca Renner, "Conflict Brewing over Herbicide's Link to Frog Deformities," *Science* 298, no. 5595 (2002): 938–9.

has been difficult to get reproducible results at low doses of atrazine. They would provide more reliable answers than continued efforts to duplicate Hayes' work.

The reason that these mechanistic studies have not been conducted comes back to the fact that atrazine research is primarily funded by contracts from Syngenta through EcoRisk. Under most contracts, study design is clearly laid out and the work must follow predetermined protocols. These constraints impede investigators from running additional studies to determine why results were different from those expected. To conduct mechanistic work, scientists must find funding from other sources, which is no easy task at a time when federal research budgets are shrinking.

## Perchlorate

Perchlorate is another controversial environmental contaminant with possible neurodevelopmental effects at low exposure doses. Perchlorate, a component of rocket fuel, has seeped into drinking water supplies throughout the country. The primary known mode of action of perchlorate (an anion composed of chlorine and oxygen [$ClO_4^-$]) is the inhibition of iodide uptake by the thyroid gland. This uptake is required for the synthesis of thyroid hormones ($T_3$ and $T_4$). In addition to its role in many other functions, thyroid hormones are required for normal neurological development in utero and in young children.[15] Alteration of this function appears to be the most sensitive effect at low-dose exposures to perchlorate.

Over the past few years, the EPA risk assessment for perchlorate has undergone review after review. The controversy has revolved around results showing greater adverse effects at lower doses than at higher doses with respect to the size of the brain regions of offspring of the mothers that ingested the chemical. Some scientists have argued that the non-linearity of the dose-response curve raises a flag regarding the validity of the data. On the other hand, some scientists have suggested different hypotheses for those results that should be tested, because, once again, the regulation of hormone levels and the hormonal regulation of fetal development are sensitive to many balancing factors that are both known and unknown.

---

[15] R. Thomas Zoeller et al., "Thyroid Hormone, Brain Development, and the Environment," *Environmental Health Perspectives* 110, no. S3 (2002): 355–61.

The freedom and the funding to conduct research addressing hypotheses that could explain the low dose, non-linear responses observed for perchlorate would greatly help move the risk assessment process forward and give greater confidence in its conclusions. The determination of what studies are funded for perchlorate research to address gaps in our knowledge, however, is under the control of the Interagency Perchlorate Steering Committee.[16] This Committee decides what studies should be conducted to finalize the perchlorate risk assessment, taking control of experimental design away from the research scientists conducting the studies. Unfortunately, the Committee includes representatives from the Department of Defense, which will ultimately be responsible for the expensive cleanup of perchlorate-contaminated surface and groundwater because it was the major purchaser and user of the rocket fuel that is the source of such contamination. The control exerted by the military and its contractors over the way this research is conducted inserts the potential for bias in the planning and decision-making process.

## Restoring Scientific Independence

As the preceding examples illustrate, we have made the mistake of letting risk assessment needs drive the science that supports our understanding of chemical health effects rather than ensuring that scientific research drives improvements in our ability to assess risks associated with chemical exposures correctly. To return to a strong science-based paradigm, we need to change the way research needs are identified and funded.

The primary reason that a large portion of our toxicology and environmental health research today is conducted under restrictive contracts rather than grants, which allow researchers greater freedom to develop hypotheses and design studies in response to their results, is that federal regulatory agencies such as EPA and FDA do not have sufficient research budgets to support all the research needed to address the environmental health problems facing our nation. Thus, the financial burden of establishing safe exposure doses of chemicals has been placed on corporations that are seeking approval for marketing new chemicals or negotiating permits for chemical releases to the environment, or that are responsible for cleaning up chemically contaminated environmental resources.

[16] Environmental Protection Agency, "The Interagency Steering Committee (IPSC)."

While this burden shifting seems, at first, to make good economic sense, it has created a situation in which money spent to obtain knowledge about the toxicity of a chemical supports only studies that address specific needs rather than independent research. These needs are generated by the way we regulate risk rather than what we need to know to assess it accurately. There is a much stronger emphasis on simply testing to determine dose-response relationships of known effects of chemicals, as opposed to basic research into mechanisms that can explain discrepancies in standard dose-response studies and possibly identify unknown effects. And, as Professor John Applegate explains in Chapter 12 of this book, even this type of applied research is scant when the laws do not mandate that it be produced. A more careful balance between standard dose-response toxicity testing and mechanistic research must be established.

The potential for bias in the interpretation of results and study design also creeps in when groups with vested financial interests control research decisions. Companies funding the research have far too many opportunities to obtain results favorable to their interests by supporting certain studies and not others. Often it is the absence of information that increases our vulnerability to new or unknown chemicals. We need to review existing laws and regulations to ensure that opportunities to control study protocols do not prevent thorough investigations of toxicological effects. An important step in devising a solution is to require the incorporation of mechanistic research into risk assessment studies. Federal agencies must also have greater control over defining research needs and making funding decisions.

In addition to increasing federal funding for mechanistic research, another important reform would be to mandate that research funds provided by regulated companies be administered by an impartial board in consultation with the appropriate federal regulatory agency. To coordinate studies and share risk information, the board should integrate its activities with the National Toxicology Program (NTP), a federal program within the Department of Health and Human Services (DHHS). The NTP was formed in 1978 with a charge that included the coordination of toxicology testing programs within public health agencies and the strengthening of the scientific basis of toxicological knowledge.[17] Its mission is to integrate

---

[17] Victoria McGovern, "National Toxicology Program: Landmarks and the Road Ahead," *Environmental Health Perspectives* 112, no. 15 (2004): A874–8.

the activities of other federal agencies involved in protection of public health, including the National Institute of Environmental Health Sciences (NIEHS), the National Institute for Occupational Safety (NIOSH), and the Food and Drug Administration (FDA) National Center for Toxicological Research (NCTR). This mission should be expanded to include oversight of research boards to ensure that toxicology research is protected from restrictions and undue bias.

# 3

## Publication Bias, Data Ownership, and the Funding Effect in Science: Threats to the Integrity of Biomedical Research

Sheldon Krimsky, Ph.D.

### The Social Context of Science

The noun *science* and all of its adjectival forms confers a sense of authority to its associated activities. Nearly everyone wants to be on the side of "good science." Environmental agencies speak of "science-based" policy, while the Food and Drug Administration (FDA) and many professional societies identify themselves with "evidence-based" medicine. Strong disagreements among scientists can create a cognitive dissonance within the popular culture. Yet, despite its authoritative position, the system of science – consisting of research and educational institutions, certified practitioners, journals and funding agencies – is embedded in a social context. The elements that make up this context can influence the questions that get asked, the studies that get funded, the results that get published, and the biases that enter into scientific practice and impair its quality.

The normative structure of science has evolved over centuries, beginning with the Enlightenment, continuing through the development of nation-states and the rise of international scientific societies, and during the current era of globalization. That structure includes a shared set of goals for uncovering the truths about the natural world, the recognition that science is a social activity that demands openness and transparency of claims and evidence, and the commitment to an epistemology that embodies a standard of empirical verifiability for certifying knowledge claims.

The pursuit of objective and verifiable knowledge can be derailed by social determinants and ideology that view science as a means to an end, rather than as an end in itself. For this reason, when science serves more than one master or when the pursuit of truth is only one of several motivations, deviance from the normative standards can be observed.

This chapter examines some of the essential requirements for the healthy functioning of science and draws attention to the deviance from those conditions, with special consideration given to the biomedical sciences. The chapter applies the overarching principles of scientific independence that are a major element of the framework for this book: To produce "healthy science," scientists must be able to conduct research without unjustified restrictions from private sponsors or government, including unwarranted influence in the research protocols, the data analysis, and the interpretation or publication of results. This means that research must never be suppressed because it produces results that are adverse to a sponsor or other interested party. Scientists should remain free to time the disclosure of data or the results of ongoing research unless the research could help address pressing public health problems or is otherwise submitted to the government as a basis for regulatory decisions. Clinical investigators must be free to report adverse effects of experimental drugs or to withdraw human subjects from a trial without fear of being sued. Sponsors must never place restrictions or otherwise influence the design or conduct of a study in an attempt to obtain results favorable to their interests. No publication or summary of research should ever be influenced – in tone or content – by the sponsoring entity. And finally, vested interests, who use the legal system to harass scientists whose research or expert testimony calls into question the safety of their practices or products, must be held accountable with sanctions and, in some cases, must compensate injured scientists for the resulting interference with their research and damage to their reputations.

This chapter begins by establishing the foundation for these principles of healthy science with a review of what philosophers and sociologists of science have contributed to our understanding of the nature of scientific knowledge and its normative structure. Second, the chapter discusses some recent trends that intrude on the integrity of science, such as the loss of disinterestedness, the lack of openness, and the commingling of science with the production of wealth. Third, it explores the "funding effect" in science and discusses its implications in the social enterprise of knowledge production. The funding effect provides empirical evidence of some adverse consequences that flow from recent intrusions on healthy science. Finally, the chapter suggests some remedies to restore integrity to the biomedical sciences.

## Normative Underpinnings of Science

### Community of Inquirers

Science is a way of knowing and generating reliable knowledge about the physical universe, including both natural and social phenomena. It is one of several ways of fixing belief about the empirical world, as noted by philosopher Charles Pierce in his famous essay, "The Fixation of Belief."[1] Pierce contrasted science with authoritarianism, intuition, and folk knowledge. We can add to that list sacred texts or knowledge by plebiscites.

Science has several features that distinguish it from the other forms of fixing belief. Unlike the fixation of belief by appeal to authority, scientific claims must be certified through a community of inquirers. For each subfield of science, the community of inquirers shares a methodology that might include measuring instruments, theoretical frameworks, nomenclature, quantitative methods of analysis, and canonical principles for interpreting data.

In contrast to intuitive ways of knowing or the appeal to sacred texts, scientific methodology must be transparent and available to anyone familiar with the art of inquiry for that subdiscipline. The democracy of science demands a transparency of methods and data. This transparency is the premise behind open publication. Where possible, those properly trained in the art of scientific inquiry should be able to replicate the outcome of an experiment, which implies a sharing of techniques and materials.

In science there is no room for "unquestionable authority." No one in science can claim infallibility. Biologist Howard Temin underscored this point in an interview with historian Horace Freeland Judson. "When an experiment is challenged no matter who it is challenged by, it's your responsibility to check. That is an ironclad rule of science, that when you publish something you are responsible for it... even the most senior professor if challenged by the lowliest technician or graduate student, is required to treat them seriously and to consider their criticisms."[2]

---

[1] Charles Pierce, "The Fixation of Belief," *Popular Science Monthly* 12 (Nov. 1877): 1–15.
[2] Horace Freeland Judson, *The Great Betrayal* (New York: Harcourt, 2004), 242.

## The Private Use of Science

The methods or discoveries of science should not be restricted to private use. That outcome is inconsistent with its communitarian enterprise. The commercialization of some areas of science can occur more readily under the newly liberalized intellectual property rules. For example, when Stanley Cohen of Stanford and Herbert Boyer of the University of California at San Francisco discovered a method of recombining and transferring DNA (recombinant DNA molecule technology), their respective institutions took out a patent for the technique. The institutions decided against restrictive licensing of the technique, which made it available to all users at a modest fee. Had they decided to offer restrictive licenses for the genetic engineering technique to a few companies, the progress of science would have suffered severely.

In her book *University, Inc.*, Jennifer Washburn reminds us of the work of Richard Nelson and Kenneth Arrow regarding the economic benefits of treating scientific methods and discovery as a nonrivalrous good that should be part of the knowledge commons. Nelson and Arrow reasoned that the public interest would be best served if most of this nonrival, basic science remained in the public domain, because any policies restricting access to that knowledge (such as exclusive licenses or secrecy provisions) would only impose substantial costs on the excluded parties, and on the economy as a whole, by stifling open competition and invention activity.[3] When scientific methods or seminal discoveries are patented, academic scientists, wishing to use the results, are not protected by a legislated research exemption, as they are in other countries. The concept of a free and open scientific inquiry has been hampered by patenting of genes and other techniques, particularly when exclusive licenses are issued.

## Freedom to Advance Theories

Science must be open to alternative hypotheses, interpretations of data, and theories that account for similar observations or facts. In a healthy scientific environment, even the marginalized and unpopular theories should have access to publications because those theories and explanations may

---

[3] Jennifer Washburn, *University, Inc.* (New York: Basic Books, 2005), 62.

someday become the orthodoxy. This access was the case when two relatively unknown Australian physicians, Barry Marshall and Robin Warren, formulated the hypothesis that gastritis and peptic ulcers were caused by the colonization of H. pylori bacteria in the intestinal tract.

The physicians met enormous opposition to their theory. To test his belief, Marshall had infected himself with the bacteria to demonstrate the cause. His published account of his self-induced ulcers and their successful treatment with antibiotics was not sufficient in itself to change the entrenched beliefs among gastroenterologists that ulcers were a stress-related disease. Skepticism toward the bacterial theory persisted until a controlled study comparing acid blockers and a placebo clearly demonstrated the success of antibiotics in the treatment, corroborating the bacterial theory of ulcers.[4] Marshall and Warren were awarded the 2005 Nobel Prize in Physiology or Medicine.

## Self-Correction

Science must be able to correct itself. It is thus unlike religion or political ideology, which are static, doctrinaire belief systems that are immutable to new information, and refractory to contradictory evidence. Science must be self-reflecting of its own biases and limitations and of its own errors. Unlike political institutions, scientific culture must have a systematic process of admitting mistakes and reporting them.

Science must strive for logical consistency. The fundamental rules of logic tell us that from a contradiction, you can derive any proposition. We cannot have a reliable system of beliefs where everything holds, where both P and not-P are true at the same time. Just as nature abhors a vacuum, science abhors a contradiction.

## Universal Truths

In healthy science, the results must stand as universal rather than as supporting distinct truths about natural phenomena according to different cultures. The physical and toxicological properties of benzene are not

---

[4] Terrence Monmaney, "Marshal's Hunch: Annals of Medicine," New Yorker (Sept. 20, 1993): 64–72.

culture-specific. Although the effects of benzene may be genotype-specific, there is no male science and female science, or Japanese science and American science as regards the knowledge of the physical world. However, there may be different cultural paths of inquiry or alternative means (models and metaphors) to describe the physical world.

Healthy science distinguishes the path to truth claims from the validation of those claims. According to the philosopher Karl Popper, the source of the origin of a hypothesis is distinct from the conditions of its validity. He wrote in *The Logic of Scientific Discovery*, "I shall distinguish sharply between the process of conceiving a new idea, and the methods and results of examining it logically."[5] Revelation or divine inspiration may be a means to discover scientific truths, but it is not a satisfactory test of their soundness. "So long as a theory [or hypothesis] stands up to the severest tests we can design, it is accepted; if it does not, it is rejected."[6]

Trust plays an essential role in the healthy functioning of science. We trust that researchers will record their data accurately and that they will not fabricate data or fudge results. Replication of studies is costly and rarely done. In his book *Real Science*, Dr. John Ziman notes: "Amongst working scientists, this trustworthiness is part of the moral order of each research community. The complex interplay of originality and skepticism that operates in such groups requires absolute impersonal trust on matters of empirical 'fact.'"[7] Trust can be undermined when scientists are working in an environment replete with incentives for secrecy or misconduct. Any confounding interests that can compromise the penultimate goal of getting at the truth will begin to diminish the integrity of and public confidence in the scientific enterprise.

## Tendencies Toward Deviant Science

The social system of science and the society in which it is embedded must be concordant with the general principles behind healthy science. An authoritarian and undemocratic society will not be compatible with open,

[5] Karl R. Popper, *The Logic of Scientific Discovery* (New York: Harper, 1959), 3.
[6] Karl R. Popper, *Conjectures and Refutations: The Growth of Scientific Knowledge*, 54.
[7] John Ziman, *Real Science* (Cambridge, UK: Cambridge University Press, 2000), 98.

unfettered science. More than likely, such societies will impose false beliefs such as "abortions result in higher rates of breast cancer," or "small doses of dioxins are actually good for our health," regardless of what the data show. The factors that foster deviance within science are complex. In different historical periods, ideology, the exigencies of war, the lust for power and prestige, and the pursuit of wealth have all contributed to aberrant behavior with respect to the normative structure of science. This section explores how commercial interests in the biomedical sciences have preempted the traditional norms of scientific practice.

## Withholding Scientific Data and Discoveries

Withholding of information violates the communitarian norm of science. It also limits the possibilities for self-correction. Among the major tributaries of biomedical science are drug companies that sponsor clinical trials. Withholding of clinical trial data that would be financially harmful to a company seems to be commonplace. It has added to publication bias in certain fields of clinical medicine. In March 2004, the *Canadian Medical Association Journal* reported that one of the world's largest drug companies withheld clinical trial findings in 1998 that indicated the antidepressant paroxetine (known as Paxil in North America) had no beneficial effect on treating adolescents. A company memorandum (revealed from discovery documents in litigation) stated: "It would be commercially unacceptable to include a statement that efficacy had not been demonstrated, as this would undermine the profile of paroxetine."[8]

Drug manufacturers also withheld trial results of antipsychotic drugs that showed increases in suicidal behavior and other adverse side effects. It is well documented that there is a preponderance of positive company-sponsored studies, with no clear explanation – only the plausible hypothesis that companies suppress results that are not in their financial interests. Occasionally, companies have used legal threats to prevent publication of negative data in studies they had sponsored.

[8] Wayne Kondro and Barbara Sibbald, "Drug Company Experts Advised Staff to Withhold Data about SSRI Use in Children," *Canadian Medical Association Journal* 170, no. 5 (2004): 783.

Because drug companies sponsor many multistage clinical trials, these companies can restrict scientific communication between sites. This practice can sometimes lead to missed opportunities to protect human subjects from dangerous drug side effects. One company stated publicly that it adopted guidelines in which it would commit to publish the results of certain clinical trials involved in hypothesis testing – which excludes testing the safety of the drug.[9]

The new guidelines issued by the pharmaceutical industry organization PhRMA states that

> Individual investigators in multi-site clinical trials will have their own research participants' data...any investigator who participated in the conduct of a multi-site clinical trial will be able to review relevant statistical tables...for the entire study at the sponsor's facilities...Sponsors have the right to review any manuscripts, presentations, or abstracts that originate from our studies or that utilize our data before they are submitted for publication or other means of communication.[10]

These are supposedly the "best" guidelines in the industry – and they are purely voluntary.

Data ownership and control by sponsors of clinical trials circumvent the authority and responsibility of the investigator and may compromise the care given to human subjects involved in the trial. Many institutions continue to permit contracts that allow sponsors to review research before it is published, to edit the prepublication manuscript, and to decide when the study should be released for publication. One survey of biomedical scientists found that those who received funding from industry were "significantly more likely to delay publication of their research results by more than 6 months to allow for the commercialization of their research."[11]

---

[9] Laurence Hirsch, "Randomized Clinical Trials: What Gets Published, and When?" *Canadian Medical Association Journal* 170, no. 4 (2004): 481.

[10] Pharmaceutical Research and Manufacturers of America, "Principles on Conduct of Clinical Trials and Communication of Clinical Trial Results," 22–3 (June 30, 2004) (available at http://www.phrma.org/publications/publications//2004–06–30.1035.pdf).

[11] Eric G. Campbell et al., "Managing the Triple Helix in the Life Sciences," *Issues in Science and Technology* 21, no. 2 (2005): 50; Richard A. Knox, "Biomedical Results Often Are Withheld: Study Examines Researchers' Financial Links to Corporations," *Boston Globe*, April 16, 1997, sec A.

Betty Dong and Nancy Olivieri are two scientists who signed "gag-clauses" in clinical trial agreements[12] but refused to compromise their right to communicate research results while they were under contract with a for-profit sponsor. Dong, a pharmacologist at the University of California, San Francisco (UCSF), investigated the bioequivalency of a trade and generic drug for hypothyroidism, expecting to find the trade drug superior. When her investigation revealed that the drugs were bioequivalent but substantially different in price, her sponsoring company threatened to sue her for publishing her results.[13]

Dr. Olivieri, a hematologist and specialist in the treatment of rare blood diseases at the University of Toronto Medical School, participated in a clinical trial to test an oral drug that seemed like a promising therapy to reduce tissue iron loading in transfusion-dependent thalassemia patients. During the trial, Dr. Olivieri identified an unexpected risk and a loss of sustained efficacy of the drug. When she was about to report those results to her colleagues and to inform patients of the risk, her sponsoring company stopped the trial and threatened to take legal action against her.[14] Both Dr. Dong and Dr. Olivieri were eventually recognized by their respective institutions for acting properly in not permitting the contractual language of their clinical trial agreement to preempt their fiduciary responsibilities as scientists and, in Dr. Olivieri's case, as a physician. How can scientists be epistemologically disinterested in the research and yet be sponsored by a for-profit entity? The next section explores the concept of "disinterestedness" in sponsored research.

Fortunately, there is a growing interest in establishing researchers' rights to communicate and publish scientific and clinical data collected under their supervision. A dozen journals associated with the International Committee of Medical Journal Editors have set a new standard for medical publications that requires authors to disclose whether or not they had full responsibility for the conduct of the trial, had access to the data, and controlled the decision to publish. Individual scientists are also resisting pressure to withhold data and results.

---

[12] Robert Steinbrook, "Gag Clauses in Clinical-Trial Agreements," *New England Journal of Medicine* 352, no. 21 (2005): 2160–2.

[13] Drummond Rennie, "Thyroid Storm," *Journal of the American Medical Association* 277, no. 15 (1997): 1238–43.

[14] Jon Thompson et al., *The Olivieri Report* (Toronto: James Lorimer, 2001).

## Scientific Bias

Columbia University sociologist Robert K. Merton cited "disinterestedness" along with "universalism," "communalism," and "organized skepticism" as comprising norms of scientific inquiry. He might have added "trust," "openness," and "honesty" to his list.[15] By "disinterestedness," Merton did not mean that scientists are neutral with respect to their choice of hypotheses or that they are impartial to one theory or another. The preference for scientists to exhibit, either overtly or tacitly, support for a hypothesis that explains a physical effect is part of the lifeblood of scientific investigation. A hunch turns into an obsession. Scientific passions are what drive discovery. So where does "disinterestedness" enter?

"Disinterestedness" implies that scientists apply their methods of inquiry, make observations, take readings, perform their analysis, and execute the interpretation of results without consideration of personal gain, ideology, or fidelity to any cause other than the pursuit of truth. Scientists may not be disinterested in learning that their empirical findings do not corroborate their hypothesis. They must, however, behave *as if* they were disinterested by allowing the data to determine the fate of their hunch.

Typically, scientists possess an intellectual standpoint in their work. They may be centrists who support a generally accepted theory or they may be renegades who back a new and controversial theory. The affinities of scientists toward one theoretical approach or another are obvious to anyone familiar with the literature of a field. For example, during the development of Quantum Theory in physics in the early part of the twentieth century, some physicists were opposed to an interpretation of the data that embodied indeterminism as a core principle.

A scientist who allows nonintellectual factors, such as religion or commerce, to influence his or her science is not disinterested in the sense I have described. Some observers have concluded that the new entrepreneurial revolution in academic science has eliminated disinterestedness as an operating norm. Ziman, a Fellow of the Royal Society, physicist, and sociologist of science, has written about the demise of "disinterestedness" as a core norm in science.

---

[15]  Robert K. Merton, "Science and the Social Order," *Philosophy of Science* 5 (1938): 321–37.

What cannot be denied is that the academic norm of disinterestedness no longer operates. Even the genteel pages of the official scientific literature, where feigned humility is still the rule, are being bypassed by self-promoting press releases. In any case, scientific authors indicate by the "affiliations" and "acknowledgments" in their papers that interests other than their own personal advancement have had a hand in the research.[16]

The question then arises: does the loss of disinterestedness affect the objectivity of science "which is usually attributed to the detached, impartial, unbiased, dispassionate (etc., etc.) attitude with which scientists undertake their research?"[17] Can science still remain healthy despite the loss of "disinterestedness"? Dr. Ziman argues that the demise of "disinterestedness" will affect the public's confidence in science, or what he calls "social objectivity." But he claims that science will continue to produce reliable knowledge. The production of objective knowledge thus depends less on genuine personal disinterestedness than on the effective operation of other norms, especially the norms of communalism, universalism, and skepticism. So long as post-academic science abides by these norms, its long-term cognitive objectivity is not in serious doubt.[18] Dr. Ziman's conclusions about the loss of disinterestedness presupposes one or both of the following premises: (1) Skepticism in science will cancel out any short-term effects on objectivity brought about by the loss of disinterestedness; (2) the self-correcting power of science will, over time, identify and correct error and bias.

In the biomedical sciences, the time it might take to correct errors or to discover bias resulting from covert commercial interests has a cost in morbidity and mortality. Even if it were the case that science would eventually correct itself, the human toll could be considerable until the time that false knowledge is discovered. The central question is whether commercial interests in science and the growth in academic-industry partnerships have an effect on the objectivity of outcome and eventually on human well-being. We shall return to this question in the section on the "funding effect" in science. Meanwhile, scientific journals, the gatekeepers of certifiable knowledge, are also tied to the commercial world by the advertising

16 Ziman. *Real Science*, 174.
17 Ibid.
18 Ibid.

they receive. Can journals be immunized against the influence of their advertisers?

## The Negative Influence of Marketing

It is generally recognized that drug company advertisements support the existence of many specialized journals and contribute to the financial viability of the leading general medical journals. David Orentlicher and Michael K. Hehir II have outlined the conflicts of interest that arise for journal editors and professional societies from advertising.[19] The prestigious, high-impact journals claim to have erected a firewall between their business and editorial divisions. The less prosperous journals are vulnerable both to potential litigation and withdrawal of lucrative advertisers. A survey of 350 journal editors who are members of the Committee on Publication Ethics found that 40 percent of biomedical journals have no declared policy on separating editorial and commercial matters.[20]

Consider the following case. In January 2004, the *British Medical Journal* reported that the California-based nephrology journal *Transplantation and Dialysis* rejected a peer-reviewed editorial – reviewed favorably by three experts – on the grounds that the marketing department rejected the article. The article questioned the survival benefits of a drug treatment on end-stage renal disease. The author of the editorial received a letter from the editor indicating that he had been overruled by his marketing department.[21]

This is an unusual case because the editor of the journal disclosed the influence of the marketing department to the author. There is no indication of how commonly or infrequently marketing plays a role in editorial decisions. But what we do know is that in the biomedical field, where new therapeutics can be worth billions of dollars in revenue, companies will make great efforts to bias the outcome of the results in their favor either

---

[19] David Orentlicher and Michael K. Hehir II, "Advertising Policies of Medical Journals: Conflicts of Interest for Journal Editors and Professional Societies," *Journal of Law, Medicine and Ethics* 27, no. 2 (1999): 113–21.

[20] Jim Giles, "Journals Lack Explicit Policies for Separating Eds from Ads," *Nature* 434, no. 7033 (2005): 549.

[21] Owen Dyer, "Journal Rejects Article after Objections from Marketing Department," *British Medical Journal* 328, no. 7434 (2004): 244.

by adding "spin" to an article, not reporting negative results, or keeping a drug on the market despite information about adverse effects.

Some observers have noted the impact that advertisements have on medical journals and have called for more stringent ethical guidelines on publishing drug advertisements, which in some cases make up 30–40 percent of the pages devoted to the journal. In a letter to the *British Medical Journal*, a writer noted:

> Drug companies' advertisements in medical journals may pose an even greater threat to medical practice and education than pharmaceutical funding of medical research because of the industry's use of the latest "technology" in advertising methods. Surely another mechanism to fund medical journals should be investigated.[22]

Some new experiments in funding journal publication have been introduced by public access electronic journals such as *Public Library of Science* (PLOS), which have no advertisements. But what about the numerous investigators who receive funding from for-profit companies? Can they remain disinterested in the outcome of their studies? Can we get objective science through private sponsorship of research?

## The Funding Effect in Science

As I explained in the preceding section, an increasing number of studies show that deviations from the principles of healthy science take their toll on the results of scientific research. Specifically, this empirical research reveals that privately funded research biases the results toward the financial interests of the sponsors.[23] The poster child of advocacy science is the tobacco industry as revealed in a thoroughly researched report issued by the World Health Organization.[24] But the funding effect on science is also showing up in the pharmaceutical, chemical, and oil/energy industries.

---

[22] S. Sussman, "Conflicts of Interest Drug Advertising Corrupts Journals," *British Medical Journal* 308, no. 6939 (1994): 1301.

[23] Justin E. Bekelman et al., "Scope and Impact of Financial Conflicts of Interest in Biomedical Research: A Systematic Review," *Journal of the American Medical Association* 289, no. 4 (2003): 454–65.

[24] World Health Organization, Committee of Experts on Tobacco Industry Documents, *Tobacco Company Strategies to Undermine Tobacco Control Activities at the World Health Organization* (July 2000) (available at http://www.who.int/genevahearings/inquiry.html).

Frederick vom Saal and Claude Hughes report a striking pattern of bias in research findings on the toxicology of the chemical bisphenol A, which is ubiquitously used in plastics. They found that, of 115 relevant studies published, none of the 11 funded by for-profit companies reported adverse effects at low-level exposures, whereas 94 of 104 government-funded studies reported such effects at extremely low doses.[25] In a metastudy of conflict-of-interest papers in biomedicine, Bekelman et al. concluded: "evidence suggests that the financial ties that intertwine industry, investigators, and academic institutions can influence the research process. Strong and consistent evidence shows that industry-sponsored research tends to draw pro-industry conclusions."[26]

Because real science does not selectively publish data skewed only toward one hypothesis, it must address the issue that researchers supported by private sponsors or who have financial interests in the subject matter of their study are subject to a subtle form of bias. Healthy science requires that this potential biasing effect be made known to reviewers, editors, and readers of the article. The *Washington Monthly* quoted Drummond Rennie, deputy editor of the *Journal of the American Medical Association (JAMA)*, responding to the conflicts of interest in the life science: "This is all about bypassing science. Medicine is becoming a sort of Cloud Cuckoo Land, where doctors don't know what papers they can trust in the journals, and the public doesn't know what to believe."[27]

Conflicts of interest in producing research are exacerbated by the fact that the pharmaceutical industry is in control of vast amounts of information, much of which remains secret or is shared as privileged business information with regulatory agencies. The practice of suppressing data unfavorable to industry's bottom line is not prima facie illegal, but it delays the science and can cost lives. Science is self-correcting, but it may take years for that correction. The cost in lives that may result from sequestered data must be weighed against the rights of companies to their confidential business information.

---

[25] Frederick S. vom Saal and Clause Hughes, "An Extensive New Literature Concerning Low-Dose Effects of Bisphenol A Shows the Need for a New Risk Assessment," Environmental Health Perspectives Online (April 13, 2005).

[26] Bekelman et al., 463.

[27] Shannon Brownlee, "Doctors without Borders: Why You Can't Trust Medical Journals Anymore," *Washington Monthly* 36, no. 4 (2004): 38.

## Redeeming Biomedical Science

The redemption of drug science will be a challenging task given the structure of the industry – which is all but vertically integrated. Companies pay for most of the drug testing; they control the data; they contract out with academic scientists and in some cases with for-profit clinical trial companies. Sometimes these contracts permit sponsor control over publications and statistical analysis of results.[28]

The drug industry is also in control of much of the market for its products. The industry uses several methods to exert such control. Drug companies support journals through ads and pay high premiums for journal supplements, provide the main financial support for the continuing education of doctors, market directly to consumers, lobby Congress and state legislators in setting drug prescription guidelines, pay generous speaker fees to scientists who promote their drugs, provide all sorts of gifts to physicians, and serve as the primary source of drug information for clinicians. In addition, they sponsor panels to develop clinical guidelines and choose panelists with company affiliations.

Getting healthy science from a system replete with conflicts of interest is truly a challenge, especially where the sector boundaries between drug development and drug evaluation have become blurred. Yet reform must begin somewhere. Four important changes are required to improve the integrity of drug science: (1) guaranteeing the openness of all clinical trial data; (2) developing a firewall between the drug manufacturers and the drug testers; (3) establishing a national, comprehensive system of postmarketing drug evaluation; and (4) mandating comprehensive and transparent disclosure policy for drug journals, clinical guidelines, and federal advisory committees.

### Openness of Clinical Trial Data

*Obstacles to Disclosure*
Perhaps the most obvious reform is to require that clinical trial data be shared openly with the scientific community and the public. This is not as

---

[28] Michelle M. Mello et al., "Academic Medical Centers' Standards for Clinical-Trial Agreements with Industry," *New England Journal of Medicine* 352, no. 21 (2005): 2202–10.

easy as it sounds since the science applied to drug safety and efficacy trials has its own idiosyncratic structure. Most of the studies are contracted out to academic centers or the burgeoning for-profit clinical research organizations (CROs) by the drug industry.[29] Clinical trials are not designed to contribute to basic knowledge but rather to supply data that pharmaceutical companies can use to bring drugs to market. Privately funded drug studies stop short of pursuing scientifically interesting questions that have no commercial value. Most drugs tested in clinical trials never reach the market. Yet, positive results in drug testing are more likely than negative outcomes to get published.

Several reasons might explain this result. First, journals have a strong preference for publishing positive rather than negative studies. Second, companies undertake in-house studies to screen out drugs that would prove ineffective in humans, weighting the drugs they contract out for external trials toward positive outcomes. Third, many corporations that fund drug studies exhibit a bias toward publishing only those results that elevate the potential market of their products. Sponsor bias has been confirmed by the appearance of secret covenants in research contracts that give the private funder of the study control over the data and/or publication of the results. Richard Friedman noted in a *New York Times* guest column that "a drug company can cherry-pick favorable studies for publication and file away studies that show its drug in a negative light."[30] In another example, Eli Lilly allegedly withheld clinical trial data on the drug fluoxetine (aka Prozac) that linked it to suicide attempts and violence.[31]

## Two Case Studies

Two cases illustrate how companies with a vested interest in certain findings seek to suppress negative outcomes. As mentioned earlier, a pharmacologist at the University of California named Betty Dong signed a contract with Flint Laboratories to undertake a six-month clinical trial comparing the company's popular thyroid drug against a generic competitor. The

---

[29] It has been estimated that industry funds 70 percent of the clinical trials in the United States. Ibid., 2202.

[30] Richard Friedman, "What You Do Know Can't Hurt You," *New York Times*, Aug. 12, 2003, Op-Ed sect.

[31] Jeanne Lenzer, "FDA to Review 'Missing' Drug Company Documents," *British Medical Journal* 330, no. 7481 (2005): 7.

contract contained the following clause: "Data obtained by the investigator while carrying out this study is also considered confidential and is not to be published or otherwise released without written consent from Flint Laboratories."[32] Unaware of the clause, Dr. Dong submitted the results for publication in the *Journal of the American Medical Association*, where her paper was refereed and accepted for publication. When the paper appeared in galleys, Dr. Dong requested that it be withdrawn in the wake of threatened legal action by Knoll Pharmaceuticals, a company that had taken over the rights to the drug and which declared Dong's results in error.[33]

In a second case, Attorney General Eliot Spitzer of New York State charged the pharmaceutical company GlaxoSmithKline (GSK) with concealing information about the safety and effectiveness of an antidepressant. The company conducted at least five studies with children and adolescents as subjects on its antidepressant Paxil (also known as paroxetine). The lawsuit alleged that GSK suppressed the negative studies that showed Paxil was no more effective than placebo and that it increased the risk of suicidal ideation. These cases, among others, have created a ground swell of interest in public databases for registering clinical trials. Currently, there are hundreds of online registers that provide different information formats, and together do not account for all the trials.[34]

## Centralized Registry

In June 2004, the American Medical Association called upon the Department of Health and Human Services to establish a centralized clinical trials registry. The International Committee of Medical Journal Editors (ICMJE), representing a dozen prestigious medical journals, issued a statement in September 2004 that their journals would not publish clinical trial results if the trials were not posted on a public database. A House bill (HR 5252) introduced by Edward Markey (D-MA) and Henry Waxman (D-CA), titled "Fair Access to Clinical Trials Act," would require any recipient of a federal grant, contract, or cooperative agreement for the conduct of a

---

[32] Rennie, 1239.

[33] Dorothy S. Zinberg, "Cautionary Tale," *Science* 273, no. 5274 (1996): 411.

[34] Eric Manheimer and Diana Anderson, "Survey of Public Information about Ongoing Clinical Trials Funded by Industry: Evaluation of Completeness and Accessibility," *British Medical Journal* 325, no. 7363 (2002): 528–31.

clinical trial to register the trial on a database to be established by the secretary of Health and Human Services.[35]

Pharmaceutical Research and Manufacturers of America (PhRMA), the trade organization for major pharmaceutical companies, recently came out in support of a voluntary system of posting, in a standardized industry-approved format, "timely communication of meaningful results of controlled clinical trials of marketed products or investigational products that are approved for marketing, regardless of outcome."[36]

These proposals differ in many important details, especially the following: which trials would be posted (hypothesis-driven, exploratory, inconclusive, aborted); when they would be posted (at inception; at conclusion); which databases would be acceptable (single or multiple databases); what type of information should be included (protocols, raw data, analyzed data, interpretation of data); in what format should the information be posted; and within what time period after a trial has begun and/or ended should a posting be required.

The ICMJE proposal requires posting the protocols of all clinical studies designed to determine the cause-effect relationship between a medical intervention and a health outcome. It excludes phase I trials that focus exclusively on drug pharmacokinetics and toxicity. The congressional bills and American Medical Association (AMA) proposal include a requirement that a summary of results of all completed trials should be posted as well. The central rationale behind the public databases was stated by the ICMJE: "If all trials are registered in a public repository at their inception, every trial's existence is part of the public record and the many stakeholders in clinical research can explore the full range of clinical evidence."[37]

For the postings to have value to the clinical community and the public, a summary of results should be a part of the mandatory registration. The raw data by itself would not be useful to those who cannot undertake the statistical analysis indicated in the protocol. Under the New York State–GSK settlement, GSK is required to post a *clinical study report*, a type of detailed abstract, defined as "a description of the protocol, all the data,

---

[35] Senator Christopher Dodd (D-CT) introduced a companion bill to the Senate (S. 2933).

[36] Pharmaceutical Researchers and Manufacturers of America, 19.

[37] Catherine DeAngelis et al., "Clinical Trial Registration: A Statement from the International Committee of Medical Journal Editors," *New England Journal of Medicine* 351, no. 12 (2004): 1250–1.

and the clinically relevant conclusions drawn from the data, including the answers to the questions posed in the protocol."[38]

Posting every trial report on a database presents problems, however. How do readers of the posted study know whether the study was well conceived, and whether the statistics were executed correctly? One well-designed negative study may be more valuable than two poorly designed positive studies. If the statistics for a particular study are standardized and stipulated by the protocol, concerns about post-trial selection of statistics to get the "best" outcome will be minimized.

Some studies posted on the registry will be published; others will not. Will the unpublished trials be included in review articles, given that unrefereed studies are rarely included? Could the pharmaceutical industry gain some market power from poorly designed studies merely by being posted on the registry? Would they be unfairly penalized from studies that are inconclusive and would ordinarily not get published even if well executed? This raises the question of whether all studies appearing on the database, but especially those that are unpublished, should receive a rating. Without some rating system, weaker studies may have an undue influence on readers untrained in biostatistics and research methodology.

The mandatory registration of all clinical trial protocols in a standardized format will be of unequivocal benefit to the medical community. But a consensus must be reached about the form in which the results of clinical trials (raw and analyzed data) should be presented in a registry that will be recalcitrant to the sponsor's interpretive bias and transparent to the power and the quality of the science.

## A National Institute of Drug Testing

In *Science and the Private Interest*, I identified three ethical norms that should serve as the standards for the integrity of clinical and environmental research.[39] These norms are that: (1) the roles of those who produce knowledge in academia and those stakeholders who have a financial

[38] Press Release, Department of Law, State of New York, "Settlement Sets New Standard for Release of Drug Information" (Aug. 26, 2004) (available at http://www.oag.state.ny.us/press/2004/aug/aug26a_04.html).

[39] Sheldon Krimsky, *Science and the Private Interest* (Lanham, MD: Rowman and Littlefield, 2003), 227.

interest in that knowledge should be kept separate and distinct; (2) the roles of those who have a fiduciary responsibility to care for patients while enlisting them as research subjects, and those who have a financial stake in the specific pharmaceuticals, therapies, products, clinical trials, or facilities contributing to patient care, should be kept separate and distinct; and (3) the roles of those who assess therapies, drugs, toxic substances, or consumer products and those who have a financial stake in the success or failure of those products should be kept separate and distinct.

In the case of drug testing, it is difficult to fulfill these norms without a structural change of the system currently in place. To establish a firewall between the drug manufacturers and the drug testers, an intermediary agency is needed to distance the sponsors of drugs tests from the scientists who undertake the testing and who are paid directly by the drug manufacturers. The "funding effect" shows us that without such a firewall, scientists will likely internalize the values of their private funders, resulting in biased outcome. This is a population effect and is not observed for each scientist. But the effect demonstrates that privately funded studies are skewed toward the sponsor's interests. My proposal is to establish a National Institute of Drug Testing (NIDT).[40]

The function of the NIDT would be to serve as the firewall between the drug companies and the researchers who study the safety and efficacy of their products. Using fees from drug companies that are based on the real costs of carrying out a clinical trial, the NIDT would screen and select qualified scientists to undertake the study. In addition, the NIDT would ensure that drug testing met high ethical standards while protecting confidential business information.

The data from such tests, whether favorable or unfavorable to the manufacturer, would be fully accessible to the drug company, other researchers, health care providers, and the general public once the investigators publish the results. It is also expected that the trial results would be posted on a public database. The NIDT would reinstitute the concept of independent and disinterested science in drug testing by establishing a separation between drug manufacturers and testers that would prevent even the appearance of conflict of interest. This proposal will respond to recent criticisms and lawsuits directed at drug companies.

[40] Ibid., 229.

A year after I published the concept of the NIDT, a similar idea was proposed by Marcia Angell in her book *The Truth about the Drug Companies*.[41] Angell wrote:

> I propose that an Institute for Prescription Drug Trials be established within the National Institutes of Health (NIH) to administer clinical trails of prescription drugs. Drug companies would be required to contribute a percentage of revenues to this institute, but their contributions would not be related to particular drugs (as in the case with FDA user fees). The institute would then contract with independent researchers in academic medical centers to conduct drug trials. The researchers would design the trials, analyze the data, write the papers, and decide about the publications. The data would become the joint property of the NIH and the researchers, not be controlled by the sponsoring company.[42]

One of the benefits of an agency like the NIDT is that it can set parameters on what data are necessary to evaluate a drug fully for efficacy and safety. There is a great difference in the effort taken to gather pre-marketing as contrasted with post-marketing data for drug studies. In the next subsection, I discuss how the science can be skewed by this difference of effort and what can be done about it.

## Comprehensive System of Post-Marketing Drug Evaluation

Post-marketing drug evaluations have not caught up with the information age, and this is thus another important area for reform. It is generally acknowledged that drug testing is never complete until a product is evaluated when it is used in large populations. Clinical trials that involve several hundred to a few thousand subjects cannot assess the drug's effect over the range of diversity that is manifest in the human genome. Therefore, clinical trial data can be considered preliminary only until the drug is tested over a sizable human population of drug users. The science of drug testing demands post-marketing data, both for evidence of efficacy and safety. If that data are not forthcoming, then there is a serious limitation to the science.

---

[41] Marcia Angell, *The Truth about the Drug Companies* (New York: Random House, 2004), 245.
[42] Ibid.

The current system of reporting adverse drug reactions in the United States is decentralized, haphazard, and purely voluntary. Physicians typically do not take the time to investigate and report adverse drug reactions to the FDA or a drug company. Therefore, valuable data necessary for self-correcting science are lost.

With current information technology, it would be possible to establish a central data bank managed by a federal agency for all drugs approved by the FDA. Physicians would have to be given an incentive or a mandate to report adverse drug incidents. Only then would we be able to realize fully the benefits of the data possibilities in drug evaluations.

Several years ago, the Japanese Ministry of Health and Welfare (MHW) revised its Good Post-Marketing Surveillance Practice with a new reporting system for adverse drug reactions. Immediately following drug approval, medical representatives are responsible for visiting each institution using the new drug periodically for six months to remind health care professionals of their obligation to report adverse events. Under the new regulations, physicians, dentists, and pharmacists as well as pharmaceutical companies are all required to submit adverse drug reports to the MHW.[43]

## Mandating Disclosure

The recognition and acknowledgment of potential bias in scientific studies are essential parts of healthy science, and requiring conflict disclosures is another obvious area for reform. Increasingly, we are learning that having a financial interest in the subject matter of one's research can bias the outcome. Catherine D. DeAngelis, editor of *JAMA*, noted that: "when an investigator has a financial interest in or funding by a company with activities related to his or her research the research is: lower in quality, more likely to favor the sponsor's products, less likely to be published, and more likely to have delayed publication."[44] Thus, the disclosure of potential conflicts of interest must be transparent.

---

[43] Ames Gross, "Regulatory Changes in Japan's Pharmaceutical Industry," *Pacific Bridge Medical* (Nov. 1998) (available at http://www.pacificbridgemedical.com/publications/html/JapanNov98.htm).

[44] Catherine D. DeAngelis, "Conflict of Interest and the Public Trust," *Journal of the American Medical Association* 284, no. 17 (2000): 2237–8.

The journal *Nature* was the last of the prestige science journals to adopt an author disclosure policy. In explaining the reasons for adopting the policy, the editor of the journal wrote, "There is suggestive evidence in the literature that publication practices in biomedical research have been influenced by the commercial interests of authors."[45] It is estimated that at least 60 percent of the English-language medical journals have a conflict of interest policy for contributors of original research.[46] Using *Ulrich's Periodicals Director*, I conducted a survey of English-language psychiatry journals that published drug studies and found 42 percent had conflict-of-interest (COI) policies.[47]

In addition to influencing authors, financial ties might also bias the decisions of reviewers and editors. Some journals, therefore, extend their COI policies to others involved in journal publications.

Two other areas where disclosure is deemed important in revealing potential biases in medical science are in clinical guidelines and in recommendations of federal advisory committees. Many journals neglect to disclose the financial interests of biomedical scientists whose names are listed on an expert panel signing off on the recommendations cited in the guidelines.

Only in the past few years, however, has any attention been given to the transparency of financial interests of those participating in the development of clinical guidelines for preventative and therapeutic interventions. In one study of 191 clinical guidelines published in six major medical journals between 1979 and 1999, only 7 published guidelines disclosed the potential COIs of the expert panel members.[48]

---

[45] Philip Campbell, "Declaration of Financial Interests: Introducing a New Policy for Authors of Research Papers in *Nature* and Nature Journals," *Nature* 412, no. 6849 (2001): 751.

[46] Richard M. Glass and Mindy Schneiderman, "A Survey of Journal Conflict of Interest Policies," talk given at the International Congress on Biomedical Peer Review and Scientific Publication, Prague, Czech Republic (Sept. 18–20, 1997).

[47] Using the search terms "psychiatry and drugs," "psychopharmacology," "drugs and mental illness," and "psychiatry and medication" in *Ulrich's Periodicals Directory* when restricted to descriptors "active," "academic/scholarly," "English language," and "refereed journals," the search yielded forty-five journals of psychiatry. Of those, nineteen had conflict-of-interest policies.

[48] George N. Papanikolaou et al., "Reporting of Conflicts of Interest in Guidelines of Preventive and Therapeutic Interventions," *BMC Medical Research Methodology* 1, no. 3 (2001) (available at http://www.biomedcentral.com/1471–2288/1/3).

Clinical guidelines are most often published under the auspices of professional medical associations, government agencies, or health promotion organizations such as the American Heart Association. These guidelines play an integral role in the practice of medicine. Most physicians do not have the time to undertake the type of comprehensive and critical review of medical evidence that is expected of panels of experts. If a financial conflict of interest among medical researchers can bias the outcome of a study (as recent research shows),[49] there is as much reason to believe it can also bias the recommendations in a clinical guideline. In one study, University of Toronto researchers surveyed 192 medical experts who participated in writing forty-four sets of guidelines for the treatment of asthma, coronary artery disease, depression, high cholesterol, and pneumonia. One hundred respondents indicated that nine out of ten had some type of relationship with a drug manufacturer. About six out of ten had financial ties to companies whose drugs were either considered or recommended in the guidelines they wrote. Of the forty-four guidelines, just one reported a potential COI.

A 2001 study examined six influential medical journals that published clinical guidelines from 1979–99. The journals were *Annals of Internal Medicine, British Medical Journal, NEJM, JAMA, Pediatric*, and the *Lancet*. Of the 115 guidelines that were published when the journal disclosure policies were in effect, only seven guidelines disclosed potential COIs.

The importance of protecting the integrity and public trust in scientific and medical advisory committees has been widely discussed.[50] Yet, there remains a lack of transparency of advisers with financial COIs, despite the fact that such disclosures have become standard procedure in the major medical publications.[51]

## Conclusion

It is impossible to remove science from its social context. Healthy science depends on the funding it receives from the government, other nonprofit

---

[49] Bekelman, 454.

[50] Sara Schroter et al., "Does the Type of Competing Interest Statement Affect Readers' Perceptions of the Credibility of Research? Randomised Trial," *British Medical Journal* 328, no. 7442 (2004): 742–3.

[51] Sheryl Gay Stolberg, "Study Says Clinical Guides Often Hide Ties of Doctors," *New York Times*, Feb. 6, 2002, sec. A.

institutions, and for-profit institutions. But the health and integrity of science must be protected from its capture by private interests. The independence of academic science from its for-profit sponsors must be a national goal shared by all professional societies, journals, academic institutions, and government agencies. This chapter has discussed some of the challenges facing that goal and made recommendations designed to insulate science from those tendencies of society that seek to exploit it for personal gain or for interests other than those that support its role as a generator of trustworthy and reliable knowledge.

4

## Science and Subpoenas

### When Do the Courts Become Instruments of Manipulation?

Paul M. Fischer, M.D.[1]

### The Beginning

On December 11, 1991, the *Journal of the American Medical Association* (JAMA) published three studies that examined the effect of the Camel cigarette "Old Joe" advertising campaign on adolescents and children.[2] I was lead author on the study that showed that "Old Joe" was nearly universally recognized by six-year-old children, a level of awareness that matched the logo for the Disney Channel. Because cigarette smoking is the leading preventable cause of death and disease in this country, I recognized that this research might play a prominent role in the subsequent debate about tobacco advertising. As a scientist, I naively assumed that this discourse would be conducted in academic journals based upon rigorous research and leading to an improved understanding of whether and how advertising influences adolescent experimentation with cigarettes. To date, most of the subsequent debate has occurred in court.

From the beginning, the tobacco industry attempted to discredit this research and harass the researchers. My experience in confronting the tobacco industry has taught me how easily the courts can become the unwitting accomplices of an industry whose goal is profit, not the

---

[1] This chapter was first published in the summer of 1996 in the legal journal *Law and Contemporary Problems*, 59: 159–67. It is reprinted here with permission from that journal's editors.

[2] Joseph R. DiFranza et al., "RJR Nabisco's Cartoon Camel Promotes Camel Cigarettes to Children," *Journal of the American Medical Association* 266, no. 22 (1991): 3149; Paul M. Fischer et al., "Brand Logo Recognition by Children Aged 3 to 6 Years: Mickey Mouse and Old Joe the Camel," *Journal of the American Medical Association* 266, no. 22 (1991): 3145; John P. Pierce et al., "Does Tobacco Advertising Target Young People to Start Smoking?" *Journal of the American Medical Association* 266, no. 22 (1991): 3154. 48.

identification of scientific truth. Michael Traynor has written that with "common sense and goodwill in every quarter," there should be few problems due to compelled discovery of scholarly research.[3] Unfortunately, in some cases, neither common sense nor goodwill prevail. In such cases, the court can become an instrument of abuse.

In this chapter, I share my experience with the judicial system and its inadvertent facilitation of one industry's effort to violate the basic principle that scientists must be able to conduct research without unjustified restrictions. Without the courts' authority, the most severe intrusions into my research and the privacy of my subjects would not have occurred. I begin the chapter by detailing the course of my research and how it threatened the tobacco industry, leading its attorneys to attempt to subpoena all records and documents involved in my studies. I then discuss the harm this excessive, court-backed effort to access research did to the course of my research and my career. I close the chapter with suggestions for reform.

## My Introduction to Subpoenas

### A Chronology of Events

The "Old Joe" studies were published in a *JAMA* theme issue dealing with tobacco research.[4] The American Medical Association also held a press conference in New York to present the findings,[5] which received wide coverage in the press.[6]

On March 9, 1992, the American Medical Association, the Surgeon General, the American Cancer Society, the American Heart Association, and the American Lung Association called for a ban on "Old Joe" advertising attractive to children.[7] The following day, James Johnson, C.E.O. of the R.J. Reynolds Tobacco Company (RJR), defended "Old Joe" in an interview

---

[3] Michael Traynor, "Countering the Excessive Subpoena for Scholarly Research," *Law and Contemporary Problems* 59, no. 3 (1996): 148.

[4] DiFranza, 3149.

[5] Stuart Elliott, "Top Health Official Demands Abolition of 'Joe Camel' Ads," *New York Times*, March 10, 1992, sec. A.

[6] Jane E. Brody, "Smoking among Children Is Linked to Cartoon Camel in Advertisements," *New York Times*, Dec. 11, 1991, sec. D.

[7] Elliott, sec. A.

published on the editorial page of *U.S.A. Today*.[8] In this interview, he attacked the "Old Joe" studies and its researchers. Mr. Johnson argued that the "studies are flawed in very serious ways. The scientists who wrote these studies are not unbiased." He made two specific claims about our research that were not true. He stated that the sample size was 23 people when in reality it was 229 people. He also claimed that we called the parents of the three- to six-year-old children in our study the night before the data collection and asked them only about cigarette use.[9] This statement was a total fabrication. Such a call to the parents would have obviously biased the results.

On March 27, 1992, I was served a *subpoena duces tecum* by RJR.[10] A suit had been filed in California by Janet Mangini against RJR, based on RJR's failure to place health warnings on promotional products such as Camel caps and tee-shirts.[11] I received the subpoena even though my research had not been named in the Mangini complaint, I was not a witness to either side in the case, and my 1991 *JAMA* research had no bearing on the issue of health warnings.

The subpoena ordered me to produce the following: the names and telephone numbers of all of the children who participated in the study; all drafts of the study design; all notes, memos, and videotapes pertaining to the study; the names, addresses, telephone numbers, background information, and occupations of all interviewers; hard copy tabulations and data tapes; originals of all test materials; all correspondence relating to the research; the names, addresses, and background information of all consultants; the names and addresses of all funding sources; and the names and telephone numbers of all respondents who were excluded from the study.

Given the published implications of my research, I had assumed that I might at some point be deposed about the study. I was, however, not prepared to receive a subpoena of this breadth and one that would require turning over the names of three-to-six-year-old children. Such disclosure

---

[8] *U.S.A. Today*, "R.J. Reynolds: Ads Do Not Cause Kids to Smoke," March 10, 1992, sec. A.
[9] Ibid.
[10] Defendant's Notice of Out of State Deposition on Oral Examination and Request for Production of Documents and Things, *Mangini v. R.J. Reynolds Tobacco Co.*, No. 939359 (Super. Ct., San Francisco Cty., Cal., March 30, 1992).
[11] *Mangini v. R.J. Reynolds Tobacco Co.*, 21 Cal.Rptr.2d 232 (Cal. Ct. App.), rev. granted and opinion superseded, 859 P.2d 672 (Cal. 1993), cert. denied, 875 P.2d 73 (Cal. 1994) (en banc), cert. denied, 115 S. Ct. 577 (1994).

would have violated written confidentiality agreements that I had signed with each parent before conducting the research.

I had also anticipated that the Medical College of Georgia (MCG), on whose faculty I was a full professor and under whose auspices the research had been conducted, would provide appropriate legal support for my position. However, Michael Bowers, the attorney general of the State of Georgia and the official counsel for the medical school, took the position that the prevailing legal issue was not human subject confidentiality, academic freedom, or the reasonableness of the subpoena power, but rather the Georgia Open Records Act, a law designed to permit public access to "official records."[12] Mr. Bowers took this position even though RJR did not, at that time, request the records via the Open Records Act. I refused to comply with the subpoena, and MCG refused to provide me with legal assistance.

I contacted my own lawyer, Robert W. Hunter, III, who prepared a motion to quash the RJR subpoena.[13] On April 28, 1992, Chief Superior Court Judge William M. Fleming, Jr., ruled in favor of our motion to quash.[14] RJR immediately appealed the ruling to the Georgia Court of Appeals, but that court, on February 9, 1993, ruled in our favor arguing that the requested documents were beyond the bounds of reasonable discovery.[15]

Two weeks later, in an article in a local newspaper, MCG lawyer Clay Stedman stated that the school had not supported my legal efforts because of its position on the Open Records Act.[16] Stedman said that MCG "decline[d] to object to [the] release of this information on the basis that although it was not an Open Records [Act] request, Open Records would have required us to release it."[17] Ironically, RJR attorneys did not know of MCG's position on this issue and had previously admitted in their Court of Appeals brief that they believed the records were not accessible to them

---

12  Open Records Act, GA. CODE ANN. § 50–18–70 to –76 (Supp. 1996).
13  Motion to Quash, *Fischer v. R.J. Reynolds Tobacco Co.*, No. 93-RCCV-230 (Ga. Super. Ct. Richmond County, April 16, 1992).
14  *Fischer v R.J. Reynolds Tobacco Co.*, No. 93-RCCV-230 (Ga. Super. Ct. Richmond County, April 28, 1992) (order granting motion to quash).
15  *R.J. Reynolds Tobacco Co. v Fischer*, 207 Ga. App. 292 (Ga. Ct. App. 1993).
16  Kathleen Donahue, "Researcher Has Hefty Legal Fees," *Augusta Chronicle*, Feb. 27, 1993, Metro sec.
17  Ibid.

under the Open Records Act because the research had not been supported by state funds.[18]

One week after the publication of this article, James R. Johnson, legal counsel for RJR, sent a letter to H. Dean Propst, chancellor of the University System of Georgia, and subsequently to Francis Tedesco, president of MCG, requesting that my research records be released to RJR under the Open Records Act.[19] I was given forty-eight hours to turn over all of the previously described records with the exception of the children's names. Stedman, as MCG legal counsel, indicated that I would be suspended if I did not turn over the documents. MCG president Tedesco indicated that the attorney general would have me arrested if I did not comply with the request.

At the advice of my lawyer, I turned all of the documents over to the court for protection until such time as the legal issues relating to the Open Records Act, academic freedom, and human subject confidentiality could be resolved. The court accepted the documents and approved a temporary restraining order against the Open Records request.[20]

One month later, RJR petitioned the court to assist MCG and the attorney general in the action against me.[21] Both the attorney general's office and MCG supported RJR's compelled disclosure motion.[22] Ironically, this action united the medical school and a tobacco company against one of the school's own faculty members.

On August 12, 1993, I received a nine-page letter listing documents and data requested by RJR through the Open Records Act.[23] It stated that RJR wanted all documentation related to the study regardless of when it was generated or by whom.[24] In response to a 1993 change in the Open

[18] Petitioner's Brief, *R.J. Reynolds Tobacco v. Fischer*, 207 Ga. App. 292 (Ga. Ct. App. 1993).
[19] Letter from James R. Johnson, Legal Counsel, RJR, to Francis J. Tedesco, President, MCG (March 10, 1993) (on file with the author).
[20] Motion for Temporary Restraining Order, *Fischer*, No. 93-RCCV-230 (Ga. Super. Ct. Richmond County, March 12, 1993).
[21] James R. Johnson's Motion to Intervene as a Defendant, *Fischer*, No. 93-RCCV-230 (Ga. Super. Ct. Richmond County, April 22, 1993).
[22] Letter from David M. Monde, Attorney, Jones, Day, Reavis & Pogue, to Kathryn L. Allen, Senior Assistant Attorney General (April 20, 1993) (on file with the author).
[23] Letter from RJR to Author (Aug.12, 1993) (on file with the author).
[24] Ibid.

Records Act that excluded release of the names of research participants, RJR did request that the subject names be redacted from the submitted documents.

On December 1, 1993, I resigned from the faculty of MCG and entered private practice in Augusta. On July 20, 1994, Judge John H. Ruffin signed an RJR request to release all of the records held by the court. The records were released to an RJR lawyer before we were notified of the decision, making an appeal of this decision moot.

## Lessons Learned

Every day in every academic institution, people request information from scientists. Most of the time, these requests are made by fellow scientists during the process of scientific research. For example, after the publication of the "Old Joe" study, I received requests from other researchers for specific information about our study and how it was done. Such requests are usually limited to information that would permit replication of the research. Successful replication is essential to establish scientific validity, and therefore scientists are usually pleased to share information.

Scientists do not use subpoenas to seek scientific truth. Thus, the subpoena of a researcher's files is evidence that the process has moved outside of the realm of scientific inquiry. As the cases cited in this chapter illustrate, a subpoena usually means that the research in question has commercial implications and that a company has decided that its lawyers, rather than its scientists, are in the best position to protect the company's interests.

Nevertheless, many subpoenas for research are routine. For example, a medical researcher might discover and report a series of side-effects in patients taking a new drug. The pharmaceutical company that manufactures the drug may then subpoena the records to see if there is an alternative explanation for the patients' symptoms. Other than concerns about patient confidentiality, such a subpoena would be handled in a routine fashion.

However, not all compelled disclosure is routine. In the extreme, subpoenas can be unwittingly used in a manner that is damaging to the researcher, the scientific process, and the greater public good.

## Damaging Effects

### Discredit the Research: Discredit the Researcher

It was clear from the *U.S.A. Today* interview that RJR wanted to discredit me and my research.[25] Furthermore, this refutation would not follow the usual "rules" of science.

The standards for a published scientific paper require that the report include sufficient detail about the scientific methods utilized so that another individual in the field could duplicate the study. This was precisely what *Advertising Age* did after initially expressing reservations about the "Old Joe" research. The journal commissioned research that was published five months later and showed that the Camel campaign was indeed highly effective in reaching young people, especially children younger than age thirteen.[26] The president of the research company said, "I was blown away by the number of smaller kids who could name cigarettes."[27] Had RJR been concerned about the veracity of our findings, it could have duplicated our research in several weeks for a few thousand dollars. Instead, the corporation spent two and a half years, and a great deal more money, in an attempt to access every page in my files.

Why would RJR be interested in every scrap of paper in a research file? The answer to this question became clear from the experience of Dr. Joseph DiFranza, the lead author of one of the "Old Joe" studies.[28] His research showed that Camel cigarettes' share of the youth market increased from a mere 0.5 percent to a substantial 32.8 percent following the "Old Joe" advertising campaign.[29] Dr. DiFranza received a similar subpoena and turned over his records to RJR. In one of the letters to a colleague that was included in the disclosed documents, Dr. DiFranza wrote, "I have an idea for a project that will give us a couple of smoking guns to bring to the national media."[30] RJR released this letter to the press and claimed

---

[25] "R.J. Reynolds: Ads Do Not Cause Kids to Smoke."
[26] Gary Levin, "Poll: Camel Ads Effective with Kids," *Advertising Age*, April 27, 1992, 12.
[27] Ibid.
[28] DiFranza, 3149.
[29] Ibid.
[30] Marcia Barinaga, "Who Controls a Researcher's Files? Tobacco Company R.J. Reynolds Subpoenas Research Study Data," *Science* 256, no. 5064 (1992): 1620.

that it proved that the researchers were biased and that the research was fraudulent.[31]

It is easy to characterize any scientist as being biased. The public assumes that scientists enter into research without a point of view. Nothing could be further from the truth. Science is impossible to do without passion about an idea. Scientists are not without opinions, but they agree to subject these opinions to objective experiments to see whether they are true. In every researcher's files, there are notes that could be taken out of context and characterized as proving bias.

In addition, every research study represents a series of methodological decisions about how data are collected and analyzed. These decisions require expert judgment, and each of these judgments, when viewed in isolation, could be challenged. It is precisely because of this that the final published paper becomes the record of the research. In the published manuscript, the researcher must describe the findings, discuss their meaning, and, most importantly, identify the study's limitations.

The broad subpoena filed by RJR is akin to requiring a Supreme Court justice to report every private note made and every comment spoken in considering a case, rather than merely being responsible for the contents of the final opinion. It would be quite easy to discredit the decisions of even the best judges if their private notes and thoughts were publicly open on demand.

## Human Subject Confidentiality

The conduct of research on human subjects requires that the public have confidence that its best interests will be protected and that its confidentiality will be preserved. In the case of our research, RJR requested the names and addresses of 239 three-to-six-year-old children whose parents had signed agreements in which we promised complete confidentiality. According to Peggy Carter, an RJR spokesperson, the company intended to use this information to contact the research subjects.[32] Her reason for requesting this breach of confidentiality was that "[t]here have been a number of stories that have come up in recent years where scientists claimed to have

[31] Maria Mallory, "That's One Angry Camel," *Business Week*, March 7, 1994, 94.
[32] Barinaga, 1620.

produced research that . . . was never done at all."[33] While this reasoning is paranoid at best, it would not be necessary for RJR to knock on children's doors at night to prove that the data in question were collected rather than fabricated.

The issue of subject confidentiality took an interesting legal turn in my case. MCG initially acknowledged the potential for abuse. In a letter from Carol Huston, one of the school's attorneys, to the attorney general's office, she stated that

> [Fischer's] concern, which I believe is well founded, is that Reynolds is attempting to harass him (and other researchers) through tactics such as this in order to discourage future research, the results of which may not be favorable to the tobacco industry. . . . We also believe if [RJR] obtains the names of the respondents, it seems very likely that [it] may contact them and attempt to harass them. This, in turn, may discourage other individuals from participating in future research projects.

Despite these observations by an MCG lawyer, the attorney general's position prevailed, and the school insisted that all names be released.

As a general matter, institutions that participate in federally funded medical research must sign agreements with the Department of Health and Human Services (DHHS), by which they agree to conduct research according to federally established guidelines. Human subject confidentiality is well protected by these standards. My study, however, was not federally funded and was subject to these guidelines only because of contractual agreements between DHHS and MCG.

On September 8, 1992, I was contacted by the acting chief of the Office of Protection from Research Risks of the National Institutes of Health. He had heard of my case and wanted information about any breach of human subject protection. He subsequently sent a letter to the school alleging noncompliance with its DHHS contract because of the school's position requiring release of my subjects' names. The school responded that it could avoid the federal regulations because my research was not federally funded. DHHS and MCG subsequently signed a revised contract in which federal regulations regarding subject confidentiality governed only federally funded research.

---

[33]  Ibid.

## Harassment

The tobacco industry approach to litigation has been described by Lawton M. Chiles, Jr., former governor of the State of Florida, as "designed to confuse the medical evidence, stone-wall, delay, refuse reasonably to settle claims, and to run up plaintiffs' attorneys' fees in a war of attrition."[34] He cites a memo written by J. Michael Jordan, an attorney for RJR:

> The aggressive posture we have taken regarding depositions and discovery in general continues to make these cases extremely burdensome and expensive for plaintiffs' lawyers, particularly sole practitioners. To paraphrase General Patton, the way we won these cases was not by spending all of Reynolds' money, but by making the other son of a bitch spend all his.[35]

This same approach was used to wear down my resources, including my time, attention, and money. The ultimate goal is to make the process sufficiently painful so that the researcher cannot complete further research and so that other scientists are discouraged from conducting similar studies.

Scientists are perfect subjects for harassment by litigation. They often have little knowledge of the law and little patience for the slow and subtle workings of the legal system. The distraction and anxiety caused by depositions, legal costs, and court appearances can easily put an abrupt end to a promising line of research or a research career.

It should be noted that RJR did not limit its harassment efforts to the use of the press and the courts. It also attempted to conscript the institution at which I worked. Bernard Wagner, M.D., Professor at the New York University School of Medicine and paid consultant to RJR, contacted my research colleagues and the president of MCG with accusations of scientific fraud.[36] A similar letter was sent to the University of Massachusetts regarding Dr. DiFranza's "Old Joe" study.[37] While MCG did not respond, the University of Massachusetts used these baseless accusations to initiate scientific misconduct hearings against Dr. DiFranza. He was eventually found innocent of these charges.[38]

---

[34] Complaint, *Florida v. American Tobacco Co. et al.*, No. CL-1466A0 (Circuit Ct., 15th Circuit, Palm Beach, Fla., April 18, 1995).

[35] Ibid., 28–9 (quoting Memorandum from J. Michael Jordan, Legal Counsel, RJR).

[36] Letter from Bernard Wagner to Tina Rojar (March 29, 1993) (on file with the author).

[37] Based on the author's conversations with Dr. DiFranza.

[38] Ibid.

## Suggestions

As a researcher who has been through the experience of compelled disclosure, I do not find many of the suggestions that I outline in this section to be viable solutions to the problem that I faced. I would not argue that scientists deserve special protection under the law in the same way that lawyers, priests, or journalists have claimed the need for protection of their relationships with clients, parishioners, and confidential sources. Science, after all, is based on a shared and open search for truth. I am not, however, so naive as to believe that most subpoenas for research records are based on goodwill, public interests, or the search for truth. I offer the following thoughts:

First, if a request for compelled disclosure has been made, realize that the process has moved outside of the normal exchange between scientists. It is likely that a commercial entity and its profits are at stake. It is also likely that the company will have greater legal resources and experience than the scientist, who may never have stepped foot inside a courtroom.

Second, despite institutional affiliation and responsibilities to protect academic freedom, universities may provide poor legal counseling to scientists facing compelled disclosure. This problem may become greater due to the increased reliance of universities on corporate support. We might expect to see university presidents siding with corporate contributors rather than their academic faculty.

Next, if an industry requests a subpoena, consider the industry's past record in dealing with the scientific community. Consider whether the industry has used the legal system to discourage good science in the past.

Also, consider the breadth of the request. If it goes far beyond what a reasonable scientist would require to duplicate the research, then there may be other ways that the company could validate the research findings without violating the privacy of the scientist's records.

Ask the scientist to identify specifically how compelled discovery could impede his research. It is impossible for the court to balance the rights of the company with those of the scientist unless it understands the implications of the legal process on the scientist's time, attention, and financial resources.

Finally, human subject confidentiality, promised as part of the research process, must be protected at all costs. There are excellent ways to identify scientific fraud without violating anonymity, such as the use of an independent review panel of scientists.

## Conclusion

The uneasy relationship between law and science regarding disclosure of scientific research materials is likely to continue. Law and science are worlds apart in terms of values that they hold and the rules that they follow. Whether it be DNA evidence or silicone breast implants, it appears that these two worlds will collide with ever-increasing frequency. This inevitable collision will require that scientists have a better understanding of the legal implications of their research and that judges have a better understanding of the impact of their decisions on the progress of science.

# TRANSPARENCY AND HONESTY

The five chapters in this second part consider the next logical step in our mission to rescue science from politics: the challenge of ensuring that when science enters the policy-making arena, it is explained honestly, considered objectively, and used in a process that is as transparent as possible. The transparency principles state:

- Researchers and those using their research must be careful to represent the findings accurately. When science is used for policy making, the limits of the scientific studies and judgments should be explicit so that the science does not serve as cover for underlying policy judgments. The data and methods of research that inform regulatory decisions must also be communicated honestly and expeditiously to the research community and broader public.
- Researchers and those using their data must be honest about the limits of the research and remaining uncertainties. If others misrepresent research to suggest an outcome not supported by the study, researchers must correct these misstatements as soon as they become aware of them.
- Research must never be dismissed or excluded because it does not provide a complete answer to a larger policy or science question. Research, by its nature, is incomplete, and to dismiss research because it does not provide a definitive answer could result in the exclusion of valuable science from regulatory decision making.
- The data underlying a published study, as well as a comprehensive description of the methods, must be available to other scientists and the public at large upon publication of the study or submission of

the results to a federal agency, in compliance with prevailing rules for preserving the privacy of human research subjects. Regulatory agencies should rigorously review and challenge exaggerated claims that underlying data must be kept confidential for business or other, however reasons.

The basic inquiry uniting all five chapters is whether and how science is misrepresented in formulating environmental and public health policy. The chapters conclude that scientific knowledge is often misused in one of two ways. In some cases, policy makers or special interests argue that science is only "sound" – and therefore reliable – when it is conclusive. If scientific research is uncertain or limited in scope, they argue, the science must be excluded or, at the very least, ignored. In other cases, affected parties or policy makers pretend that scientific research completely resolves policy controversies, even though the final decision in reality is based on considerations that go well beyond the available data. Either way, the outcome is the same: Underlying scientific knowledge is misrepresented and its value to policy making is undermined.

The book's survey of the ways that scientific research is misunderstood and sometimes misrepresented begins with Professor Hornstein's examination of the "sound-science" campaign, which has gained significant momentum in recent years. This sound-science narrative insists that science be conclusive before it is used to support regulatory or judicial decisions. Professor Hornstein shows how the sound-science movement neglects the reality of how science works. High-quality scientific research arises from a flexible, adaptive approach to scientific discovery, particularly in the trial-and-error work of applied science used for regulation. To suggest that the science instead must produce "the" definitive answer before it can be integrated into policy ignores the realities of scientific discovery, as well as the limits of scientific knowledge. It also means that less, rather than more, science will influence policy making, a result that is precisely the opposite of what sound-science proponents advocate.

Dr. Cranor explores a parallel problem occurring in the judicial system. In response to a series of Supreme Court decisions issued a decade ago, some judges have excluded scientific expert testimony that is based on research that, standing alone, cannot definitively resolve complex causation questions. These exclusions occur even though the underlying research does provide valuable insights into causation. Rejecting expert testimony on causation simply because it does not meet unrealistic judicial standards of scientific certainty not only excludes important knowledge that science can provide to juries in answering difficult causation questions, but it may deny injured individuals their constitutional right to a jury trial.

This tendency of legal institutions to exclude science because it is not definitive lies at one end of the spectrum of violations of the honesty and transparency principles. At the other end of the spectrum is an equally damaging tendency to exaggerate the information that science does offer to the resolution of policy questions. Rather than excluding scientific research from policy-making projects until it is conclusive, this type of institutional practice ignores the limits of science by purporting to base decisions on science when the policies transcend the limits of science and must also be resolved using values.

In the third chapter of this section, Dr. Holly Doremus discusses the exaggeration of the scientific support for political decisions in the context of natural resource policy. She concludes that political pressures, court rulings, and even professional allegiances are in unhealthy alignment in the area of endangered species protection, leading agencies to overstate the extent to which scientific research informs their policy decisions. Compounding the damage to scientific credibility and integrity created by such exaggerations, these distorted claims allow policy makers to escape public accountability for their decisions.

Dr. Vern Walker considers analogous types of transparency problems in the international arena, especially in the resolution of trade disputes. Dr. Walker argues that the law makes unrealistic demands on science when it insists on explicit chains of logic to justify its findings, with further demands that each link in the chain be supported by empirical scientific evidence. In these settings, scientists sometimes succumb to the pressure to overstate their findings in an effort to answer policy makers' questions, and the limits of science are lost or glossed over in the course of integrating science into policy. The result is that scientific knowledge is forced into a rigid mold, obscuring uncertainties and limitations.

Just as Dr. Walker considers the costs to scientists arising from violations of the transparency principles, Dr. David Adelman looks specifically to the scientific community's own internal struggle in articulating the limits of research. The conflict between scientists who use Bayesian statistics versus frequentist statistics is fundamentally a debate among scientists regarding how best to communicate research limitations. By probing the assumptions behind the two methodologies, Dr. Adelman identifies ways that scientists can improve their own communication of uncertainties and suggests parallel reforms of the legal system to better represent the underlying limitations of scientific research. Such reforms respond to the tendency of the legal system to ignore the limits of science, as documented in the previous four chapters.

# 5

# The Data Wars, Adaptive Management, and the Irony of "Sound Science"

Donald T. Hornstein, J.D.

## The Sound-Science Crusade versus Adaptive Management

What science has to tell policy makers has always been contested terrain. Rachel Carson, in the *New Yorker* essays from which her classic book *Silent Spring* was drawn, questioned the government's manipulation of science to support the toxicological safety of pesticides. Carson included a charge that a panel of toxicologists at the National Academies of Science (NAS) had been stacked by industry-sponsored experts. Later, when the publication of *Silent Spring* itself ignited a public controversy over the integrity of science, President John F. Kennedy was forced to bypass the NAS to receive advice from the President's Science Advisory Committee (PSAC), which issued a report in 1963 largely supporting Carson. There followed counterattacks on the findings of the PSAC by the NAS, counter-counterattacks against the scientific integrity of the NAS by analysts at the Audubon Society, a proliferation of studies by other researchers, and over a dozen separate congressional pesticide-related hearings by the Eighty-Eighth Congress between 1963 and 1964.[1]

In the ensuing forty years, there have been so many other episodes in which science is said to have been misused by policy makers that it is possible today for commentators to identify different *patterns* of distortion and to argue over which pattern best captures the current state of science–policy interaction. This argument matters because, depending on which

---

[1] This synopsis is taken from Donald T. Hornstein, "Lessons from Federal Pesticide Regulation on the Paradigms and Politics of Environmental Law Reform," *Yale Journal on Regulation* 10, no. 2 (1993): 369, 426. The full story is recounted in Christopher J. Bosso, *Pesticides and Politics: The Life Cycle of a Public Issue* (Pittsburgh, PA: University of Pittsburgh Press 1987).

pattern is perceived to describe reality, entirely different narratives about regulatory science can emerge. And these narratives in turn can lead to radically different political prescriptions for reshaping the connections between science and policy.

The first section of this chapter discusses the emergence of one such narrative, the "sound-science" story, and the even-more-recent emergence of two legislative prescriptions that follow the sound-science script. These legislative measures, known as the Shelby Amendment and the Data Quality Act (hereinafter the Data Amendments), were adopted by Congress in the late 1990s but have only more recently begun to exert influence on the regulatory landscape through aggressive implementation during the Bush Administration. Although it remains to be seen whether the Data Amendments will have a lasting effect on the landscape, one can only hope not. So far, the regulatory regime they seek to inaugurate resembles a dreary world of bare-knuckled trench warfare, in which interest groups are armed with mechanisms to challenge, in the name of sound science, any scientific research with which they disagree. The result is that the normal level of disputation over regulatory science disintegrates into a form of perpetual hazing in which science may not be used (nor possibly even referenced) unless it first passes through a gauntlet of repetitive challenges.

Rather than reflecting principled science, the Data Amendments are designed to be used as a political weapon in contravention of legitimate scientific principles. The principle of transparency, in particular, requires that "research must never be dismissed or excluded because it does not provide a complete answer to a larger policy or science question." As discussed in this chapter, both the Shelby Amendment and the Data Quality Act are tools used to exploit the inevitable uncertainties in most science, and to impugn as "unsound" any science in which uncertainties can be found. This approach violates the core principles that are the framework for this book, specifically the principle that research by its nature is incomplete and to dismiss research because it does not provide a definitive answer could result in the exclusion of valuable science from regulatory decision making.

The irony is that the data wars unleashed by the sound-science narrative are taking shape contemporaneously with the emergence of a potentially more hopeful and optimistic model for science–policy interactions. The second section of this chapter sketches the outlines of adaptive management, an approach to scientific uncertainty that has been used occasionally, but with increasing frequency, among regulators and scientists who are tasked with managing natural resources such as watersheds, forests, and wildlife. Adaptive management seeks to structure regulatory decision making in the style of systematic experimentation, with an eye toward the development of knowledge over time by careful measurement of regulatory outcomes and the iterative adjustment of regulatory policy making to reflect what has been learned from previous successes and failures.

To be sure, it is important to see whether adaptive management can actually live up to its promises. But for present purposes, the contrast in its approach to science and scientists with that taken by the Data Amendments could not be more stark. As the Data Amendments go about setting up the apparatus for an extremely adversarial system, adaptive management has been experimenting with decision-making structures that allow science to be vetted but through less confrontational means. Adaptive management practitioners, moreover, have also experimented with structures that seek to address the science–policy chasm, such as by the creation of independent science advisory bodies that are deliberately insulated from overt political interference while at the same time creating mechanisms for collaborative interactions between scientists and nonscientific policy makers. These kinds of independence, iteration, and transparency, of course, are features that have long characterized science itself.

Recently, as challenges under the Data Amendments have begun to seep into natural resources management, special interest adversarialness has begun to operate side by side with these other, more collaborative, open, and scientific approaches. As the contrast unfolds, the deeper irony of the Data Amendments is revealed: that the sound-science narrative is itself antiscientific. Science involves constant hypothesis testing by disinterested observers. In contrast, the sound-science narrative is predicated on the worldview that nothing can be known or even repeated until it can be officially challenged by nonscientists or otherwise certified as perfect.

## Of Narratives, Counternarratives, and the Data Wars

### The "Science Charade" Narrative

In 1995, Professor Wendy Wagner documented how, in environmental regulation, administrators can overrely on science (and scientists) to implement statutory programs through which Congress demands public protection against the risk of serious harm even when the extent of the risk is highly uncertain. This overreliance can occur inadvertently. For example, it can occur when administrators delegate regulatory standard setting to scientists who are influenced by scientific norms demanding high confidence levels before acting, and thus who often fail to develop timely standards – precisely because the data are uncertain. Such a failure occurs despite the political norm adopted by Congress in the overarching statute that action be taken even without satisfaction of such high confidence levels. The resulting regulatory inaction leaves the precautionary statute poorly implemented, as the public faces the underlying risk of harm while regulatory scientists study the issue indefinitely and wait for scientific certainty to emerge. Professor Wagner argued that the agency, by viewing the problem as one solely for scientists (and the traditional norms of science) to resolve, is engaging in a charade to camouflage the agency's own failure to make the necessary "trans-scientific" policy judgments that the situation demands.[2]

Wagner also argued that the science charade can be intentional. This occurs when administrators take action but exaggerate the extent to which their decisions are mandated by science, precisely to avoid political accountability for what in reality are their own trans-scientific policy judgments. Wagner illustrates this variation with the decision of the federal Environmental Protection Agency (EPA) in 1979 to relax the ambient air pollution standard for ground-level ozone from 0.08 parts per million (ppm) to 0.12 ppm. In an interview given two years later in 1981, the EPA administrator, Douglas Costle, admitted that he was aware of the political pressure the agency would face in selecting the 0.12 ppm standard from the leading alternatives of 0.08, 0.10, and 0.15: "[I]t was [going to be] a political loser no matter what you did . . . the minute you picked a number . . . everybody can argue that it can't be that number, or it could just as easily be another number . . . *[I]t was a value judgment*."[3] In contrast to the candor of this statement, in 1979 EPA camouflaged its decision with a

[2]  Wendy E. Wagner, "The Science Charade in Toxic Risk Regulation," *Columbia Law Review* 95, no. 7 (1995): 1613.
[3]  Ibid., 1641 (emphasis added) (citing Marc K. Landy et al., *The Environmental Protection Agency: Asking the Wrong Questions* (New York: Oxford University Press, 1990), 71 (quoting interview with Doug M. Costle, EPA administrator, in Cambridge, MA, July 31, 1981).

"mind-numbing" fifteen-page scientific justification that, while acknowledging that the science behind the agency's selection was not "undisputed," nonetheless insisted that in making his choice, the administrator was exercising his "informed scientific judgment."[4] The science charade in this case was intentional.

Finally, Wagner also warned that the science charade could be premeditated. This variation occurs when the government or others manipulate science to justify predetermined regulatory ends. It was precisely this kind of charade that Rachel Carson alleged in the 1960s when she pointed to NAS pesticide panels "stacked" with industry-sponsored toxicologists. In the 1970s, it was alleged that EPA drastically overstated the science on sulfur dioxide pollution in order to justify its politically aggressive air pollution reduction agenda. In the 1980s, it was alleged that EPA refused to regulate formaldehyde under the Toxic Substances Control Act based on science that "deviated significantly from both the prevailing scientific evidence regarding health effects of formaldehyde and accepted EPA risk assessment assumptions."[5] And, more currently, there is criticism from groups such as the Union of Concerned Scientists that the Bush Administration regularly manipulates science to suit its political ends in numerous areas across the policy spectrum.[6] What matters here is the typology of the allegations rather than their particular merits – if true, the allegations reflect the most cynical, premeditated variation of the science charade.

Depending on which of the science charades is detected, a wide variety of corrective measures could address the problem. To correct the unproductive delay caused by the inadvertent charade, for example, policy makers could establish (and have established) regulatory deadlines for risk-based determinations or minimized the importance of such determinations in the first place by charging the agency simply to oversee the installation of the best available pollution-control equipment. To discourage the intentional charade, agencies could be forced on judicial review to identify both the limits of the science at issue and the permissibility of the trans-scientific

[4] Ibid., 1642.
[5] Ibid., 1647.
[6] Union of Concerned Scientists, "Scientific Integrity in Policy Making: Investigation of the Bush Administration's Abuse of Science," Union of Concerned Scientists, http://www.ucsusa.org/global_environment/rsi/page.cfm?pageID=1641.

policy judgments that may have been made. To combat premeditated manipulation, policy makers could prohibit the stacking of scientific panels with those who might have financial conflicts of interest, strengthen civil and criminal penalties for deliberate data omissions and falsifications, and/or enhance the legal protection given to whistleblowers.

## The "Sound-Science" Narrative

Beginning in the 1980s, a consistent counternarrative to the science charade arose: Decision makers were not using enough science, or not enough "rigorous" science. Initially, the focus was aimed at what was alleged to be the institutional shortcomings of courts in their use of science in tort litigation. In 1985, Peter Huber singled out tort litigation against the childhood pertussis vaccine as a "case study" in which courts were alleged to be less capable than administrative agencies of making sound comparative risk decisions when the evidence showed "particularly precise risk figures" for this vaccine.[7] In 1991, in a popular book, Huber coined the phrase "junk science," and both revised his argument as to the pertussis vaccine litigation (he now claimed that the data linking the pertussis vaccine to brain damage were junk science rather than "particularly precise") and expanded his institutional critique of courts to argue that tort litigation spawned decisions based on non-peer-reviewed science introduced into evidence by scientists out of the mainstream.[8]

As Professor Carl Cranor discusses in Chapter 6 of this book, in 1993 the Supreme Court handed down *Daubert v. Merrell Dow Pharmaceuticals, Inc.*,[9] a tort case involving claims against Bendectin, an antinausea

[7] Peter W. Huber, "Safety and the Second Best: The Hazards of Public Risk Management in the Courts," *Columbia Law Review* 85, no. 2 (1985): 277, 288. Huber's institutional argument was that the administrative agencies, rather than courts, were better suited to make the "aggregative calculus of risk created and risk averted that progressive public-risk management requires." Ibid., 278. Huber's particular case history of the relative risks of the childhood pertussis vaccine is addressed and criticized in Donald T. Hornstein, "Reclaiming Environmental Law: A Normative Critique of Comparative Risk Analysis," *Columbia Law Review* 92, no. 3 (1992): 562, 621–4 (noting that the litigation led to development of safer vaccines that seemed capable of reducing the side-effects of the traditional whole-cell vaccine while still maintaining efficacy against the underlying whooping cough disease itself).

[8] Peter W. Huber, *Galileo's Revenge: Junk Science in the Courtroom* (New York: Basic Books, 1991), 174–5. At the time he wrote this book, Huber had become a Senior Fellow at the conservative-leaning Manhattan Institute.

[9] 509 U.S. 579 (1993).

medication administered to pregnant women, and adopted mechanisms designed to enhance the reliability of scientific information introduced into evidence in federal courts. *Daubert* was read by its proponents to endorse the efficacy of peer-reviewed epidemiological studies, which they argued did not show a statistically significant link between Bendectin and birth defects.[10]

Whatever its beginnings as a critique of tort litigation, the junk science story soon expanded into a somewhat nebulous claim that much public health and environmental *regulation* was unscientific. The expansion of the claim beyond courtrooms and tort litigation was apparent as arguments were made to *"Daubertize"* regulatory agency decision making.[11] The nebulousness of the claim was also apparent. Sometimes critics merely postured for rhetorical advantage by claiming that adherents to the science charade narrative, rather than identifying the limits of science, were calling for its abandonment – something that was not the case.[12] Other times, critics argued that agencies such as EPA were too slow to recognize new scientific findings that were alleged to disprove conservative default policies that the agency had previously made.[13] Yet other times, critics were actually second-guessing Congress for repeatedly enacting precautionary statutes that protect people from public-health and environmental risk even when science does not allow for those risks to be characterized with scientific certainty. In the 1990s, these claims began to be described as the "sound-science" argument and, despite itself being the subject of heavy factual criticism, coalesced into an overarching notion: " that agencies like EPA and [the Occupational Safety and Health Administration] ignore 'sound science' in their zeal to write stringent regulations to implement ultra-protective regulatory policies."[14]

---

[10] Leslie Morsek, "Get on Board for the Ride of Your Life! The Ups, the Downs, the Twists, and the Turns of the Applicability of the 'Gatekeeper' Function to Scientific and Non-Scientific Expert Evidence: *Kuhmo's* Expansion of *Daubert*," *Akron Law Review* 34, no. 3 (2001): 689, 704 n. 58.

[11] Alan Charles Raul and Julie Zampa Dwyer, "'Regulatory *Daubert*'": A Proposal to Enhance Judicial Review of Agency Science by Incorporating *Daubert* Principles into Administrative Law," *Law and Contemporary Problems* 66, no. 4 (2003): 7.

[12] James W. Conrad, Jr., "The Reverse Science Charade," *Environmental Law Reporter* 33, no. 4 (2003): 10306.

[13] Ibid. But see Wendy E. Wagner, "EPA's Lag in Responding to Scientific Advances: A Reply to Conrad," *Environmental Law Reporter* 34, no. 2 (2004): 10497.

[14] Thomas O. McGarity, "MTBE: A Precautionary Tale," *Harvard Environmental Law Review* 28, no. 2 (2004): 281, 318 (citations omitted).

In the two sections that follow, I discuss how the Data Amendments have become two of the more concrete manifestations of the sound-science narrative.

## The Data Amendments

### Shelby Data Disclosure

As the science-charade and sound-science narratives unfolded in the 1990s, the Republican-controlled Congress adopted two measures that, at least as seen by their proponents, reflected the sound-science story. The Shelby Amendment itself was born with virtually no legislative fanfare, as discussed in this section. But it is not difficult, and in fact quite revealing, to consider the episode that prompted Senator Richard Shelby (R-AL) to introduce it.

The episode centered on EPA's regulation of ground-level ozone and airborne particulate matter, thus involving the same regulatory regime that Professor Wagner used to illustrate the "intentional" science charade where the agency implied in 1979 that its choice of a 0.12 ppm ozone standard was largely a "scientific" exercise. Eighteen years later, in 1997, it had become plain to EPA that its earlier standards for ozone and particulates were not stringent enough. The agency reached this conclusion in part by the sort of scientific evidence that the *Daubert* Court in 1993 was understood to have endorsed: published, peer-reviewed evidence. Indeed, if *Daubert* had implied that the gold standard for scientific evidence was peer-reviewed epidemiological evidence, then EPA in the mid-1990s had before it solid gold evidence that particulate levels theretofore thought to be healthy in fact were not.

Among the evidence before EPA "was the so-called 'Six Cities Study,' a twenty-year longitudinal collection of studies measuring air-pollution effects among thousands of people in diverse settings – a massive research effort that alone had spawned over one hundred publications."[15] As Dr. Douglas Dockery, a Harvard researcher and one of the study's principal investigators, later testified, "what we found was that, even as we adjusted

---

[15] Donald T. Hornstein, "Accounting for Science: The Independence of Public Research in the New, Subterranean Administrative Law," *Law and Contemporary Problems* 66, no. 4 (2003): 227, 238.

for sex, age, and cigarette smoking, occupation, education, obesity, and chronic disease history, people living in areas with higher . . . particle concentrations had a shorter life expectancy than people living in the cleaner cities."[16]

Because EPA's stricter particulate standards threatened to impose costly remedial measures, EPA faced a barrage of organized opposition, including highly visible congressional oversight hearings and the introduction of legislation that specifically would have postponed EPA's proposed revision. The legislation failed. But during the congressional hearings Senator Shelby and others demanded access to the raw data underlying the Six Cities Study, including the detailed confidential medical information provided to the researchers by thousands of citizen-participants.[17]

Dr. Dockery refused in order to protect the medical privacy of the study's subjects. Under further congressional pressure, he finally agreed to allow an independent scientific body, the Health Effects Institute (HEI), access to the underlying data under conditions of confidentiality. HEI confirmed the basic legitimacy of both the methodology and substantive results of the Six Cities Study.[18] The Six Cities Study was further reviewed by a panel from the National Research Council, and in 2002 the panel issued tentative findings that EPA's epidemiological studies were "generally defensible."[19]

In the meantime, unsatisfied with Dockery's refusal to provide access to the raw data, Senator Shelby introduced a one-sentence amendment, later called the "Data Access" or "Shelby Amendment," into a four-thousand-page fiscal year 1999 appropriations bill. The Shelby Amendment was not the subject of any contemporaneous committee hearings, and its sparse legislative history "consisted mostly of staged colloquies and a few cursory sentences in the various committee reports that accompanied the massive budget bill."[20] The statute allows any person to demand under the Freedom of Information Act "all data" produced by researchers operating under any federally financed award from grantors such as the National Science Foundation, National Institutes of Health, or other "awarding agencies." The statute is entirely asymmetrical, and does not allow access to the data

---

[16] Ibid.
[17] Ibid.
[18] Ibid.
[19] Ibid., 236.
[20] Ibid., 230–1.

underlying research financed by corporations, even when this research is submitted to federal agencies for use in decision making that has health, safety, or environmental ramifications. Senator Shelby later wrote that his amendment was designed to minimize "the use of junk science."[21]

Senator Shelby's statement is, to say the least, revealing. What it reveals, however, is nothing pertinent to the scientific validity of the Six Cities Study. That study, whether measured by the preference for peer-reviewed data suggested in *Daubert* or by the preference for empirical data encapsulated in Peter Huber's writings on junk science, passes muster with flying colors. Rather, what it reveals is that the term "junk science," like the broader sound-science narrative of which it is a part, had become unmoored from any neutral concern for scientific validity. Thus, it is hardly surprising that scientific institutions with a longstanding interest in the integrity of science, such as the National Academies of Science, soon called for the repeal of the Shelby Amendment.[22]

And little wonder. The Shelby Amendment is a thinly disguised political tool to be used by those who oppose a particular government regulation. Accordingly, after Congress refused to prevent EPA from revising its ozone and particulate standards, after the Six Cities Study had been corroborated twice by scientific institutions, and after both the Supreme Court and the D.C. Circuit Court of Appeals had rejected legal challenges brought against EPA's ozone and particulate revisions,[23] William Kovacs, vice president of the United States Chamber of Commerce, suggested candidly that he might nevertheless like to apply the Shelby Amendment to the Six Cities Study, and "reanalyze it."[24]

## The Data (Information) Quality Act

Two years after passage of the Shelby Amendment, a short rider was introduced to another massive appropriations bill, adding Section 515 to the Treasury and General Government Appropriations Bill for Fiscal Year 2001.

[21] Senator Richard Shelby, "Accountability and Transparency: Public Access to Federal Funded Research Data," *Harvard Journal on Legislation* 37, no. 2 (2000): 369, 376.
[22] Hornstein, "Accounting for Science," 231.
[23] *Whitman v. Am. Trucking Ass'ns*, 531 U.S. 457 (2001); *Am. Trucking Ass'ns v. Environmental Protection Agency*, 238 F. 3d 355 (D.C. Cir. 2002) (on remand from the Supreme Court).
[24] Pat Phibbs, "OMB Guidelines on Quality of Information Seen as Having Profound Impact on Agencies," *Environmental Reporter* 33, no. 3 (2002): 146.

As with the Shelby Amendment, Congress held no hearings on the bill. A Washington lobbyist named Jim Tozzi later claimed credit for conceptualizing the bill as part of his paid work during the 1990s for cigarette companies that were under pressure from adverse health and safety data.[25] But the bill, referred to after enactment as either the Data Quality Act (DQA) or Information Quality Act, went well beyond data relating to cigarettes.

The new law directed the White House's Office of Management and Budget (OMB) to issue procedural guidance to all federal agencies for "ensuring and maximizing the quality, objectivity, utility, and integrity of information . . . disseminated by Federal agencies." The statute further directed OMB to require that all federal agencies adopt their own data quality guidelines within one year and establish administrative mechanisms by which any "affected persons" could seek and obtain "correction" of information "that does not comply with the guidelines."[26]

There has never been a statute like the DQA – one anchored by virtually no legislative history yet seemingly applicable across all federal agencies whenever "data" are involved.[27] It soon became clear that OMB would fill the empty spaces of this statute with pages from the sound-science narrative. Thus, rather than limit who could seek "correction" of "disseminated" governmental data to those about whom the government had produced and disseminated poor-quality information, OMB defined the terms so broadly[28] that, in 2003, a business organization known as the Competitive Enterprise Institute could use the DQA to demand in the name of "quality" that the federal government retract *even its reference* to a report known as the "National Assessment on Climate Change" – despite the fact that the report had been peer-reviewed by over three hundred scientific and technical

[25] Chris Mooney, "Paralysis by Analysis: Jim Tozzi's Regulation to End All Regulation," *Washington Monthly* 36, no. 5 (2004): 23. As to the lack of congressional consideration of the Data Quality Act, Dr. John Graham, the official later tasked with administering the statute, conceded that "the law was enacted as a rider to an appropriations bill without any hearings or extensive legislative history." National Research Council, *Ensuring the Quality of Data Disseminated by the Federal Government* (Washington, DC: National Academy Press, 2002), 9.

[26] Treasury and General Government Appropriations Act for Fiscal Year 2001, Pub. L. No. 106–554, § 515, 114 Stat. 2763 (2000).

[27] Thomas O. McGarity et al., *Truth and Science Betrayed: The Case against the Information Quality Act* (available at http://www.progressiveregulation.org/articles/iqa.pdf).

[28] Guidelines for Ensuring and Maximizing the Quality, Objectivity, Utility, and Integrity of Information Disseminated by Federal Agencies, 66 Fed. Reg. 49,721 (Sept. 28, 2001) (defining "affected persons" to include anyone "who may benefit or be harmed. . . . as well as persons who use information that is disseminated").

experts and assembled under the supervision of experts convened by the President's Committee of Advisors on Science and Technology.[29]

Not content with empowering citizen vigilantes to challenge agencies for using even peer-reviewed science, OMB also found in the DQA another page from the sound-science narrative: that Congress should not have authorized federal agencies to take precautions against risk even when the precise dimension of the risk could not be characterized at a high level of confidence. In 2002, OMB insisted that the DQA also mandated all federal agencies to "adopt or adapt" an especially stringent and time-consuming protocol for risk analysis theretofore found only in the federal Safe Drinking Water Act, a unique requirement that was, of course, not referenced at all by Congress when the DQA was enacted.[30]

OMB also found in the DQA the same asymmetrical concern for sound science that had been hard-wired into the Shelby Amendment. OMB's implementing regulations exempted concern for the quality of data submitted by companies in "adjudications," which could include studies submitted in support of a product or pollution permit, and "public filings," which seems to include companies' evidence of compliance with legal requirements as well as evidence supporting companies' submissions under the federal Toxic Release Inventory.[31]

In short, the DQA was an almost perfect invention for those subscribing to the sound-science narrative – a statutory fountain from which could pour an almost limitless array of obstacles against the science used by the government in its regulation of health, safety, and the environment.

## Another Narrative? Adaptive Management and Agency Learning

Despite the important differences between the sound-science and science charade narratives, there is one area of overlap: Both narratives view science

---

[29] For information on the National Assessment, see U.S. Global Change Research Program, *Climate Change Impacts on the United States: The Potential Consequences of Climate Variability and Change* (Cambridge, UK: Cambridge University Press, 2001) (available at http://www.usgcrp.gov/usgcrp/Library/nationalassessment/foundation.htm).

[30] Guidelines for Ensuring and Maximizing the Quality, Objectivity, Utility, and Integrity of Information Disseminated by Federal Agencies; Republication, 67 Fed. Reg. 8452, 8458 (Feb. 22, 2002).

[31] Wendy Wagner and David Michaels, "Equal Treatment for Regulatory Science: Extending the Controls Governing the Quality of Public Research to Private Research," *American Journal of Law and Medicine* 30, nos. 2–3 (2004): 119.

in fairly fixed, static terms. Sound science operates as if there exists a perfect factual "answer" to most regulatory questions that needs to be obtained, or at least approached, before regulators can take action. The science charade operates as if the answers that science provides also are knowable, albeit incomplete because they cannot shed light on the trans-scientific value judgments implicit in the questions asked. But especially in the field of natural resources management, both narratives fail to capture another, increasingly common reality: that we will not, indeed cannot, obtain the knowledge we need until we attempt solutions, measure their effectiveness (or, as likely, ineffectiveness), integrate that knowledge into redesigned approaches, and then continue the iterative process of learning.

In a 2005 report, the National Academies of Science's National Research Council (NRC) described a system of regulatory problem solving known as "adaptive management" that seeks to address just this kind of situation.[32] To be clear, adaptive management "does not postpone actions until 'enough' is known about a managed ecosystem,"[33] nor is it simply a "trial and error" process."[34] Instead, it represents a more systematic "learning while doing" approach that involves choosing actions likely to generate meaningful and positive results, monitoring the actual results of those actions, and subsequently learning from analysis of the data how to improve the design of the next generation of actions.[35]

In contrast with the sound-science narrative, adaptive management recognizes the need for responsible regulators to take action in the face of uncertainty. And, in contrast to the science charade narrative, adaptive management heavily emphasizes a scientific process of iterative hypothesis testing. Although its use in natural resources management is relatively new, it has a history of use in business, engineering, military planning, and public administration.[36]

To be sure, the role for adaptive management in natural resources decision making remains highly uncertain. Although Congress explicitly authorized its use in the late 1970s for salmon restoration programs in the Columbia River watershed, adaptive management's track record in the

---

[32] National Research Council, *Adaptive Management for Water Resources Project Planning* (Washington, DC: National Academy Press, 2004).
[33] Ibid., 19.
[34] Ibid., 22.
[35] Ibid., 22–4.
[36] Ibid., 28.

ensuing twenty years has been poor. Nonetheless, there continues to be a high level of enthusiasm for the concept. Adaptive management currently plays a role in the U.S. Army Corps of Engineers' Comprehensive Everglades Restoration Plan (the most ambitious natural resources restoration plan in history), in several forest management plans adopted by the U.S. Forest Service, in dozens of Habitat Conservation Plans developed under Section 10 of the Endangered Species Act, and in numerous other natural resources applications. It gained special visibility in the mid-1990s when the Glen Canyon Adaptive Management Program released high water from the Glen Canyon Dam, simulating a spring flood to determine whether manufactured pre-dam conditions, including transported sediment, could help restore beach habitat critical to the Colorado River's riparian ecology.[37]

Adaptive management, of course, is much easier said than done. A recent NRC report noted that, although some progress had been made, the adaptive management program for the Everglades restoration effort had not yet sufficiently developed "key tools" for comprehensive monitoring of outcomes, for regional assessments of current environmental pressures, and for the integration of monitoring and research feedback into the planning process.[38] Indeed, these criticisms seem so central to the adaptive management exercise that one wonders whether the NRC isn't dangerously optimistic when it concludes that "these early evaluations . . . not only provide an opportunity for mid-source correction, but also serve as important lessons for adaptive ecosystem restoration in other parts of the nation."[39] And if adaptive management is making such a mediocre showing in the Everglades project, it is not difficult to imagine adaptive management failing altogether – or worse, being actively manipulated – in projects with far less political visibility.

That said, however, there are also signs that adaptive management represents a bona fide innovation, especially to the extent that there may be simply no escaping the "regulatory learning" narrative. Particularly in this regard, there are positive signs that adaptive management represents a marked improvement in integrating science into policy over the endless data wars promised by the sound-science narrative. Consider, as a case in

---

[37]  Ibid., 80.
[38]  Ibid., 57–8 (citing a detailed 2003 assessment by the U.S. General Accounting Office).
[39]  Ibid., 59.

point, a comparison of the two narratives as applied to the restoration of ecological integrity in the West.

One of the flashpoints for conservation in the American Southwest involves efforts to save the southwestern willow flycatcher, a species of bird listed under the federal Endangered Species Act. To see what the sound-science narrative has to offer, one need go little further than a petition from an Arizona rancher filed under the Data Quality Act in 2003 demanding that the U.S. Forest Service "correct" a specific portion of a "guidance document" that notes how livestock grazing during the flycatcher's breeding season can increase cowbird parasitism on the flycatcher's nests.[40] The rancher's lawyer demanded this portion of the Forest Service's scientific guidance be changed because, under the DQA, it is not "objective" science until it has cited other studies that the rancher believed to be applicable and is "capable of being reproduced" by other scientists.[41] In short, habitat protection was to be altered or suspended until the science was perfect.

In contrast, consider the regulatory learning narrative underlying the Glen Canyon Adaptive Management Program that is experimenting with simulated floods on the Colorado River in part to restore the riparian habitat needed by the southwestern willow flycatcher. There, a working group of stakeholders with diverse (and often conflicting) interests in the Grand Canyon and Glen Canyon Dam operations meets regularly to collaborate over possible measures that can improve habitat protection while still addressing power, recreational, and water-supply economic interests. The stakeholder group is advised by a Technical Work Group that features a Science Center with a full-time staff known as the Grand Canyon Monitoring and Research Center.[42] Although this program is far from perfect, it has moved beyond endless data wars and conducted experiments on dam releases, the results of which "were extensively monitored and ... used in subsequent deliberations about dam operations."[43]

---

[40] Formal Request for Correction of USDA Information from Eddie Johnson, Johnson Ranch, to John King, Assistant Director of the Information Resources Management, Department of Agriculture (March 21, 2003) (available at "Docket of Data Quality Petitions," OMB Watch, http://www.ombwatch.org/article/articleview/2668/1/231).

[41] Ibid.

[42] National Research Council, "Adaptive Management for Water Resources Project Planning," 79.

[43] Ibid., 80 (noting both positive and negative aspects of the Glen Canyon Adaptive Management Program).

Take one more example, this one involving efforts to conserve habitat for rare species of butterflies. The sound-science approach is exemplified in another petition under the Data Quality Act, this one sent in June 2004 to the Department of the Interior. The petition opposed efforts to list (under the Endangered Species Act) the Sand Mountain blue butterfly because, among other things, of assertions in a one-page petition that "habitat loss evidence is exaggerated and riddled with inapplicable and misapplied science. Photographic evidence is skewed. [And] status cannot be determined from data."[44] In contrast, an article in the journal *Conservation Biology* documents how an adaptive management approach was used to redesign the Monarch Butterfly Biosphere Reserve in Central Mexico.[45] Among other things, this approach took care to structure scientific experts "into three working groups to prevent dominant personalities or authorities from biasing the judgments of the entire group." Using this structure, the experts reviewed the results of sequential "spatial analysis in an iterative way until [scientific] consensus was attained."[46]

## Conclusion

I seek to make two points in this chapter. First, the sound-science narrative, especially as it has been unleashed through the recently enacted Data Amendments, represents bad public policy. It is bad policy because its premise, in contravention of the principle of transparency, is that our understanding of public-health and environmental risks must (or even can) approach perfection before we take measures to protect ourselves or conserve natural resources. It is bad policy because its approach to science is one of extreme adversarialness. And it is bad policy because it has developed in the subterranean world of last-minute, politically invisible riders to appropriations bills, and in the overreaching of executive branch administrators in their implementation of the Data Amendments.

---

[44] Information Quality Act Petition Challenging the Service's Use and Interpretation of Available Information for the Sand Mountain Blue Butterfly (*Euphilotes pallescens arenamontana*) as a Threatened or Endangered Species to Gale Norton, Secretary of the Interior, Department of the Interior (June 21, 2004) (available at "Docket of Data Quality Petitions," OMB Watch, http://www.ombwatch.org/article/articleview/2668/1/231).

[45] Luis A. Bojorquez-Tapia et al., "Mapping Expert Knowledge: Redesigning the Monarch Butterfly Biosphere Reserve," *Conservation Biology* 17, no. 2 (2003): 367.

[46] Ibid., 370.

Second, and perhaps even more tragically, the sound-science narrative threatens to blind us to the possibilities of an emerging regulatory learning narrative that would allow policy makers to engage science more constructively. Adaptive management and the regulatory learning narrative plainly are at this point only works in progress. They portend, however, the possibility of real progress away from the corrosive data wars currently promised us by those who claim only to advocate "sound science."

# 6

# The Dual Legacy of *Daubert v. Merrell-Dow Pharmaceutical*

## Trading Junk Science for Insidious Science

Carl F. Cranor, Ph.D.

## Judicial Distortion of Science

*Daubert v. Merrell-Dow Pharmaceutical* and its progeny are Supreme Court cases that aim at improving the quality of scientific expert testimony admitted into evidence in federal litigation[1] and respond to the perceived threat posed by the use of "junk science" in the courtroom.[2] In resolving a challenge to the validity of a scientific experts' testimony in a tort case, the Supreme Court in *Daubert* held that judges in reviewing expert testimony should follow the Federal Rules of Evidence, not *Frye v. U.S.*[3] Moreover, in order for testimony to be admitted, it must be "reliable" and fit the facts of the case.

Despite the Supreme Court's laudable goals of improving the quality of the science in litigation, however, lower courts still seem to be struggling with scientific evidence in legal cases; judges often fail to review the science in toxic tort cases as scientists would have done, thus frustrating the aims of *Daubert* and two key subsequent decisions. These decisions reveal views that are contrary to sound scientific principles. Mistaken court conceptions of reasonable scientific evidence or of good scientific argument often then

---

[1]  *Daubert v. Merrill Dow Pharm., Inc.*, 509 U.S. 579 (1993); *General Elec. Co. v. Joiner*, 522 U.S. 136 (1997); *Kumho Tire Co. v. Carmichael*, 526 U.S. 137 (1999).
[2]  The term "junk science" was introduced to suggest that testimony and evidence from suspect or dishonest scientists led to mistaken legal verdicts in favor of plaintiffs, driving good products, such as the anti–morning sickness drug Bendectin, off the market. Michael D. Green, *Bendectin and Birth Defects: The Challenges of Mass Toxic Substances Litigation* (Philadelphia, PA: University of Pennsylvania Press, 1996), 20–1 (citing Peter Huber, *Galileo's Revenge: Junk Science in the Courtroom* [New York: Basic Books, 1991]; Peter Huber, *Liability: The Legal Revolution and Its Consequences* [New York: Basic Books, 1988]).
[3]  *Frye v. U.S.*, 293 F. 1013 (D.C. Cir. 1923).

are propagated through the legal system by precedent or by merely following the Joneses of brethren courts. As a result, in their efforts to avoid junk science, or being misled by persuasive but suspect scientists, courts have done violence to the scientific process, constructed views of science that are not accurate, appeared not to have understood scientific reasoning, and lessened protection of the public's health.

This chapter considers the courts' struggle with several important scientific issues and shows how they have violated two of the scientific principles spotlighted in this book: First, research should not be dismissed or excluded simply because it does not represent a complete or definitive answer to a larger policy or science question; second, the limits of scientific research and its resulting uncertainties should not be misrepresented. The approaches taken by the courts diverge, sometimes significantly, from those utilized by the scientific community.

While a primary goal of this chapter is to alert those engaged with the judicial system about the pitfalls of such mistakes, in the context of the scientific principles that are the foundation of this book, such trends have even more important implications for the scientists who are paid to testify as expert witnesses and the lawyers who hire them. Scientists, both those testifying for plaintiffs and those testifying for defendants, are or should be aware of the various reasons that judicial use of science conflicts with bedrock scientific methodologies, practices, and assumptions. When they permit lawyers to construe their testimony in a manner that ignores or denies such scientific conventions, their testimony misrepresents their research and borders on professional dishonesty. The lawyers themselves are responsible for the same breach.

The chapter analyzes four typical scientific errors that courts make in their rulings on the admissibility of expert testimony and causation. First, and contrary to prevailing views within the scientific community, courts often insist that expert testimony on causation must be supported with epidemiological studies that reveal a relative risk that is twice the background rate. Second, courts sometimes exclude animal and other studies as appropriate support for expert testimony that a substance causes human harm, especially when human studies are not available. Third, courts often treat "no effect" epidemiological studies as definitive evidence of no adverse effect, even though scientists would not accept this simple inference. Finally, "weight of the evidence" arguments – or, as I will call them, "inferences to the best explanation" – the essence of scientific reasoning, have posed difficulties for courts leading to judicial confusion and often the exclusion of reasonable scientific arguments.

These judicial errors have important consequences for policy and science. Legal endorsement of mistaken science, together with the enhanced screening required by *Daubert*, encourage parties to litigation (usually defendants) to repeat mistaken views and further contaminate the legal system with a new kind of insidious science. The result is that valuable scientific knowledge is excluded from judicial decision making and the best experts are likely discouraged from participating in the law, a role they often do not relish in the first place. The legitimacy of the law as an institution is being threatened; legal decisions are vulnerable to challenges of being illegitimate, incomplete, or, too often, just wrong.

## Relative Risk Rules

One significant issue between scientists and some courts is the necessity of epidemiology studies that demonstrate a relative risk of twice the background rate or a disease rate two times higher than the disease rate in the unexposed population. Numerous courts have adopted this screening principle for determining whether evidence is admissible and for satisfying the causation test, despite the fact that such an approach directly conflicts with the views of many scientists and consensus scientific committees.

In a recent study of all of the cases in which the relative risk standard was addressed, Russellyn Carruth and Bernard Goldstein found thirty-one cases in state and federal courts up to 2001 in which relative risks greater than two (RR > 2) were discussed. In twenty-nine cases, courts addressed whether RR > 2 is a threshold for *proof of causation* to the satisfaction of a jury, with twelve (almost 40 percent) saying that RR > 2 "was required to support a reasonable inference of causation," while fourteen indicated that it was not.[4] In addition, twenty-one of the opinions addressed whether RR > 2 is a threshold for the admissibility of an expert opinion on causation, with ten (virtually half) saying that "RR > 2 is required," and eleven that

---

[4] Russellyn S. Carruth and Bernard D. Goldstein, "Relative Risk Greater Than Two in Proof of Causation in Toxic Tort Litigation," *Jurimetrics: The Journal of Law, Science, and Technology* 41, no. 2 (2001): 200–1.

it is not. This demanding judicial standard appears to be increasingly used over time.[5] Both pre- and post-*Daubert* courts, as well as commentators, have endorsed the relative-risk-greater-than-two approach.[6]

Within these decisions, there is some variation in how strong the requirement is. Some courts require that the research show a relative risk of two before it will be admitted, dismissing cases that do not meet this requirement, while other courts require such evidence for the ultimate standard of proof. My focus here will be on the admissibility issue.

Courts may well be tempted to adopt this judicially constructed requirement for causation because it establishes a bright line standard that seems to track the legal principle that plaintiffs prevail if they make their case by a preponderance of the evidence. A judicial rule that makes having a RR > 2 necessary for expert testimony seems to provide an evidentiary foundation for testimony that is objective and directly pertinent to human harm. The rule also appears to provide a scientific answer to the standard of proof that must be met for general or specific causation. Yet, even this assumption is mistaken. As discussed by Professor David Adelman in Chapter 9 of this book, the rule depends on the erroneous notion the statistics alone indicate that a randomly chosen diseased person in the exposed group "more probably than not" had his or her disease caused by the substance.

The courts' insistence on epidemiological evidence showing a relative risk of two or greater raises several scientific problems. Even if requiring epidemiological studies showing an actual RR > 2 were justified for some ideal purpose, which is doubtful, many quite probative studies simply fall well short of that standard. (Often such studies are not even available.) Such studies are likely to be rare for most toxic chemicals because a chemical

---

[5] Carruth and Goldstein, 202. (After Daubert, ten courts required RR > 2, six did not, and one did not consider the requirement.)

[6] *Daubert v. Merrell Dow Pharm., Inc.*, 43 F.3d 1311, 1320–1 (9th Cir. 1995), on remand from 509 U.S. 579 (1993); In re *Joint E. & S. Dist. Asbestos Litig.*, 758 F. Supp. 199, 203 (S.D.N.Y. 1991), aff'd, 52 F.3d 1124 (2d Cir. 1995); *Merrell Dow Pharm., Inc. v. Havner*, 953 S.W.2d 706 (Tex. 1997). Commentators who argued early on for requiring a relative risk even greater than two are Bert Black and David E. Lilienfeld, "Epidemiologic Proof in Toxic Tort Litigation," *Fordham Law Review* 52, no. 5 (1984): 732, 769. More recently, defense attorneys in the *Parlodel* litigation argued for the same point: Joe G. Hollingsworth and Eric Lasker, "The Case against Differential Diagnosis: *Daubert*, Medical Causation Testimony and the Scientific Method," *Journal of Health Law* 37, no. 1 (2004): 85–112.

must be sufficiently potent to produce such results.[7] For example, substantial cigarette smoking increases the risks of lung cancer by about ten times (from 19/100,000 to 190/100,000), indicating that it is a quite potent carcinogen, while secondhand smoke increases lung cancer rates approximately 1.3 times compared with unexposed populations.[8] Yet society's acceptance of the proposition that the level of relative risk posed by secondhand smoke is unacceptable is manifest in smoking bans in work and other public places. There seems to be little question that secondhand smoke causes cancer, but the rate is much lower than that for direct smoke and it is more difficult to identify individuals who have contracted cancer as a consequence of exposure.

Further, there are a variety of reasons to believe that published epidemiological studies systematically underestimate the actual risks to those exposed compared to what one might consider very good or ideally accurate epidemiological studies. When this underestimation occurs and judges preclude such studies because the relative risk is too low, plaintiffs will be deprived of scientifically relevant and legally probative evidence of causation that might be quite helpful to the court and juries.

Epidemiological studies are ordinarily conducted to identify public-health problems from environmental or workplace exposure. Once a causal relationship is suspected between exposure and disease, if preventive actions can be taken for those who continue to be exposed, they ordinarily will be. An epidemiological study is essentially as early a snapshot in time as might be helpful for public-health purposes.[9] Consequently, for illnesses with any significant latency period, such studies will miss additional adverse effects and will suffer from an "incomplete accrual" of diseases.[10]

Often epidemiological studies are done in occupational settings. Those who are employed tend to be healthier than the general population, producing a "healthy worker effect." Thus, "comparing exposed workers to

---

[7] James Huff and David P. Rall, "Relevance to Humans of Carcinogenesis Results from Laboratory Animal Toxicology Studies," in *Maxcy-Rosenau-Last: Public Health and Preventive Medicine*, ed. John M. Last and Robert B. Wallace (Norwalk, CT: Appleton and Lange, 13th ed., 1992), 433, 439; Lorenzo Tomatis et al., "Avoided and Avoidable Risks of Cancer," *Carcinogenesis*, 18, no. 1 (1997): 97, 100.

[8] Patricia A. Buffler, "Uses of Epidemiology in Environmental Medicine," in *Environmental Medicine*, ed. Stuart M. Brooks et al. (St. Louis, MO: Mosby, 1995), 46–62, esp. 55.

[9] Carruth and Goldstein, 207.

[10] Ibid.

the general population tends to understate relative risk," because the general population has a greater variability and wider range of susceptibility to diseases than healthy workers.[11] In addition, human studies that are conducted too long after exposure (often on former employees) can also result in underestimations of risks.[12]

A study typically reports an average relative risk from exposure to a toxic substance; this convention may disguise higher or lower relative risks in subgroups, either because of differences in levels of exposure or because the sample disguises the effect of exposure on more sensitive or vulnerable individuals. For example, in one study higher exposures might result in relative risks of four, while lower exposures might reveal relative risks of only 1.7. The weighted average of the different relative risks might yield an overall average relative risk for the study of less than two. If such a study cannot be used, individuals who had been subjected to higher exposures than the average in the reference study, and who might have individual relative risks above two, would be precluded from providing that evidence of their likely harm.

As scientists become increasingly aware of sensitive subpopulations – for example, those resulting from genetic or other susceptibilities[13] – they have found that average relative risks inadequately reveal the risks posed to sensitive subgroups. Reporting only the average results from a study may conceal the distribution of disease in differentially exposed or differentially sensitive subgroups, thus underestimating their disease rates.

Tort law clearly protects sensitive subgroups by stating it will take the victim as the tortfeasor finds him – that is, if the victim is particularly vulnerable (for example, if he or she has an abnormally fragile, or "eggshell" skull), the defendant cannot escape liability by arguing that the victim

---

[11] Ibid., 208 (noting that a 1.5 relative risk in an exposed worker population might well reflect a doubling of the disease rate compared to the appropriate unexposed population).

[12] Robert A. Rinsky et al., "Benzene Exposure and Hematopoietic Mortality: A Long-Term Epidemiological Risk Assessment, *American Journal of Industrial Medicine* 42, no. 6 (2002): 474–480; Sharon R. Silver et al., "Effect of Follow-Up Time on Risk Estimates: A Longitudinal Examination of the Relative Risks of Leukemia and Multiple Myeloma in a Rubber Hydrochloride Cohort," *American Journal of Industrial Medicine* 42, no. 6 (2002): 481–9.

[13] Frederica P. Perera, "Molecular Epidemiology: Insights into Cancer Susceptibility, Risk Assessment, and Prevention," *Journal of the National Cancer Institute* 88, no. 8 (1996): 496–509 (discussing the interaction of environmental factors and genetic and acquired susceptibilities to cancer).

would not have been hurt if he or she were "normal." Overly stringent admissibility rules risk frustrating such protections by precluding expert testimony based on a full range of studies, including those with overall relative risks less than two.[14] This result fails to reflect accurately the subtlety and complexity of the science involved and will unfairly disadvantage some plaintiffs.

Finally, there is a subtler theoretical point about relative risks of two that causes underestimation of risks. In a series of papers, Sander Greenland and James Robins have argued that it is difficult to determine how much disease to attribute to an exposure. Exposure to a toxicant might cause new cases of disease – that is, diseases in individuals who would not have contracted the disease at all – or it might accelerate the onset of disease in individuals who would have contracted the disease in any case, but not as early. Both contributions to disease should be attributed to the exposure. However, epidemiological studies ordinarily would only record the new cases of disease, thus underreporting the disease-causing potential of the substance.[15]

Reliance on epidemiological studies and the requirement that they demonstrate a relative risk of two also raise serious ethical and policy issues. A demand for human epidemiological studies commits the tort law to the view that other people must have suffered serious diseases or death at a high enough rate from a similar exposure before a plaintiff at the bar even has a chance at a jury trial and just compensation. While tort law is not on the front line of protecting the public's health by preventing exposure, deterrence of conduct that can injure others is a substantial justification of torts.

A striking example from radiation epidemiology illustrates the shortcomings of a RR > 2 screening rule. Ionizing radiation, a known carcinogen, causes cancer in many human organ systems. One study shows that atomic bomb survivors from Hiroshima and Nagasaki contracted leukemia and multiple myeloma, as well as cancer of the esophagus, stomach, colon,

---

[14] *Prosser and Keeton on the Law of Torts*, ed. W. Page Keeton (St. Paul, MN: West, 5th ed., 1984), 291–2 .

[15] Sander Greenland, "Relation of Probability of Causation to Relative Risk and Doubling Dose: A Methodologic Error That Has Become a Social Problem," *American Journal of Public Health* 89, no. 8 (1999): 1166; Sander Greenland and James M. Robins, "Epidemiology, Justice, and the Probability of Causation," *Jurimetrics: The Journal of Law, Science, and Technology* 40, no. 3 (2000): 321.

other segments of the digestive system, urinary tract, lung, lymph nodes, and a number of other sites.[16] Surprisingly, the radiation exposures for many in these study populations were relatively low.[17] Yet these findings show, with 90 percent confidence, that all malignant neoplasms taken together, except leukemia, have a relative risk of less than two. Only radiation exposure that causes leukemia, multiple myeloma, urinary tract cancer, and colon cancer has a relative risk greater than two.

Given this carcinogen, should judges rule as inadmissible evidence for each neoplasm for which there is not a relative risk greater than two or engage in the more subtle task of assessing and weighing the evidence that radiation caused the cancer? The latter course ensures that relevant and quite significant scientific evidence is admitted into trial and that those possibly harmed by radiation receive a fair (if complex) assessment of the evidence of the causes of their harm.

## Rejection of Animal Studies and Other Evidence

A second problem with the judiciary's temptation to rely on epidemiological studies, with or without RR $>$ 2 as a necessary condition of admissibility, is that the requirement precludes admitting expert testimony largely supported by other kinds of evidence, such as animal and molecular evidence. This approach constitutes a quite serious scientific mistake, despite its superficial plausibility.

Consider animal evidence. Obviously, animals are not humans; they have different biology and they do not have the same physical characteristics as humans. These dissimilarities make it more difficult to evaluate what experts can infer from animal studies in order to assess risks for humans. Courts that reject expert testimony based on such evidence often stop right there. However, good toxicologists would go on to discuss and assess what could be inferred from animal studies. In fact, consensus scientific committees widely rely upon such studies for inferring human harm

---

[16] H. Kato, "Cancer Mortality," in *Cancer in Atomic Bomb Survivors*, ed. Itsuzo Shigematsu and Abraham Kagan (Tokyo: Japan Scientific Societies Press, 1986), quoted in Arthur K. Sullivan, "Classification, Pathogenesis, and Etiology of Neoplastic Diseases of the Hematopoietic System," in G. Richard Lee et al., *Wintrobe's Clinical Hematology* 2 (Philadelphia, PA: Lea and Febiger, 9th ed., 1993), 1725, 1750.

[17] Julius C. McElveen and Chris Amantea, "Legislating Risk Assessment," *University of Cincinnati Law Review* 63, no. 4 (1995): 1553, 1556.

from exposures. The scientific literature generally contains a series of more reasonable principles to guide the understanding of animal studies.[18] For example, well-known scientists have concluded that

> [f]rom data available so far, therefore, it appears that chemicals that are carcinogenic in laboratory animals are likely to be carcinogenic in human populations and that, if appropriate studies can be performed, there is qualitative predictability. Also, there is evidence that there can be a quantitative relationship between the amount of a chemical that is carcinogenic in laboratory animals and that which is carcinogenic in human populations.[19]

Others have concurred, including the National Academy of Sciences.[20] Utilizing specifically the language of rebuttable presumptions, the NAS notes that "in the absence of countervailing evidence for the specific agent in question, it appears reasonable to assume that the life-time cancer incidence induced by chronic exposure in man can be approximated by the life-time incidence induced by similar exposure in laboratory animals at the same total dose per body weight."[21] Quite distinguished researchers

---

[18] Carl F. Cranor, *The Science Veil over Toxic Tort Law* (forthcoming); Carl F. Cranor and David A. Eastmond, "Scientific Ignorance and Reliable Patterns of Evidence in Toxic Tort Causation: Is There a Need for Liability Reform?" *Journal of Law and Contemporary Problems* 64, no. 4 (2001): 42–3.

[19] Huff and Rall, 437.

[20] Victor A. Fung et al., "The Carcinogenesis Bioassay in Perspective – Application in Identifying Human Cancer Hazards," *Environmental Health Perspectives* 103, no. 7–8 (1995): 682 (chemicals shown unequivocally to induce cancer in laboratory animals, especially in multiple species, must be considered capable of causing cancer in humans). Moreover, a group of researchers from the National Institute of Environmental Health Sciences, the University of North Carolina, the International Agency for Research on Cancer (IARC), the Linkoping University in Sweden, the National Cancer Institute, and National Institute of Occupational Safety and Health, have concluded that experimental results, in particular long-term carcinogenicity tests, have proven to be valid predictors of human risk. Tomatis et al., 103).

[21] Huff and Rall, 437 (quoting the National Research Council, *Pest Control: An Assessment of Present and Alternative Technologies*, Vol. 1, *Contemporary Pest Control Practices and Prospects* [Washington, DC: National Academy Press, 1975], 66–83). See also Curtis C. Travis, "Interspecies Extrapolation of Toxic Data," in *Health Risk Assessment: Dermal and Inhalation Exposure and Absorption of Toxicants*, ed. Rhoda G. M. Wang et al. (Boca Raton, FL: CRC Press, 1993), 387–410, recommends a slightly different scaling factor on which there is considerable consensus. IARC concurs in the principle: ". . . it is biologically plausible . . . to regard agents for which there is sufficient evidence of carcinogenicity in experimental animals as if they presented a carcinogenic risk to humans." International Agency for Research on Cancer, "Preamble to the IARC Monographs, Sect. 9: Studies of Cancer in Experimental Animals," International Agency for Research on Cancer, http://www-cie.iarc.fr/monoeval/preabmle.html.

from around the world agree that animals studies are valid predictors of human risk.[22]

The specific evidence supporting the similarity between animal and human with regard to carcinogenicity is quite extensive. First and perhaps most compelling, "experimental evidence to date certainly suggests that there are more physiologic, biochemical and metabolic similarities between laboratory animals and humans than there are differences."[23] Further, "biological processes of molecular, cellular, tissue, and organ functions that control life are strikingly similar from one mammalian species to another. Such processes as sodium and potassium transport and ion regulation, energy metabolism, and DNA replication vary little in the aggregate as one moves along the phylogenic ladder."[24] Indeed, the more scientists "know about the similarities of structure and function of higher organisms *at the molecular level*, the more [they] are convinced that mechanisms of chemical toxicity are, to a large extent, identical in animals and man."[25] Other experts have observed, "[t]here is overwhelming evidence that, at the cellular level, humans . . . do not differ qualitatively from experimental animals in their response to carcinogens. Furthermore, processes operative in humans that lead to cancer induction are also operative in rodent systems."[26]

Even though there are differences in carcinogenic responses from one species to another, particular patterns of responses in animals greatly increase the likelihood that a carcinogenic response in one mammalian species will produce a carcinogenic response in another mammalian species. Cross-species carcinogenic responses constitute evidence that scientists utilize to help conclude that substances with these properties in animals are more likely to be carcinogenic in humans.[27]

---

[22] Tomatis et al., 97, 100.

[23] David P. Rall et al., "Alternatives to Using Human Experience in Assessing Health Risks," *Annual Review of Public Health* 8 (1987): 355–6.

[24] Huff and Rall, 434. ("Significant scientific understanding of neural transmission, renal function and cell replication and development of cancer have come from non human species, often species far removed phylogenetically from humans.")

[25] Ibid., 204.

[26] J. S. Bertram et al., "Rationales and Strategies for Chemoprevention of Cancer in Humans," *Cancer Research* 47, no. 11(1987): 3012.

[27] George M. Gray et al., "An Empirical Examination of Factors Influencing Prediction of Carcinogenic Hazard across Species," *Regulatory Toxicology and Pharmacology* 22, no. 3 (1995): 283–4, 287.

Taken together, the principles just reviewed and others support inferences about adverse effects in humans, unless there is good substance-specific evidence to the contrary, and they help make inferences reliable concerning the toxicology of carcinogens.[28] The evidence constitutes what Ellen Silbergeld has called the "vertical integrity" of organisms: "... mechanistic explanations at the most basic level of biological organization do not lose their validity for explaining and predicting as molecular events are organized into cells, cells into organs, organs into organisms and organisms into populations."[29]

For the preceding reasons, consensus scientific committees, such as the International Agency for Research on Cancer and the National Toxicology Program,[30] routinely utilize a wider variety of scientific evidence than epidemiological studies to draw conclusions about the likelihood of human harm.[31] They rely upon lifetime studies of substances in animal experiments, "mode of action" studies in animals, mechanistic information, chemical structure–biological activity relationships, and human case studies. The U.S. EPA and the Federal Judicial Center Manual on Scientific Evidence come to the same conclusions.[32] Judges and ultimately juries

[28] There are some exceptions to these presumptions, but they are recognized as such. In rare circumstances, for example, the IARC will deviate from its presumption about animal carcinogens. Jerry M. Rice et al., "Rodent Tumors of Urinary Bladder, Renal Cortex, and Thyroid Gland in IARC Monographs Evaluations of Carcinogenic Risk to Humans," *Toxicological Sciences* 49, no. 2 (1999): 171. Other scientific bodies disagree with this, indicating that such issues are not fully settled. For example, the California Environmental Protection Agency disagrees with some reclassifications of animal carcinogens on the basis of mechanistic information and would continue to treat them as potential human carcinogens. Personal Communication with Lauren Zeise, Chief, Reproductive and Cancer Hazard Assessment, California Environmental Protection Agency (Sept. 20, 2000).

[29] Ellen K. Silbergeld, "The Role of Toxicology in Causation: A Scientific Perspective," *Courts, Health Science and the Law* 1, no. 3 (1991): 374.

[30] See Cranor and Eastmond for examples of such patterns of evidence (citing evidence assessments of carcinogens from the IARC and the U.S. National Toxicology Program).

[31] Ibid., 5–48; Carl F. Cranor, "Justice, Inference to the Best Explanation and the Judicial Evaluation of Scientific Evidence," in *Topics in Contemporary Philosophy: Vol. III: Law and Social Justice*, ed. Joseph Keim Campbell et al. (Cambridge, MA: MIT Press, forthcoming 2005); Carl F. Cranor, "The Science Veil over Toxic Tort Law: How Should Scientific Evidence Be Used in Toxic Tort Law?" *Law and Philosophy* (forthcoming 2005); Carl F. Cranor, "Scientific Inferences in the Laboratory and the Law," *American Journal of Public Health* (forthcoming).

[32] Proposed Guidelines for Carcinogen Risk Assessment, 61 Fed. Reg. 17,960, 17,977 (April 23, 1996) ("[T]here is evidence that growth control mechanisms at the level of the cell are

should make similar assessments based upon all the scientifically relevant evidence, both for purposes of admissibility and proof of causation.

While it is understandable, albeit unfortunate, that untrained judges can be misled about these issues, scientists retained by plaintiffs and defendants alike certainly should be aware of the scientific consensus on these points. If experts argue against the use of animal evidence, without qualification and without speaking to the preceding plausible scientific principles, they do not speak candidly to the validity and subtleties of animal research, its scientific relevance, it pertinence to humans, and its considerable biological value. They would be emphasizing only outliers, not its central scientific plausibility. Moreover, such failures may border on misrepresentation of studies in the field. Because they are largely dependent on incomplete and often imbalanced expert evidence for their understanding of scientific evidence, courts are often misled and the stage is set for them to commit these scientific errors.

The courts' preclusion of nonepidemiological evidence not only contradicts scientific practice, it will lead to systematic asymmetries in the outcome of cases that strongly favor the defense. I argued earlier that courts might be tempted to require epidemiological studies with relative risks greater than two in order to provide a bright line and simplify evidentiary rulings. Defendants clearly have ample incentives to urge them to extend this approach (epidemiological studies are insensitive and often not available) and to urge great skepticism toward animal and other nonepidemiological data.

## "No Effect" Epidemiological Studies

A third issue where the courts' approach to scientific evidence diverges from the approach taken by scientists involves epidemiology studies that show "no effect." Some courts appear to assume because an epidemiological study shows "no effect" on humans, there is no causal link between a

homologous among mammals, but there is no evidence that these mechanisms are site concordant [i.e., must be in the same tissue in rodents and humans]."); Bernard D. Goldstein and Mary Sue Henifin, "Reference Guide on Toxicology," in *Reference Manual on Scientific Evidence* (2nd ed., 2000), 419 (available at http:/www.fjc.gov/public/home.nsf/ autoframe?openform&url_r = pages/556&url_l = index).

substance and a particular disease.[33] That is, courts may believe that negative epidemiological studies trump all other kinds of evidence and prove the absence of causation. This too would be mistaken.

The courts' reliance on "no effect" epidemiology studies to conclude that an exposure did not cause plaintiff's disease oversimplifies the science since there are at least two possible interpretations of what such studies show. A study might only show no evidence of an effect or it might show that there is evidence of no effect – a much more difficult point to establish. On the first possibility, one might say that there is not or perhaps not yet any human epidemiological evidence of an adverse effect. On the second, there is more affirmative evidence of no effect.

These two judgments are clearly different, as the following analogy suggests. Suppose that I am looking over a large plain at some distance. If someone asks me if there are people down on the plain, and I do not see any, I might say, "There is no evidence that there are." However, this response does not mean that there are none. I might not have good evidence that no one is on the plain. I might not have had good enough eyesight or I might not have used a telescope with sufficient magnification to reveal people at such a distance, and I might not have investigated the issue in any other way. Consequently, I would not have very good evidence that no people were on the plain.

I could somewhat better support a claim that no one was on the plain below if I had a telescope that I knew would permit me to see them, but still was unable to see anyone. However, even a high-magnification telescope might be insufficient, depending upon my purposes for wanting to know whether there were people below. If I wanted to be highly certain that there was no one on the plain, then I might need to undertake a number of other investigations, such as leaving my vantage point and going to investigate at a much closer range.

Judges need to learn to distinguish much more carefully between the statement "there is no evidence for an effect" and the statement "there is evidence of no effect." Defendants' evidence could trump plaintiffs' other

---

[33] *Chambers v. Exxon Corp.*, 81 F. Supp. 2d 661, 665–66 (M.D. La. 2000) (holding that expert testimony that benzene exposure causes chronic myelogenous leukemia [CML] was inadmissible for lack of scientific reliability, in the absence of an epidemiological study that conclusively established a statistically significant risk of contracting CML from exposure to benzene).

evidence of an adverse effect, but only if defendants' evidence could sufficiently establish that there was evidence of no effect from good, sensitive human studies. It is extremely difficult to establish such evidence. In most cases, even if defendants present studies showing no evidence (yet?) of human harm, plaintiffs might well have other kinds of evidence revealing an adverse effect on humans. Considering those pieces of diverse evidence, the question becomes whether the testimony offered by plaintiffs' experts has a reasonable enough foundation to support their causes of action.

If plaintiffs have offered some evidence of an effect based on other kinds of studies – such as animal studies, good human case reports, molecular studies, mode of action studies, and structure activity relationships – one issue is whether such evidence is sufficient to satisfy admissibility reviews (this decision should be made independent of the defendant's evidence). The fact that defendants have pointed out that there is no evidence of an effect in particular human epidemiological studies should not trump plaintiffs' evidence that there may be some effect. Beyond admissibility decisions, if defendants have epidemiological studies that provide a plausible argument that there is evidence of an adverse effect, and the court has admitted plaintiffs' expert testimony, the court must then decide whether plaintiffs have offered enough evidence to survive a directed verdict when evidence conflicts.

In sharp contrast to these judicial approaches, scientists are extremely careful to avoid inferring from the fact that there is "no evidence of effect" that there is "evidence of no effect." To have a study that shows evidence of no adverse effect is so difficult to establish that most reputable consensus scientific bodies – such as the International Agency for Research on Cancer – require that some highly specific and detailed conditions be met before any such conclusion is drawn. Even then the results apply only to the disease endpoint of interest and not to unrelated diseases.[34]

There are also more generic concerns related to "no effect" studies. Most judges do not comment on and appear to be insensitive to a wide range of scientific reasons that human studies might be negative even though an exposure in fact contributes to a disease. For example, if studies are shorter than the latency period of disease, if sample sizes are too small to detect an

---

[34] International Agency for Research on Cancer, "Preamble to the IARC Monograph Series, Sect. 8: Studies of Cancer in Humans."

adverse effect, or if a disease endpoint is so common that it will be difficult to identify new causes of that condition, then epidemiological studies have substantial chances of not detecting adverse effects even when they are in fact caused by exposures. "No effect" outcomes would simply be artifacts of the studies, and not necessarily results of exposure to a property of the substance.

Judges should learn from scientists and be quite skeptical of what "no effect" epidemiological studies show.[35] If they do not make more sophisticated distinctions, they will continue to reward counsel for misrepresenting the implications of "no effect" findings and reward experts for confusing the court and jury.

## "Weight of the Evidence" or "Inference to the Best Explanation"

Beyond their problematic reviews of individual types of evidence, some courts commit a much more systemic error by admitting or excluding individual scientifically relevant studies rather than assessing them as a collective whole. The traditional scientific approach is to gather all available scientifically relevant data and then evaluate it, developing a final judgment on the basis of the cumulative "weight of (all the relevant and reliable) evidence." In contrast, as Professor Thomas McGarity also discusses in Chapter 1 of this book, the courts have allowed experts to deconstruct the evidence by analyzing and excluding it piece by piece. As Professor McGarity has described it, this "corpuscular" approach asks that each individual piece of research be evaluated on the basis of whether it individually supports a definitive finding of causation. If an individual piece of evidence does not support causation standing alone, then the evidence is rejected as well as the expert testimony that relies on it.[36]

---

[35] See *Ambrosini v. Labarraque*, 101 F.3d 129 (D.C. Cir. 1996), for a case in which the court recognizes the need to consider statistical power in order to assess the plausibility of a negative epidemiological study. The court pointed out that the plaintiffs' expert "explained that an epidemiologist evaluates studies based on their 'statistical power.'" Statistical power, he continued, "represents the ability of a study, based on its sample size, to detect a causal relationship. Conventionally, in order to be considered meaningful, negative studies, that is, those which allege the absence of a causal relationship, must have at least an 80 to 90 percent chance of detecting a causal link if such a link exists; otherwise, the studies cannot be considered conclusive." Ibid., 136.

[36] Thomas O. McGarity, "Our Science Is Sound Science and Their Science Is Junk Science: Science-Based Strategies for Avoiding Accountability and Responsibility for Risk-Producing Products and Activities," *University of Kansas Law Review* 52 (2004): 897.

Such a process of rejecting individual scientifically relevant pieces of evidence does great injustice to scientific inferences and reveals substantial misunderstandings of arguments based on the weight of the scientific evidence.[37]

Although philosophers of science differ in their analyses of causal inferences, for practical application there is a common reasoning process. This scientific core diverges significantly from the way many courts approach the same issues. Some philosophers suggest the idea of making inferences to the best explanation,[38] some are Bayesians,[39] and so on. I do not argue for one or another of these interpretations. What is important for assessing courts' reviews of experts' reasoning is to understand some of the major steps, common to the different approaches, that scientists utilize in coming to conclusions about the causal effects of exposures to substances. Once these processes are understood, it will serve as a corrective to the views of some courts.

Scientists utilize nondeductive inferences to support their inferences about scientific claims. Sometimes they are called "inferences to the best explanation" or "diagnostic arguments," although judges, experts, and regulatory agencies often call them "weight of the evidence arguments." Such inferences have several characteristics; an obvious one is that nondeductive inferences are simply those whose conclusions are supported but not guaranteed by their premises. Nondeductive inferences contrast with deductive arguments, where the premises logically or semantically guarantee the conclusion; if the premises are true, the conclusion *must be* true (there is a logically tight relationship between premises and conclusion).

In nondeductive arguments, even if the premises are true, the nondeductive link between premises and conclusions will have varying degrees of strength, (such arguments would not be valid or invalid, but would be "strong," "weak," or fall on a continuum between these two characteristics).

---

[37] *Allen v. Pennsylvania Engineering Corp.*, 102 F.3d 194 (5th Cir. 1996); *General Elec. Co. v. Joiner*, 522 U.S. 136 (1997); *Joiner v. General Electric Co.*, 864 F.Supp. 1310 (N.D. Ga. 1994); |*Mitchell v. Gencorp In.*,| 165 F. 3d 778 (10th Cir. 1999).

[38] Gilbert H. Harman, "The Inference to the Best Explanation," *Philosophical Review* 74, no. 1 (1994): 89–90; Paul Thagard, *How Scientists Think about Disease* (Princeton, NJ: Princeton University Press, 1999), 129; Larry Wright, *Critical Thinking* (New York: Oxford University Press, 2001).

[39] *Magistrini v. One Hour Martinizing Dry Cleaning*, 180 F.Supp.2d 584 (D.N.J. 2002); Brian Skyrms, *Choice and Chance: An Introduction to Inductive Logic* (Belmont, CA: Dickenson, 1966).

If the premises are true, they may offer much, modest, or little (to no) support for the conclusion in question.

In addition, scientists conventionally follow several steps in making scientific inferences about the causes of disease. They would notice a correlation or association between some exposure or condition and a disease needing explanation. They then consider a sufficiently complete list of plausible explanations for the manifestation of disease.[40] And, typically, they would tentatively rank these explanations in order of plausibility to explain the evidence. Next, scientists would identify research, typically in the form of tests, studies, or background information that could assist the search, help discriminate between different explanations, provide more support for some explanations compared with others, and assist in arriving at the best explanation. They might conduct original research if others had not yet done pertinent studies and the time and resources were available to do so.

In coming to the best explanation of the disease, experts then consider all scientifically relevant information[41] that bears on possible explanations,[42] seeing how well it "fits together" or can be integrated to provide the most likely explanation for the phenomena in question.[43] Finally, based on all the data, an expert's search for causal understanding would then focus on

[40] One of the "most basic, . . . least understood," and difficult steps is to find a sufficiently complete list of possible explanations for the phenomena to be explained. Ibid., 107.

[41] Wright, Critical Thinking, 206–17; Larry Wright, Practical Reasoning (New York: Harcourt, Brace Jovanovitch, 1989), 104. (What is or should be less controversial for legal purposes is that what constitutes scientifically relevant information or data is a scientific matter. This is not to say that the scientific judgment that goes into this assessment is totally subjective or that it can be idiosyncratic. Scientists also may differ about relevance. However, even in cases in which ultimate scientific conclusions may be controversial, what constitutes scientifically relevant data may be less controversial than the conclusions drawn.)

[42] See, for example, Skyrms, 107; Thagard, 129. Two scientific methodologists put this point especially strongly: Tom A. Hutchinson and David A. Lane, "Standardized Methods of Causality Assessment of Suspected Adverse Drug Reactions," Journal of Clinical Epidemiology 42, no. 1 (1989): 10. ("A causality assessment method must respect Fisher's fundamental rule of uncertain inference – never throw information away. That is, any fact, theory or opinion that can affect an evaluator's belief that [a particular exposure] caused an adverse event E must be incorporable by the method into the 'state of information' on which the assessment is based.") (emphasis added).

[43] Bayesians typically would begin with a prior belief about the toxicity of a substance, and then update this belief (as more probable or less probable) as they considered other studies. Ellen Silbergeld describes this system as follows: "The reasonableness or plausibility of an explanation in science is tested by its consonance with other knowledge." Silbergeld, 376.

how much more probable an effect is with a particular causal explanation than without it or how much more plausible that explanation is compared with competing explanations. In short, the final step is a review of all the scientifically relevant information for the best explanation of the phenomena to be explained.

Some courts have failed to recognize this inferential approach in several ways. First, when courts judicially require human epidemiological studies and by implication exclude expert testimony that does not include such evidence, they are depriving scientists of some studies and data that they would typically use in nondeductive arguments for making causal judgments. Second, and more specifically, courts would not be permitting scientists to utilize all scientifically relevant data and information to draw conclusions about human harm, since implicitly they would be taking the position that such evidence collectively could not provide respectable support for a scientific inference for legal purposes. This approach places legal constraints on the range of scientific arguments that could be offered, in effect substituting their legal or personal judgments for an expert's scientific judgment about what evidence is scientifically relevant for drawing a scientific conclusion. Third, when courts exclude combinations of nonepidemiological evidence, such as animal studies, molecular evidence, and good case studies, they fail to respect evidence scientists themselves would regard as relevant and fail to respect the foundational inferences of science. They create artificial legal limits on what is considered scientifically relevant evidence and limits on the kinds of scientific arguments that can be offered, making scientific judgments that scientists should make.

Two cases and the issues they raise illustrate these points and the need for judges to be able to review complex patterns of evidence: *General Electric v. Joiner* and *Allen v. Pennsylvania Engineering*.[44] These cases have several features in common. In both, plaintiffs were forced to rely largely upon nonepidemiological evidence because human studies were insensitive, exposures were quite contaminated, or the substances in question were not the obvious object of study. Consequently, in both cases, plaintiffs had to utilize animal and other kinds of evidence.

---

[44] *Allen v. Pennsylvania Engineering Corp.*, 102 F.3d 194 (5th Cir. 1996); *General Elec. Co. v. Joiner*, 522 U.S. 136 (1997); *Joiner v. General Electric Co.*, 864 F.Supp. 1310 (N.D. Ga. 1994).

In both cases, the judges had to review evidence that was sufficiently far from the experience of lay people that the arguments seemed implausible or worse on their faces. In *Joiner*, some baby mice received what the courts called "massive" doses of polychlorinated biphenyls (PCBs) injected directly into their bodies (not the route of Joiner's exposure), the concentrations that the mice received seemed vastly higher than Joiner's, and the lung tumors induced were said to be much different.[45] Moreover, adult mice did not have the same reaction as the baby mice.

In *Allen*, rats exposed to ethylene oxide (ETO) contracted brain cancer, while mice, phylogenetically more similar to rats than rats are to humans, did not contract brain cancer. Moreover, there was molecular evidence that ETO did not need metabolic modification to reach nearly any target organ in the body and damage DNA. Since brain cancer is quite rare, there were only poor epidemiological studies available.

In both cases, the courts' simplistic reasoning resulted in rejection of the scientific arguments. In *Joiner*, the courts did not understand, or it was not explained to them, that the baby mice studies were designed to determine whether a substance was a cancer "promoter" – precisely the argument that the plaintiffs had used. Moreover, such arguments have a long and honorable scientific history.[46] Scientists believe that the carcinogenic process is a multistage one with at least three major stages identified; initiation, promotion, and progression. Some agents – "initiators" – tend to "alter the structure of DNA and/or chromosomes" in the cells. However, for cells with DNA damage to become a cancer, they must be "promoted" – that

[45] *General Elec. Co. v. Joiner*, 522 U.S. at 144–5.
[46] Samuel M. Cohen, "Alternative Models for Carcinogenicity Testing: Weight of Evidence Evaluations Across Models," *Toxicologic Pathology* 29, Suppl. (2001): 183–90 ("The neonatal mouse model has been used for more than 40 years"); Allan H. Conney, "Induction of Microsomal Enzymes by Foreign Chemicals and Carcinogenesis by Polycyclic Aromatic Hydrocarbons: G.H.A. Clowes Memorial Lecture," *Cancer Research* 42, no. 12 (1982): 4875–4917; International Agency for Research on Cancer, "Consensus Report: The Use of Short-and Medium-Term Tests for Carcinogens and Data on Genetic Effects in Carcinogenic Hazard Evaluation," *IARC Scientific Publications No. 146*, ed. D. B. McGregor et al. (1999) (available at http://www-cie.iarc.fr/htdocs/iarcpubs/pub146/pub146contents.html); *IARC Monograph* 10 (1976): 231 (Infant mice studies provided some of the evidence that safrole was a carcinogen. The National Toxicology Program also utilized such data for listing safrole.); R. Michael McClain et al., "Neonatal Mouse Model: Review of Methods and Results," *Toxicologic Pathology* 29, Suppl. (2001): 128–37; Miriam C. Poirier, "In Memoriam: James A. Miller (1915–2000)," *Carcinogenesis* 22, no. 4 (2001): 681–3 (memorialized for beginning this line of research at McArdle Laboratory for Cancer Research);.

is, "clones of spontaneously initiated cells" must expand and create many copies of the damaged cell.[47] (Some substances initiate cancer in mammals, others promote it, and some do both.) The final stage is that the cancers must progress to full-fledged tumors.[48] Joiner argued that exposure to PCBs promoted DNA damage in the lungs that had been caused by his earlier exposure to cancer initiators in cigarette smoke.

All this evidence taken together (which the court did not explicitly consider) is not obviously such a bad argument that the expert offering it should be excluded from testifying. Since toxicologists typically calculate the appropriate dose that causes cancer based on lifetime exposures, the mice did not necessarily receive "massive" doses or concentrations of PCBs that were much greater than those to which Joiner was exposed. Even if one agreed with defendant's characterization of the tumor pathology (a further issue), different pathological tumors in the mice and Mr. Joiner are what one would expect from a tumor promoter; it promotes whatever cell damage had been initiated. I do not know or argue that the plaintiffs were correct, only that once the scientific argument is understood, it is hardly as outrageous as the two courts suggested. Failure to recognize the quality of the argument may have constituted abuse of discretion on the part of the trial court, which would constitute grounds for an appellate court to overturn the decision.

In *Allen v. Pennsylvania Engineering Inc.*, the Fifth Circuit Court of Appeals first came close to imposing an epidemiological threshold for admissibility, next ruled that plaintiffs' experts' reliance on rat studies (showing ETO could case brain cancer) was "unreliable," and third ruled that molecular studies were only the "beginning not the end of scientific inquiry and proves nothing about causation without other scientific evidence."[49]

There are several problems with this opinion. Rats appear to be a better model for humans than mice in providing evidence that ETO could cause brain cancer because they have slower metabolism and breathing rates than mice, thus retaining ETO in their bodies more like humans.[50]

---

[47] Henry C. Pitot, III, and Yvonne P. Dragan, "Chemical Carcinogensesis," in *Casarett and Doull's Toxicology: The Basic Science of Poisons*, ed. Curtis d. Kaassen (New York: McGraw-Hill, 6th ed., 2001), 267, 278.

[48] Ibid., 267.

[49] *Allen*, 102 F.3d at 198.

[50] Personal Communication with David A. Eastmond (June 2003).

While rats are more similar to mice than they are to humans, in this case that similarity is misleading. Third, ETO is a multisite mutagen, a quite significant biological feature of a substance.[51] Moreover, because it is a small molecule and requires no transformation by human metabolism, it could reach nearly any target site in the body. The rat studies showed that ETO could be retained in the body, permitting the small ETO molecule to cross the blood-brain barrier, reach the brain, and cause cancer.

In *Allen* there is independent scientific evidence that the courts made mistakes. Two well-known toxicologists who are experts in ETO (one from industry, one not) judged that the plaintiffs' arguments that ETO more likely than not could cause brain cancer were quite respectable scientific arguments. (One expert found defendants offered misleading science.) Each expert had somewhat more difficulty concerning specific causation because of uncertainty about exposure, but that might be expected in a tort case where it is quite difficult to determine exposure.[52]

In sum, the courts in both *Joiner* and *Allen* excluded the plaintiffs' experts by excluding individually each kind of evidence and failed to understand how the largely nonepidemiological evidence as an integrated whole could constitute a reasonable argument in support of the plaintiffs' legal claims. Perhaps the courts uncritically accepted the defendants' characterization of the research used in expert testimony. In any case, they appeared not to have understood the arguments. The courts in both cases reviewed the evidence contrary to how good scientists would. Finally, given how few substances have been subjected to epidemiological studies, evidence like that in *Joiner* and *Allen* is more likely to be typical than cases in which good epidemiological evidence is presented. Courts must learn to review such evidence sensitively in order to preserve the justice of the legal system.

---

[51] "Mutagenicity testing, combined with an evaluation of chemical structure, has been found to identify a large proportion of trans-species, multiple-site carcinogens." R. Julian Preston and George R. Hoffmann, "Genetic Toxicology," in *Casarett and Doull's Toxicology*, 342.

[52] Peer-reviewed reports supported by the National Science Foundation Research Grant, "A Philosophic and Scientific Investigation of the Use of Scientific Evidence in Toxic Tort Law," $160,000 (2000–2004) (NSF #99–10952), Carl F. Cranor and David A. Eastmond, principal investigators.

## Conclusion

The courts' implementation of the *Daubert* trilogy of cases has fallen short of the goal of ensuring that the law better comports with the relevant science. Some judges have constructed rules about scientific evidence that do not respect the validity and subtleties of different types of evidence. They have substituted legal notions of relevant evidence for the broad range of scientific evidence scientists would utilize. They have also dismissed or excluded individual pieces of evidence that may not by themselves support plaintiffs' ultimate conclusions, but when integrated with other kinds of evidence might constitute a good nondeductive scientific argument.[53]

These mistakes are the direct result of the judiciary's understandable but regrettable lack of sophistication in reviewing such complex scientific research. More importantly, however, judges have been misled by experts or lawyers on one side of the cases. Litigants too often present views of science with a patina of respectability and consistently ignore how a conscientious scientific assessment of the same evidence would be conducted. Such constructed but mistaken views of science are much more insidious than some of the expert testimony that originally might have motivated the *Daubert* decision. Moreover, when courts accept such insidious scientific views and provide them the imprimatur of legal respectability, they leave a written record that invites a further propagation of insidious science through the legal system to be used repeatedly by other defendants and other courts.[54] These outcomes multiply the mistakes and contaminate the law, putting its legitimacy at risk.

What might be done to address these issues? Courts need to understand that scientists utilize inferences to the best explanation or diagnostic inferences. These in turn require that judges should permit expert testimony based on *all* the evidence that an expert assembles and integrates in support of his or her conclusions (and reject corpuscular assessments of evidence).

---

[53] I have not presented a comprehensive view of this problem (indeed I am not aware of such studies), but have discussed some prominent examples in which court-constructed views of science were at odds with how scientists themselves would assess the same kinds of evidence.

[54] Joe G. Hollingsworth and Eric Lasker, "The Case against Differential Diagnosis: *Daubert*, Medical Causation Testimony and the Scientific Method," *Journal of Health Law* 37, no. 1 (2004): 85–112 (arguing for their views largely by citing case law as an authority).

They need to recognize that human evidence is often unavailable, thus forcing scientists to rely upon other kinds of evidence.[55] Then they need to recognize that numerous patterns of evidence support inferences about a substance's toxicity that involve little or no human evidence and review them sensitively for admissibility. Some of these more complex patterns of evidence will not ease judges' gatekeeping duties; quite the contrary, they will be difficult to assess. If these tasks prove too daunting, courts may need to reconsider the heightened duty to review evidence for admissibility in order to preserve fairness between parties and the legitimacy of the law.[56]

[55] Cranor and Eastmond, 10–16, 34–45.
[56] Margaret A. Berger, "Eliminating General Causation: Notes towards a New Theory of Justice and Toxic Torts," *Columbia Law Review* 97, no. 7 (1997): 2135; Cranor and Eastmond, 45–8.

# 7

# Using Science in a Political World: The Importance of Transparency in Natural Resource Regulation

Holly Doremus, J.D., Ph.D.

## Shielding Science from Politics

The premise of this book is that the work of doing policy-relevant science – that is, the process of producing the data needed to support regulatory and management decisions – must be insulated to the extent feasible against the vagaries of the political world. That premise is unquestionably sound; the scientific process will generate more reliable information more quickly if it is allowed to function according to its established norms, free of external political or financial momentum pushing toward one outcome or another.

But the premise is also incomplete. "Doing science" is only one part of the policy equation. Scientific information does not directly or magically become policy; it must be interpreted and applied. There is no formula that can objectively translate scientific information into regulatory decisions. Instead, the process of using science to construct policy is a complex one necessarily involving multiple judgment steps. Some of those judgments are essentially scientific, extrapolations or inferences drawn about the natural world from limited data, but many are essentially political, involving choices and trade-offs among societal goals. These two types of judgment are often closely intertwined and difficult to separate. The fundamental challenge of using science in the policy arena is to ensure that political judgments match societal goals and remain accountable to the public, while scientific judgments match our best understanding of the natural world and remain accountable to the relevant scientific community. Politics must not be allowed to obscure a scientific consensus, but equally the technical complexities of science must not be allowed to obscure the political judgments that are ultimately at the heart of regulatory decisions.

Transparency is an important tool for ensuring accountability in both science and politics. The scientific process cannot function unless researchers forthrightly communicate their results and the methods by which those results were generated to the scientific community. Communication facilitates replication and extension of the observations, as well as review and critique of claims based on the results. Openness is just as critical to a democratic society. Voters cannot hold their representatives responsible for decisions if they do not know what decisions have been made or what trade-offs those decisions entail.

Despite its acknowledged importance to the separate worlds of science and policy, transparency has been notably lacking in the natural resource management decisions that bridge those worlds. Transparency about who makes regulatory decisions, about the scientific basis for those decisions, and especially about the value choices made in the translation step from science to policy is essential to the effective use of scientific information in the political world of policy making. In this chapter, I explain why transparency is important, why it does not come easily in this context, and what steps might be taken to increase the transparency of decisions applying scientific information to policy problems.

## The Need for Transparency in Technical Regulatory Decisions

### Transparency and Accountability

Transparency is a tool for increasing political accountability. It helps address the principal-agent problem, which is inherent in representative government and amplified in the administrative state. In a democracy, ultimately the people are supposed to determine policy choices. But they do not do so directly. Two layers intervene between the voters and key regulatory decisions. Legislators, the people's elected representatives, enact statutes and appropriate funds to implement them. Administrative agencies then make key decisions about how to implement those statutes, from giving content to vague legislative terms to choosing how aggressively to enforce regulatory requirements.

This system of delegation is unavoidable, but carries obvious costs. The goals of legislators do not perfectly correspond with those of voters, nor do those of agency personnel perfectly correspond with those of legislators.

Agencies may be subject to focused political pressures that drive their preferences in directions that reflect special interests rather than the public interest. Even if agency personnel are firmly dedicated to pursuing the public interest, intense and focused political pressures may cause them to misinterpret that interest. The result is a high potential that regulatory decisions will reflect the goals and political sensitivities of bureaucrats and legislators rather than those of the electorate.[1]

The principal-agent problem is most acute when statutes delegate power to agencies in vague, general terms. Sometimes the legislature makes very specific demands of agencies, leaving little room for judgments that might run counter to legislative goals. But for the most part that has proven impractical or politically unattractive in the natural resource context. Even the most specific natural resource statutes provide agencies with ample discretion, offering plenty of opportunities for the actions of the agents to diverge from the goals of the principals. That is not to say that agencies do not seek to promote the public interest as they see it, but for a variety of reasons their view of the public interest may diverge from that of the legislature or the public.

In order to hold agents to their goals, principals have to be able to monitor the actions of the agents. If agents can hide their decisions, or the value choices that produce those decisions, from their principals, they will be free to pursue their own values. The easier it is for the public to discover and understand the political trade-offs made by agency personnel, the easier it is to hold agencies politically accountable for the ways in which they choose to exercise their discretion.

## The Prevalence of Judgment in Science-Based Decision Making

At first glance, transparency might seem less important for science-based policy decisions than for others. After all, science itself is supposed to act as an accountability mechanism. Legislative mandates for science-based decision making proliferated in the early 1970s, an era of newly magnified distrust of government agencies. Those mandates rest on an idealized and

---

[1] Steven P. Croley, "Theories of Regulation: Incorporating the Administrative Process," *Columbia Law Review* 98, no. 1 (1998): 56; J. R. DeShazo and Jody Freeman, "The Congressional Competition to Control Delegated Power," *Texas Law Review* 81, no. 6 (2003): 1443.

optimistic picture of what science can provide; they assume that scientific information will generally supply objective, value-free prescriptions for management. If that were the case, simply requiring that decisions take into account the best available science, as many natural resource management laws do,[2] would significantly constrain agency discretion. As it turns out, though, the science is typically far less certain than that hopeful vision.

There is strong evidence that natural resource regulation is affected by the principal–agent problem, and that science mandates do not neutralize that problem. The Endangered Species Act (ESA) contains the strongest science mandates of any federal natural resource law. Nonetheless, it has never lived up to its uncompromising legislative language. The ESA requires protection of any species that is in danger of extinction throughout all or a significant portion of its range, or likely to become so in the foreseeable future.[3] A combination of political resistance and funding shortfalls, however, has guaranteed that listings have never come close to covering all the species that seem to qualify.[4] Once species are listed, the ESA requires that federal agencies, through consultation with the Fish and Wildlife Service (FWS) and the National Marine Fisheries Service (NMFS) to ensure that their actions are not likely to jeopardize the continued existence of any listed species.[5] The regulatory agencies rarely find jeopardy, however, and even when they do, they almost always offer alternatives that allow actions to proceed.[6] Finally, the Act forbids "take," broadly

[2] Among the federal natural resource management statutes that prescribe reliance on scientific information, consultation with scientists, or solicitation of outside reviews are the following: the Endangered Species Act, see 16 U.S.C. §§ 1533(b)(1)(a), 1533(b)(2), 1536(a)(2); the Magnuson Fishery Conservation and Management Act, see 16 U.S.C. § 1851(a)(2); the Marine Mammal Protection Act, see 16 U.S.C § 1373(a); and the National Forest Management Act, see 16 U.S.C. § 1604(h).

[3] These are the statutory definitions of endangered and threatened species, respectively: 16 U.S.C. § 1532(6), (20).

[4] Amy Whritenour Ando, "Waiting to Be Protected under the Endangered Species Act: The Political Economy of Regulatory Delay," *Journal of Law and Economics* 42, no. 1 (1999): 29; Andrew Metrick and Martin L. Weitzman, "Patterns of Behavior in Endangered Species Preservation," *Land Economics* 72, no.1 (1996): 1; U.S. General Accounting Office, *Endangered Species: Factors Associated with Delayed Listing Decisions* (Washington, DC: Government Printing Office, 1993); David S. Wilcove et al., "What Exactly Is an Endangered Species? An Analysis of the U.S. Endangered Species List, 1985–1991," *Conservation Biology* 7, no. 1 (1993): 87.

[5] 16 U.S.C. § 1536(a)(2).

[6] Oliver A. Houck, "The Endangered Species Act and Its Implementation by the U.S. Departments of Interior and Commerce," *University of Colorado Law Review* 64, no. 2 (1993): 278, 318.

defined, of endangered animal species without a permit.[7] But government agencies have almost never enforced this prohibition against private parties, and have granted permits on the basis of exceedingly thin information, supported by naked promises of adaptive management.[8]

Clearly, the ESA's science mandates have not tied the regulatory agencies to the mast. Science mandates in other natural resource laws have fallen similarly short, for two major reasons. First, the scientific information available to support regulatory decisions regarding natural resources falls far short of certainty. It is frequently incomplete, ambiguous, and contested. Translating that kind of science into policy requires an array of critical interpretive judgments. Second, even when the statutory prescriptions appear clear on the surface, as they do in the ESA, Congress often has not made the needed policy judgments at the level of specificity required for regulatory decisions. The result is that agencies are left to make judgments, subject only to loose constraints from the available scientific data and applicable legislative prescriptions. The political process can provide additional constraints, but only if the judgments can be made transparent. Without transparency, the agencies will have plenty of room to pursue their own goals rather than those of the public.

## A Concrete Example: The Klamath Basin Water Conflict

The Klamath Basin, straddling the Oregon-California border, contains two distinctly different parts: a high, flat, arid Upper Basin and a Lower Basin characterized by steep mountains and abundant rainfall.[9] The federal Klamath Project, operated by the Bureau of Reclamation, irrigates the highest-value farm land in the Upper Basin. The major natural waterbody in the Upper Basin, Upper Klamath Lake, serves as the primary

---

[7] The take prohibition is at 16 U.S.C. § 1538(a)(1)(B). The statutory definition of "take," at 16 U.S.C. § 1532(19), includes not only killing, wounding and capturing listed species, but also harassing or harming them. The Fish and Wildlife Service has further defined "harm" to include significant habitat modification that actually kills or injures a listed creature. 50 C.F.R. § 17.3.

[8] Holly Doremus, "Adaptive Management, the Endangered Species Act, and the Institutional Challenges of 'New Age' Environmental Protection," *Washburn Law Journal* 41, no. 1 (2001): 50, 68–74.

[9] For a detailed description of this conflict, see Holly Doremus and A. Dan Tarlock, "Fish, Farms, and the Clash of Cultures in the Klamath Basin," *Ecology Law Quarterly* 30, no. 2 (2003): 279.

storage reservoir for the project. Upper Klamath Lake is extensive but very shallow, averaging only eight feet deep. It cannot store enough water to carry over from year to year. As a result, the project's water supplies are always at the mercy of the highly variable yearly precipitation in the Upper Basin.

Three species of fish in the Klamath Basin are protected by the federal Endangered Species Act: two species of suckers in Upper Klamath Lake and other reservoirs in the Upper Basin, and coho salmon in the Klamath River and its tributaries in the Lower Basin. To fulfill its ESA obligation to ensure that operation of the Klamath Project does not jeopardize the continued existence of the listed fish, the Bureau of Reclamation is required to consult with the U.S. Fish and Wildlife Service (FWS), which is responsible for the suckers, and the National Marine Fisheries Service (NMFS), which is responsible for the salmon.

In 2001, a drought intensified competition for the basin's limited water resources. The Bureau proposed to distribute water to farmers to a degree that would reduce water levels in Upper Klamath Lake and flows in the Klamath River below those at which the project had traditionally been operated. FWS found that the Bureau's proposal would jeopardize the listed suckers; to protect them, FWS called for maintaining higher lake levels. NMFS concluded that the coho would also be jeopardized by the Bureaus proposal; it prescribed higher seasonal flows in the Klamath River. Although the Bureau believed the wildlife agencies had overestimated the needs of the fish, it agreed to follow their prescriptions.[10] Together, the mandates for higher lake levels and higher river flows left no water available from Upper Klamath Lake for delivery to project irrigators. For the first (and so far the only) time, the headgates of a federal irrigation project were closed in order to protect fish.

---

[10]   Under the ESA, a federal agency contemplating action that may adversely affect a listed species prepares a "biological assessment," evaluating the effects. After reviewing that assessment, the wildlife agency issues a "biological opinion" concluding that the action as proposed either will or will not violate the prohibition on jeopardy. If it finds jeopardy, the wildlife agency must suggest "reasonable and prudent alternatives" consistent with the purpose of the proposed action and consistent with conservation of the species. 16 U.S.C. § 1536; 50 C.F.R. § 402.02. The action agency ultimately decides whether or not to proceed with the action, and in what form, but if it decides to go ahead in the face of a jeopardy opinion, it can expect at least a skeptical review from the courts. *Bennett v. Spear*, 520 U.S. 154, 169 (1997) (explaining that a biological opinion "theoretically serves an 'advisory function,'" but actually has a powerful coercive effect because of its influence with reviewing courts).

The resulting outcry focused on the extent of scientific support for the biological opinions. The Bush Administration sought review of the science by the National Research Council (NRC), the policy advice arm of the independent National Academies of Science and Engineering. The NRC followed its usual procedure, appointing a committee of experts from a variety of disciplines to spend several months reviewing the Klamath biological opinions. The committee's preliminary report concluded that there was "no substantial scientific support" for either FWS's demands for higher lake levels or NMFS's demands for higher river flows. The committee also noted that there was no substantial scientific support for the Bureau of Reclamation's proposal to reduce lake levels and instream flows.[11] Subsequently, in a much more detailed final report, the committee reiterated and expanded upon its conclusions, but also emphasized that it was not accusing the regulatory agencies of employing junk science.[12]

Critics on both sides have argued that the regulatory decisions in the Klamath conflict were too political and insufficiently scientific. Given the limits of both the data available and the legislative prescriptions, however, a more objective decision-making process simply would not have been possible. Although neither side seems to want to admit it, judgments are inevitable. The real argument is not over whether judgments should be made, but on what terms.

In the Klamath Basin, one set of judgments was needed to interpret the available data. Judgments of this sort are a familiar part of the scientific research process. Over time, the scientific process is an extraordinarily powerful method of generating strongly reliable, objective information about the natural world. But in the early stages or at the frontiers of knowledge, science is a messy process characterized by incomplete information and competing explanations. Research scientists constantly exercise judgment— in deciding what to test, what explanations to accept, and which data to prefer when some are consistent with the scientists' preferred explanation and others are not.

[11] National Research Council, *Interim Report from the Committee on Endangered and Threatened Fishes in the Klamath River Basin: Scientific Evaluation of Biological Opinions on Endangered and Threatened Fishes in the Klamath River Basin* (Washington, DC: National Academy Press, 2002), 2.

[12] National Research Council, *Endangered and Threatened Fishes in the Klamath River Basin: Causes of Decline and Strategies for Recovery* (Washington, DC: National Academy Press, 2004).

Research judgments occur in a very different context than regulatory ones, however. Research scientists put only their own careers on the line, and can choose when to make their claims. In the regulatory context, other people's livelihoods and identities are at stake, and the luxury of time is absent. Statutory deadlines and the consequences of inaction frequently force agencies to make decisions on the basis of scanty information. Because these decisions have impacts far beyond the agencies, they should be subject to public oversight.

The most important scientific judgments in the Klamath controversy dealt with the effects of water levels in Upper Klamath Lake on the endangered suckers and of flow levels in the Klamath River on the threatened coho salmon. Hardly any information was available, because interest in the suckers and salmon was not particularly high before they were listed under the Endangered Species Act. When the controversial 2001 biological opinions were drafted, regulators knew that the suckers had experienced massive die-offs in some years, and very limited recruitment in many. They did not have a direct population count because adult fish are difficult to sample. They also did not have a strong understanding of the species' life cycle, or which life stages might be the most crucial to population success. The data they did have were equivocal. For example, there were data comparing larval abundance with spring lake levels in six years. If one year was ignored, the remaining five showed a good correlation between higher lake levels and greater larval abundance. That seemed to make conceptual sense, because water levels in the very shallow Upper Klamath Lake are strongly correlated with increased wetland habitat, thought to be important to the young fish. Nonetheless, the one anomalous data point was an extreme outlier, showing the highest larval abundance in the driest year. Including it in the analysis made the apparent correlation between recruitment and water levels disappear.[13]

Any or all of the data points might have been incorrect; sampling error was known to be high. The outlying point might have been wrong due to sampling error, incorrect procedures, or even miscalculation. It or any of the other points might also represent a chance biological anomaly, or might be attributable to some confounding factor. Perhaps the fish spawned early or late one year, for example, so that water levels were not being measured

---

[13]  Ibid., 225.

at the most critical time. The stated norms of the scientific community require that no data be ignored or rejected without a good theoretical explanation, even if it does not fit the preconceived notions of the observer or it seems out of step with other observations. In practice, however, that norm is frequently violated, at least to the extent that scientists in fact do form opinions about systems based on the subset of the available data they find most convincing.[14]

Neither an idealized version of objective science nor conventional research science practices offer a clear model in these circumstances. Ideally, the regulatory agencies would interpret ambiguous data in light of societal goals, which would illuminate the costs of potential errors. But in the Klamath situation, as is typically the case, the agencies were also left to make key judgments about societal goals because Congress had ducked those decisions.

To begin with, determining that the suckers and coho qualified for listing under the ESA required the regulatory agencies to make judgments about the degree of acceptable risk to those species. Congress has provided only the most general indication of how those judgments should be made, defining as "endangered" any species that is "in danger of extinction throughout all or a substantial portion of its range," and as "threatened" any that is "likely to become endangered in the foreseeable future."[15] These definitions could cover every species on earth, because the legislature omitted any explanation of how great a risk would qualify a species for protection, or over what time period extinction risk should be evaluated. The key policy decisions have been left to the regulatory agencies, which in turn have chosen to make them on an ad hoc basis in individual regulatory determinations rather than articulating general principles.

Once the species were listed and consultation began on the effects of the Klamath Project, NMFS and FWS had to determine what level of risk would fall below the jeopardy threshold, and what degree of scientific

---

[14] Typically, research scientists reveal and explain their rejection of any data points, but not always. Robert Milliken, who famously demonstrated that all electrons have the same charge, aggressively separated "good" data (consistent with his theory) from "bad" data, publishing only about 40 percent of his observations. Gerald Holton, "On the Art of Scientific Imagination," *Daedalus* 125, no. 2 (1996): 183, 204–6. Even Gregor Mendel may have "fudged" the data on pea inheritance that launched modern genetics. Theodozius Dobzhansky, "Looking Back at Mendel's Discovery," *Science* 156, no. 3782 (1967): 1588.

[15] 16 U.S.C. § 1582(6), (20).

certainty to require for that decision. Again, the statute is not particularly helpful; it does not define jeopardy, simply directing federal agencies to "ensure" that their actions are "not likely" to cause jeopardy.[16] The joint regulations issued by the FWS and the NMFS suggest caution in this determination, but again quite vaguely: Actions reasonably expected to "appreciably reduce the likelihood of survival and recovery in the wild" are considered to jeopardize the continued existence of the species.[17]

## The Appropriate Burden of Proof

Policy judgments about acceptable risks and necessary degrees of scientific certainty, like those required in the Klamath Basin, pervade natural resource management. Those judgments, rather than the data themselves, are at the heart of resource management conflicts. How they should be made depends upon the relative costs of different types of error, which are fiercely contested.

Because they place high importance on environmental resources, environmentalists typically regard the costs of erring on the side of under-protection of those resources as much higher than the costs of mistaken overprotection. Accordingly, they would apply a strong precautionary principle, requiring convincing evidence that proposed development actions will not cause irreversible environmental harm. Resource users, of course, take the opposite view. They may not place much value on the environmental resources, and they stand to bear the economic costs of regulation. To their eyes, therefore, it is far more important to avoid over-regulation. Accordingly, they demand strong scientific proof of harm as a prerequisite to the imposition of regulations that restrict their autonomy or earnings.

Many of the disputants may not even understand that the argument centers on the burden of proof. Almost by definition, the scientific evidence in these conflicts is limited, and subject to multiple determinations. People with a strong interest in the outcome tend to interpret ambiguous scientific evidence as supporting their favored outcome. So it is genuinely possible that people on both sides believe that putting more emphasis on the science would compel the decisions they want to see. But there are also people on

16  16 U.S.C. § 1536(a)(2).
17  50 C.F.R. § 402.02.

both sides who understand exactly what the argument is about but prefer couching their claims as scientific ones to openly arguing for their values.

Ultimately, where the burden of proof should lie and how strong that burden should be are societal choices that will depend upon societal judgments about the costs of different types of error. In a democracy, the public must be the final arbiters of the relative importance of goals that may be in tension with one another. But the public cannot make those judgments if it does not understand what burden of proof is being imposed. Transparency about these policy judgments, therefore, is an essential element of an effective political process.

## Elusive Transparency

Federal natural resource statutes including the ESA leave a great deal of discretion to the regulatory agencies. Agency decisions exercising that discretion necessarily involve multiple judgment steps, including closely intertwined judgments about scientific and political matters. If the political aspects of those decisions are hidden, the agencies have opportunities to pursue their own preferences, to be captured by those with the most at stake in the decisions, or to misinterpret the public interest. Transparency is most needed for these sorts of decisions, but it is in just these contexts that transparency is in shortest supply.

By their very nature, these decisions are difficult to make transparent. They involve the interpretation and application of complex scientific information. The American lay public is not scientifically sophisticated. The average American voter, therefore, lacks the background to unpack claims that agency decisions are required by the available scientific evidence. Public interest groups can help, but even they face substantial barriers. Both highly specialized knowledge and a substantial investment of time and effort may be necessary to evaluate the science and ferret out the judgments implicit in highly technical regulatory decisions.

The close entanglement of scientific and policy judgments further complicates efforts to understand what is really going on in regulatory decisions, or for that matter in outside evaluations of those decisions. Even when they are made with the best of intentions, scientific judgments in the regulatory context are inevitably influenced by the policy views of the people making them. For example, the NRC's Klamath Committee was asked only to review the scientific grounding of the biological opinions,[18] but its conclusions seem to have been affected by the policy leanings of Committee members. The Committee's chair proclaimed in a published defense of the Committee's work that clearer scientific support should be demanded for regulations with serious economic consequences.[19] That is a tenable policy position, albeit one that Congress rejected in the ESA, but it has no place in a strictly scientific review.

## The Agencies' Agenda

The decision-making agencies are not inclined to help the public sort out the policy judgments in their decisions. To the contrary, they have every incentive to hide those judgments.[20] They are required by vague legislation to make difficult social choices between inconsistent goals. Congress and much of the public apparently expect regulatory agencies to balance conservation perfectly with economic development, finding the magic point at which society can maximize both. Moreover, the agencies are acutely aware of the presence of extremists on both sides who firmly oppose any balancing – conservationists who assign no value to economic interests, and developers who assign no value to the environment. Whatever balance they confess to striking between economics and the environment, the agencies are sure to face criticism.

Appeals to science can deflect that criticism by making it appear that any trade-offs were necessitated by nature rather than chosen by a political actor. In addition to deflecting political criticism, claims of scientific decision making carry affirmative political power of their own. Scientific decision making appears to be free of the corrupting influences of money and special interest politics. It also appears inherently fair; if an agency simply follows the directives of science, then it cannot favor the powerful

---

[18] National Research Council, *Endangered and Threatened Fishes in the Klamath River Basin*, 379.

[19] The Committee chair wrote in an exchange in the journal *Fisheries* that "[w]here the economic stakes are high," special attention should be given to the role of speculation in regulatory decisions. William M. Lewis, Jr., "Klamath Basin Fishes: Argument Is No Substitute for Evidence," *Fisheries* 28, no. 3 (2003): 20–1.

[20] Holly Doremus, "Listing Decisions under the Endangered Species Act: Why Better Science Isn't Always Better Policy," *Washington University Law Quarterly* 75, no. 3 (1997): 1029; Wendy E. Wagner, "The Science Charade in Toxic Risk Regulation," *Columbia Law Review* 95, no. 7 (1995): 1613, 1651–1.

or politically connected. Finally, science and scientists enjoy a much higher level of public trust than do politics and politicians. Those who are adversely affected by a regulatory decision are more likely to accept it if they trust the motives of the decision maker. Decisions that appear scientific therefore inherently enjoy greater public credibility and are subject to less opposition than others.

Regulatory agencies may also believe that emphasizing the scientific nature of their decisions will immunize those decisions against judicial review. The federal courts have articulated a doctrine of great deference to technical regulatory decisions. The classic statement of this principle comes from the Supreme Court's 1983 decision in *Baltimore Gas and Electric Company v. Natural Resources Defence Council*: When examining a "scientific determination, as opposed to simple findings of fact, a reviewing court must generally be at its most deferential."[21] Established doctrine also calls for deference to agency policy choices within the range permitted by the statute that an agency implements,[22] but there is some evidence that courts do not always defer to agency policy choices.[23] In fact, it is not clear that "scientizing" their natural resource decisions gives regulatory agencies much advantage in litigation,[24] but it would not be surprising if they expected it to do so.

The key regulatory decisions in the Klamath conflict do not openly acknowledge choices about societal goals or the extent of uncertainty in the supporting data. In listing the long-lived suckers as endangered, FWS documented a precipitous decline in the population in recent years and noted that there appeared not to have been any substantial recruitment for nearly twenty years. [25] In this particular case, there was little disagreement that the suckers required protection. Nonetheless, the lack of any attempt to quantify, or even describe, the degree of risk to the species, the time

---

[21] 462 U.S. 87, 103 (1983).

[22] *Chevron U.S.A. v. Natural Resources Defense Council*, 467 U.S. 837, 844 (1984).

[23] Wagner, 1666–7.

[24] Federal agencies lose an astonishing percentage of lawsuits challenging their ESA implementing actions, despite their established practice of scientizing those decisions. Nearly 80 percent of reported decisions in litigation over listing determinations have gone against the agencies. Holly Doremus, "The Purposes, Effects, and Future of the Endangered Species Act's Best Available Science Mandate," *Environmental Law* 34, no. 2 (2004): 397, 431.

[25] Endangered and Threatened Wildlife and Plants; Determination of Endangered Status for the Shortnose Sucker and Lost River Sucker, 53 Fed. Reg, 27,130 (July 18, 1988) (to be codified at 50 C.F.R. § 17)

period over which viability was forecast, or the extent of confidence that the agency had in its estimates is conspicuous. NMFS, in the coho salmon listing, similarly glossed over the risk question. It simply stated that its listing determinations were made on the basis of population status, and noted that the current population was much reduced from its historic numbers, although it appeared fairly stable over the last twenty years.[26]

NMFS also had to explain its identification of the coho in this region as a Distinct Population Segment (DPS) qualifying for listing. (A DPS is a group that is genetically isolated from the rest of the species and of significance either biologically or ecologically.) It referred to policy statements, scientific papers, and technical memoranda, but did not address precisely how it decided these salmon were sufficiently distinct to justify separate treatment.[27] When it proposed this group for listing, NMFS had found a relatively large genetic distance between them and fish from rivers to the north and south, and had noted that tagged fish from this group were more likely to spend the ocean portion of their life cycle off the California coast than their cousins from more northerly rivers.[28] Neither of these distinguishing traits amounted to a bright line. There was also considerable genetic diversity within the recognized DPS, and the ocean distributions overlapped.[29] The agency was required to draw bright lines where nature had provided none but it did not acknowledge the policy elements of its decision.

## Stakeholder Agendas

It is not just the regulatory agencies that are inclined to overemphasize the scientific nature of natural resource regulation. Critics on both sides of natural resource conflicts buy into the paradigm of scientific decision making, downplaying the political aspects of the decisions. For these reasons, there has not been any substantial push for increased transparency.

[26] Endangered and Threatened Species; Threatened Status for Southern Oregon/Northern California Coast Evolutionarily Significant Unit (ESU) of Coho Salmon, 62 Fed. Reg. 24,588, 24,589–91 (May 6, 1997) (to be codified at 50 C.F.R. § 227).
[27] Ibid., 24,590.
[28] Endangered and Threatened Species: Proposed Threatened Status for Three Contiguous ESUs of Coho Salmon Ranging from Oregon through Central California, 60 Fed. Reg. 38,011 (proposed July 25, 1995) (to be codified at 50 C.F.R. § 227).
[29] Ibid., 38,013–14.

Critics may genuinely (but naively) believe that science alone can determine regulatory decisions, or they may believe that disguising political choices with the appearance of science will systematically work to their political advantage. Extractive interests might believe they would gain a political advantage from this approach because they have better access to the decision makers. Many natural resource management decisions are made in the field or regional offices of decentralized agencies, by people who live in the rural communities most affected by the decisions. In addition, because they stand to bear focused economic costs, extractive interests will find it worthwhile to invest the time and resources necessary to influence these decisions. They might well believe that scientific cover, which makes these decisions less politically accountable to the general public, will increase the effectiveness of their focused political pressure.

Conservation interests apparently see the political landscape differently, because they have long overemphasized the scientific nature of natural resource decisions. They may favor scientizing these decisions as a way to increase the relative power of agency scientists against political appointees in the decision-making process. The heroes of the conservation movement in the United States, from its origins to the present day, have been scientifically trained.[30] Biologists, especially ecologists and those who study endangered species or systems, tend to favor conservation more strongly than the general public. Increasing their power in decision making, therefore, should increase the likelihood of pro-conservation decisions.

It is difficult to tell how well this strategy has worked for conservation interests. The history of anemic ESA implementation previously described shows that it is hardly foolproof, but perhaps implementation would have been even weaker if these decisions were not heavily scientized. There is some evidence that giving scientists a prominent role in decisions can favor conservation. In the National Forest Management Act, Congress required that the Forest Service seek advice from a Committee of Scientists on the development of forest planning regulations.[31] The Committee deliberately did not limit itself to technical advice. Its policy recommendations resulted

---

[30] These conservation scientist-advocates include, among others, Rachel Carson, Paul Ehrlich, Aldo Leopold, Thomas Lovejoy, Gifford Pinchot, George Perkins Marsh, John Muir, Norman Myers, and Edward O. Wilson.

[31] 16 U.S.C. § 1604(h).

in a strong regulatory requirement that forest supervisors maintain viable populations of native species.[32] When the Clinton Administration decided to revise the forest planning regulations, it again empanelled a Committee of Scientists, and that Committee's report provided the justification for the Forest Service to make ecological sustainability the primary goal of forest planning.[33]

## The Implications of Opacity

Today, though, the risks of hiding political decisions behind a veneer of science are probably higher than its rewards for conservationists. First, to the extent that such a strategy allows regulatory agencies to hide their political decisions, it increases their ability to respond to the focused political pressures of extractive interests. Second, scientists rarely are the top decision makers in regulatory agencies. The political appointees who run the agencies can almost always reject the recommendations of scientists if they choose to do so. Third, the insistence that science dictate regulatory decisions requires that the certainty of the scientific information be exaggerated.

The third factor leaves conservationists vulnerable to demands that they prove those claims, precisely the demands currently being made by the "sound-science" antiregulatory movement. When closer inspection shows that the scientific information is equivocal – as it did, for example, in the Klamath conflict – anticonservation interests can turn demands for scientific decision making against conservation.

Further, exaggerating the level of scientific certainty discourages additional research that may be necessary for protection of the resource. A regulatory agency anxious to insist that survival of the endangered suckers in the Klamath Basin depends upon higher lake levels, for example, is not likely to fund, encourage, or carry out studies that might disprove

---

[32] National Forest System Land and Resource Management Planning, 47 Fed. Reg. 43,026, 43,048 (Sept. 30, 1982) (to be codified at 36 C.F.R. § 219). This viability requirement provided a key legal hook that enabled environmentalists to virtually shut down logging on national forests in the Pacific Northwest during the spotted owl wars.

[33] National Forest System Land and Resource Management Planning, 65 Fed. Reg. 67,514 (Nov. 9, 2000) (to be codified at 36 C.F.R. §§ 217, 219). The Bush Administration has now revised the rules again, without the input of scientists, eliminating both the viability requirement and the primacy of ecological sustainability. National Forest System Land Management Planning, 70 Fed. Reg. 1023 (Jan. 5, 2005) (to be codified at 36 C.F.R. § 219).

that hypothesis. But if in fact the fish are more dependent on some other environmental factor, they may go extinct while the agency enforces its ineffective regulations. Now and for the future, therefore, I believe conservation interests will be better served by bringing the political judgments inherent in regulatory decisions into the sunshine than by insisting that no such political judgments exist.

Hiding value choices inherent in seemingly technical decisions can also have costs for the scientific enterprise. It can distort the scientific process by encouraging scientists and others to frame what are really value differences as scientific ones.[34] That in turn can limit the ability of science to fulfill its role as a key source of information for the development and evaluation of policy options.[35] It may also discourage scientists from studying problems with important policy implications, because doing so may bring them into the middle of fierce political battles.[36]

## Restoring Transparency

### Congress and the Agencies

Either Congress or the regulatory agencies could readily increase the transparency and accountability of technical resource management decisions. Congress could provide greater specificity on how the necessary policy decisions should be made, or could explicitly require that agencies disclose uncertainties in the underlying data and explicitly discuss how their decisions deal with uncertainty. Agencies could openly acknowledge their policy choices, in general rule makings or in individual regulatory decisions.

But neither the agencies nor the legislature is likely to take that step. Agency incentives for hiding their policy choices behind scientific curtains have already been explained. Congress also benefits from the lack of transparency. By delegating difficult policy decisions to regulatory agencies,

[34] Eric T. Freyfogle and Julianne Lutz Newton, "Putting Science in Its Place," *Conservation Biology* 16, no. 4 (2002): 863, 871.

[35] Roger A. Pielke, Jr., "When Scientists Politicize Science: Making Sense of Controversy over *The Skeptical Environmentalist*," *Environmental Science and Policy* 7, no. 5 (2004): 405–6.

[36] Some biologists working in the Klamath Basin, for example, have described their work as "combat biology." Robert F. Service, " 'Combat Biology' on the Klamath," *Science* 300, no. 5616 (2003): 36.

and directing the agencies to make those decisions scientifically, Congress too can deflect political responsibility for the results.

## The Courts

The best hope for transparency, therefore, comes from the courts. Courts have different incentives from agencies and legislatures. They have no reason to deflect political responsibility from agency decision makers. They may even enhance their own institutional power by more closely overseeing these decisions. Moreover, while overseeing the substance of scientific decisions is institutionally uncomfortable for courts, forcing agency judgments into the open fits easily within existing doctrine.

Judges are accurately and acutely aware both that they lack specialized scientific expertise and that Congress may deliberately leave complex policy judgments to agencies steeped in the details of the specific issues. The courts therefore profess to be very reluctant to intervene substantively in highly technical agency decisions. With respect to policy judgments, they will openly step in only when regulatory agencies overstep legislative boundaries, which are often drafted broadly. With respect to scientific judgments, courts will reject them only when the agency has ignored a consensus of both its own and outside scientists, or failed to offer a coherent explanation of how the available evidence leads to its conclusion.

Substantive review, however, is not required in order for courts to enhance transparency. Courts have been much more willing to require more complete or persuasive explanations for judicial decisions. Standard "hard look" review allows courts to encourage, and even to require, that agencies reveal the value choices that determine their regulatory decisions. Courts must defer to agency policy choices within the (sometimes quite amorphous) boundaries established by Congress, but are fully entitled to demand an explanation of those choices sufficient to allow them to determine whether the agencies have kept within their boundaries.[37]

### A Model Case

A good starting point is the decision in *Fishermen's Dock Cooperative, Inc. v. Brown*.[38] In *Fishermen's Dock*, a coalition of commercial fishers challenged

---

[37]   *Citizens to Preserve Overton Park v. Volpe*, 401 U.S. 402 (1971).
[38]   75 F.3d 164 (4th Cir. 1996).

a quota for summer flounder set by the Department of Commerce under the Magnuson Fishery Conservation and Management Act.[39] A scientific advisory committee had produced the quota, with the goal of keeping mortality below a specified target level. The committee chose a quota one standard deviation below the mean estimated recruitment over the previous five years. Plaintiffs claimed that the Magnuson Act's requirement that quotas be set using the best scientific data available mandated the use of the mean annual recruitment level, which would have resulted in a higher quota.

The court disagreed. It noted that use of the best scientific data need not mandate "one and only one possible quota."[40] The committee had chosen a quota with a higher probability than that sought by the fishermen of resulting in mortality below the target level. The court noted that given the uncertainty of the data, any specific quota could be attacked as arbitrary. Under the circumstances, the agency "necessarily had some discretion to decide what precise degree of assurance it would seek within the uncertainty of the data."[41] It had explained why it chose the lower quota, essentially noting that its primary goal was to stay below the target mortality and that some assumptions in the model it used could be optimistic.

This decision is a good model in three respects. First, the court recognized that the best available science frequently will not point to a single, clearly identifiable management choice. Second, it realized that the selection of a particular choice within the range identified by the available science depended upon value choices. Third, the court gave the agency's decision greater deference because both the scientific and value bases for the particular choice within that range were explained.

### Remand as Remedy

Courts can and should take the next step, remanding decisions where such transparency is lacking. Perhaps they have not done so yet because they simply have not recognized such decisions for what they are. Courts should be on the lookout for (and litigants should point out) circumstances in which regulatory decisions necessarily involve value choices, but those choices and the grounds for them have not been explained. Agencies should have

---

[39]  Magnuson Fishery Conservation and Management Act, 16 U.S.C. §§1801–1883.
[40]  75 F.3d 164, 169.
[41]  Ibid., 171.

to provide that explanation, with reference to their goals, their understanding of the degree of uncertainty in the data, and the extent to which they have employed a precautionary approach.

This vision of judicial review does not invite "ossification" – that is, the bureaucratic paralysis that can result from agencies endlessly putting off rule making while they gather more data to satisfy too-demanding courts.[42] Technically intensive natural resource decisions, unlike the open-ended environmental and workplace regulations that have given rise to concerns about ossification, are focused on relatively narrow circumstances and are required both by law and by practical circumstances to be made quickly.

Moreover, these decisions are frequently governed by a "best available scientific information" standard that plainly contemplates some level of uncertainty. Currently, the agencies are a long way from overly detailed consideration and justification of their actions. They frequently provide absolutely no acknowledgment of political choices necessarily required by the underlying statutory regime, much less any explanation of the basis for those choices. The value choices are made almost entirely on an *ad hoc* basis, subject to the political whims of the moment, in individual regulatory decisions. Forcing those *ad hoc* value choices more clearly into the open would be the reverse of ossification. It might make regulatory agencies uncomfortable, but it would not make their decisions any more difficult than Congress necessarily contemplated.

Courts should not, however, be encouraged to interfere with agency policy judgments within boundaries left open by the legislature. Those choices are properly subject to political, rather than judicial, review. Agencies must be assured that revealing their political choices will not undermine their judicial position. Instead of effectively pressuring agencies to engage in a

---

[42] Frank B. Cross, "Pragmatic Pathologies of Judicial Review of Administrative Rulemaking," *North Carolina Law Review* 78, no. 4 (2000): 1013; William S. Jordan, III, "Ossification Revisited: Does Arbitrary and Capricious Review Significantly Interfere with Agency Ability to Achieve Regulatory Goals through Informal Rulemaking?" *Northwestern University Law Review* 94, no. 2 (2000): 393; Jerry L. Mashaw and David L. Harfst, "Regulation and Legal Culture: The Case of Motor Vehicle Safety," *Yale Journal on Regulation* 4, no. 2 (1987): 257; Thomas O. McGarity, "The Courts and the Ossification of Rulemaking: A Response to Professor Seidenfeld," *Texas Law Review* 75, no. 3 (1997): 525; Richard J. Pierce, Jr., "The Unintended Effects of Judicial Review of Agency Rules: How Federal Courts Have Contributed to the Electricity Crisis of the 1990s," *Administrative Law Review* 43, no. 1 (1991): 7.

science charade, courts should provide incentives for the agencies to reveal their political choices, thereby facilitating political accountability.

## Mandating Disclosure

Courts could also take another important step to increase transparency in science-policy decisions. Conservationists have always assumed, or at least hoped, that science mandates would strengthen the hand of conservation scientists in natural resource regulation. In practice, this effect has been limited because control of agency decisions ultimately rests with political appointees. Historically, political appointees have proven themselves quite willing to reject the recommendations of agency scientists and scientific advisory committees, a trend that continues in the current administration.[43] They can frequently do so with political impunity because the public does not have access to those recommendations, unless they are leaked to the press. Currently, agency scientific recommendations may not even be discoverable in litigation; some courts have ruled that they are covered by the deliberative process privilege,[44] which protects internal predecision discussions in order to allow agencies to engage in frank and complete consideration of the decision.

Ideally, Congress would mandate public disclosure of the recommendations or reports of agency scientists. Failing that, courts could exclude such recommendations or reports from the deliberative process privilege. Where

[43] Andrew C. Revkin, "Bush Aide Softened Greenhouse Gas Links to Global Warming," *New York Times*, June 8, 2005, sec. A. The deputy assistant secretary of interior for fish, wildlife, and parks, Julie MacDonald, has been particularly active in this respect. She has no training in biology, but she has aggressively criticized work by agency scientists that suggested, for example, that the greater sage grouse should be listed as endangered. Felicity Barringer, "Interior Aide and Biologists Clashed over Protecting Bird," *New York Times*, Dec. 5, 2004, sec. 1. Ultimately, the agency decided not to list the bird. Endangered and Threatened Wildlife and Plants; 12-Month Finding for Petitions to List the Greater Sage-Grouse as Threatened or Endangered, 70 Fed. Reg. 2244 (Jan. 12, 2005). Another example relates to the treatment of hatchery fish under the Endangered Species Act. A scientific advisory panel convened by the National Marine Fisheries Service recommended against considering hatchery fish in listing decisions. That advice not only was not followed, it was not made public by the agency, leading the panel to submit it to the journal *Science*. Ransom A. Myers et al., "Hatcheries and Endangered Salmon," *Science* 303, no. 5666 (2004): 1980. For other examples, see Laura Paskus, "Conscientious Objectors: Public Employees and Their Allies on the Outside Fight against Bush's War on Science," *High Country News*, Dec. 20, 2004, p. 10.

[44] *Center for Biological Diversity v. Norton*, 336 F. Supp. 2d 1155 (D. N.M. 2004); *Center for Biological Diversity v. Norton*, No. Civ. 01–409 TUC ACM, 2002 WL 32136200, (D. Ariz. July 24, 2002); *Greenpeace v. National Marine Fisheries Serv.*, 198 F.R.D. 540 (W.D. Wash. 2000)1.

Congress has directed agencies to use the best available scientific information in their decisions, the public is entitled to know what agency scientists think of the scientific data, without filtering by political appointees. That does not mean that agency scientists must always control the ultimate decisions, or that they can necessarily be trusted not to mix policy judgments into their scientific evaluations. But making the unvarnished recommendations of agency scientists public should help increase the transparency of science-policy decisions, even if agency scientists are just as inclined as agency politicians to hide their political judgments. If an agency must disclose internal scientific advice counter to its decision, it will face both political and judicial pressures to explain the discrepancy. That will give agency policy makers incentives to explain the policy judgments both in their decision and in the recommendations of their scientists.

## Conclusion

Natural resource management decisions, although they appear superficially to be dictated by scientific information, in fact can hide numerous judgments. Science and policy are closely intertwined in those judgments, but the regulatory agencies have strong incentives to pretend that they involve only science. That presents problems for democratic governance, because the agencies cannot be held politically accountable for hidden choices. Any steps that make it easier for the public to understand precisely who is responsible for regulatory choices, and the basis on which those choices have been made, will increase political accountability. Agencies and the legislature cannot be counted on to take those steps, but courts can and should do so.

Conservationists, who have been complicit in the pretense of scientific primacy in the past, should realize that it is not only inconsistent with democracy but likely to work against their interests in the current political climate. Instead of trying to eliminate the political elements of regulatory decisions, they should focus on making the inevitable politics more open and accountable.

# 8

# Transforming Science into Law

## Transparency and Default Reasoning in International Trade Disputes

Vern R. Walker, Ph.D.

## Transparency in Law versus Transparency in Science

The principles of transparency that are part of the framework for this book, as applied to governmental fact finding, require the fact finder to make several aspects of decision making clear to all interested parties: the evidence behind a finding of fact, the fact finder's evaluation of that evidence, and the reasoning connecting the evidence to the finding. Ideally, all parties could understand which evidence the fact finder took into account and how the fact finder assessed the probative value of that evidence in arriving at the findings. A similar ideal of transparency occurs in science. The design and analysis of empirical studies should be so transparent that other scientists can critique the methods used and replicate the research. All interested researchers should have access to the data-gathering methods, if not the data itself, and should be able to evaluate for themselves the degree of evidentiary support for the scientific findings. With regard to transparency, therefore, law and science share the same ideal. There would seem to be no conflict of principles when scientists provide the evidentiary basis for legal fact finding.

From a legal perspective, this ideal of transparency is closely connected to other ideals: the predictability and legitimacy of the law, and the rule of law itself. If legal rules transparently govern the outcomes in particular cases, and if similar cases are decided similarly, then the law is more likely to be predictable and fair. Moreover, governmental institutions are less likely to abuse their powers. A major goal in founding the World Trade Organization (WTO) was to achieve predictability and legitimacy in the resolution of international trade disputes by requiring transparent reasoning for the findings of fact that resolve those disputes. When those findings are about the risks of harm posed by imported products, the WTO relies on scientific evidence and reasoning. And if transparent scientific reasoning can help make international trade law more predictable and fair, there would seem to be no harmful downside for science.

A central thesis of this chapter, however, is that the involvement of science in legal fact finding pressures scientists to transform their reasoning patterns into those of legal reasoning, and to transform the practice of science into a regulatory enterprise. Due to the logical nature of scientific reasoning, this involvement makes the politicization of science not only likely, but inevitable and perhaps even rational. A default-logic model of legal and scientific reasoning helps us to understand why this is so, and fact finding in WTO trade disputes provides a good example of the dynamic involved.

The analysis suggests that the pressure to increase the transparency of scientific reasoning can have countervailing costs, especially in the case of fact finding about risks that have significant scientific uncertainty. Principles of transparency, however, help us to keep those costs to acceptable levels. If we are to rescue science from politics, we need to understand the underlying logic of legal fact finding, and the role of science within it. Otherwise, an unreflective pursuit of transparency runs the risk of politicizing science even further.

## Transparent Dispute Settlement in the WTO: The Role of Legal Rules

A major goal behind the establishment of the WTO in 1995 was to create a system of transparent and predictable rules governing trade.[1] Other goals were to clarify the rights and responsibilities of global trading partners

---

[1] Understanding on Rules and Procedures Governing the Settlement of Disputes, art. 3, Apr. 15, 1994, Marrakesh Agreement Establishing the World Trade Organization (hereinafter WTO Agreement), Annex 2, Legal Instruments – Results of the Uruguay Round, vol. 31, 33 I.L.M. 112 (1994) (available at http://www.wto.org/english/docs_e/legal_e/28-dsu.pdf) (hereinafter DSU Agreement); Agreement on the Application of Sanitary and Phytosanitary Measures, preamble, April 15, 1994, WTO Agreement, Annex 1A, 33 I.L.M. 1125 (1994) (available at http://www.wto.org/english/docs_e/legal_e/15-sps.pdf) (hereinafter SPS Agreement). Background information on the WTO, as well as all of the WTO documents discussed in this chapter, can be found on the WTO website (http://www.wto.org).

and to establish a dispute settlement mechanism that would adjudicate particular trade disputes using those trade rules. That dispute settlement process employs fact-finding panels appointed to decide particular cases, and a standing Appellate Body established to resolve the issues of law arising in the disputes. While a panel's decisions about issues of law are subject to reversal by the Appellate Body, a panel's findings of fact are considered final.[2]

A mechanism of dispute settlement, however, could be governed by procedural rules without satisfying transparency principles. Those principles require more than transparent procedures. They require that policy makers relying on scientific research must be careful to represent the scientific findings accurately, including the limitations of the scientific research. This principle applies to WTO fact-finding panels when they rely upon scientific research as evidentiary support for a finding of fact. Such findings are the foundation of a major WTO agreement called the Agreement on the Application of Sanitary and Phytosanitary Measures (SPS Agreement). The SPS Agreement establishes the rights and responsibilities of WTO members when they take measures to protect the health or life of humans, animals, or plants (so-called "sanitary or phytosanitary measures"). Such measures that affect international trade can include testing requirements, quarantines, or outright bans on products. The concern among trading partners is that a member state might impose restrictions on imported products in order to protect its own domestic industry from foreign competition, but try to justify those restrictions as being necessary to protect health or life.

The SPS Agreement, while acknowledging each member's sovereign right to take *legitimate* protective measures, provides that such measures are in fact legitimate only if they have a foundation in scientific fact. The SPS Agreement uses science as a "neutral arbiter" in trade disputes over sanitary or phytosanitary measures. The agreement requires WTO members to "ensure that any sanitary or phytosanitary measure is applied only to the extent necessary to protect human, animal or plant life or health, is based on scientific principles and is not maintained without sufficient scientific evidence."[3] In addition, "[m]embers shall ensure that their

---

[2] DSU Agreement, arts. 6–8, 11–12, 17.
[3] SPS Agreement, art. 2.2.

sanitary or phytosanitary measures are based on an assessment, as appropriate to the circumstances, of the risks to human, animal or plant life or health, taking into account risk assessment techniques developed by the relevant international organizations."[4] The SPS Agreement requires WTO members to justify their protective measures by means of scientific risk assessments. Two important cases explained the application of these broad standards.

## The Beef Hormones Case

In the first dispute adjudicated under the SPS Agreement, the United States and Canada complained against the European Communities over a European ban on imports of meat and meat products derived from cattle raised using certain growth-promoting hormones (the *EC – Hormones* case).[5] The European Communities argued that the hormones employed are carcinogenic and that the residues in meat products increase the risk of cancer to consumers. The WTO fact-finding panel found that the European Communities were acting inconsistently with the requirement that a measure must be based on a risk assessment.

In deciding the appeal of the case, the Appellate Body developed several new legal rules relating to the scientific basis required under the SPS Agreement. First, the banned products must pose a risk that is "ascertainable" – that is, a risk that is not merely "theoretical," although it need not be so certain as to provide "absolute certainty."[6] Second, the measure must be "sufficiently supported or reasonably warranted" by a risk assessment.[7] Third, the supporting evidence must be "sufficiently specific" to the risk posed by the particular products, although that evidence need not be quantitative or represent a consensus view among scientists.[8] Because the Appellate Body created these new rules as interpretations of the SPS Agreement, fact-finding panels are bound to apply them in deciding later cases. The final decision in the *EC – Hormones* case was

---

[4]  Ibid., art. 5.1.
[5]  WTO Appellate Body Report, EC Measures Concerning Meat and Meat Products (Hormones), WT/DS26/AB/R & WT/DS48/AB/R, para. 2 (Jan. 16, 1998) (available at http://docsonline.wto.org/DDFDocuments/t/WT/DS/26ABR.WPF).
[6]  Ibid., paras. 182–6.
[7]  Ibid., paras. 186, 193.
[8]  Ibid., paras. 187, 194, 198–201.

that the European Communities had in fact failed to base the product ban on a "risk assessment that reasonably supports or warrants the import prohibition."[9]

## The Salmon Case

A later case under the SPS Agreement (the *Australia – Salmon* case) involved a dispute over an Australian prohibition on the importation of fresh, chilled, or frozen salmon, ostensibly to protect against the spread of pests or disease within Australia's territory.[10] In addition to applying the rules developed in the *EC – Hormones* case, the Appellate Body in *Australia – Salmon* held that an adequate risk assessment must evaluate the "likelihood" or "probability" of the entry, establishment, or spread of disease, not merely the "possibility" of entry, establishment, or spread.[11] Such evidence need not be complete, however, and it can be either quantitative or qualitative.[12] The final decision in the *Australia – Salmon* case was that the report on which Australia relied was not in fact an adequate risk assessment satisfying WTO requirements. Therefore, Australia's prohibition was not consistent with its obligations under the SPS Agreement.

## Legitimate Science or Inadequate Risk Assessment?

As these two cases make clear, the SPS Agreement's approach of using scientific research as a neutral arbiter over the legitimacy of sanitary and phytosanitary measures depends upon the WTO's being able to distinguish legitimate or sound science from an inadequate risk assessment. Legal rules about trade responsibilities must rest upon legal rules about what counts as an adequate scientific assessment of risk. The WTO approach is that in a trade dispute over a governmental measure, the disputing members should lay their reasoning about the measure transparently on the table, in such a way that a fact-finding panel can inspect that reasoning and decide

---

[9] Ibid., para. 208.
[10] WTO Appellate Body Report, Australia – Measures Affecting Importation of Salmon, WT/DS18/AB/R, para. 1 (Oct. 20, 1998) (available at http://docsonline.wto.org/DDFDocuments/t/WT/DS/18ABR.DOC) (hereinafter Salmon Appellate Body Report).
[11] Ibid., para. 123.
[12] Ibid., paras.125, 130.

whether the measure is "based on scientific principles" and is supported by "sufficient scientific evidence," as required by the SPS Agreement. The legal rules presuppose, therefore, that we can make additional rules about when reasoning is scientific and sound.

## Logical Features of Legal Rules

Before analyzing scientific reasoning in contrast with legal reasoning, it is useful to summarize several logical features of legal rules. First, legal rules are *conditional* propositions of the form "if $p$, then $q$," where $p$ and $q$ stand for propositions. A legal rule states that finding proposition $p$ to be true is a sufficient condition for finding $q$ to be true. For example, "if a sanitary measure is supported by an adequate scientific risk assessment, then it satisfies the requirements of the SPS Agreement."

Second, the conditional proposition must be adopted by proper legal authority in order to have the force of law. Legal rules, in order to be valid, must be adopted by a person or institution that has the authority to adopt them, and adopted in a manner that satisfies the applicable procedural rules. Finally, legal rules must apply universally: They must govern all situations that satisfy the antecedent condition in the "if" clause. They should decide the outcomes in all cases to which they apply. Any exceptions from the rule should be identified and governed by additional rules.

In law, the goal is to use rules to decide cases objectively and consistently, not subjectively and by the inscrutable whim of the decision maker. Universal rules are also a primary method of achieving transparency. Legal fact finding is transparent to the extent that the process is governed by adopted procedural rules, the issues to be decided are determined by the substantive legal rules, and the evidence is evaluated and the findings are made by applying the evidentiary rules. To the extent that explicit legal rules govern the outcomes of the cases, the legal system operates transparently.

## Default Reasoning in Science: The Role of Generalizations

To understand the similarities and dissimilarities between legal reasoning and scientific reasoning, we can view them both as instances of what logicians call "default reasoning."[13] Default reasoning relies on available evidence to warrant probabilistic conclusions that are subject to future revision. Such reasoning is dynamic, because the degree of support provided by the reasoning and evidence to the conclusion can change over time, as we acquire new information or rethink old information. Default reasoning is also defeasible, meaning that new information or a reanalysis can defeat the prior conclusion or undermine its evidentiary support. Nevertheless, in the absence of such defeating considerations, default reasoning is presumptively valid: It is reasonable to treat the (provisional) conclusion as being probably true. That makes default reasoning practical, because we can use it to reach conclusions about objects and events in the real world, and we can rely on those conclusions to guide our decisions and actions. This section describes how scientific reasoning has these characteristics, and the role that generalizations play in that reasoning.

Scientists use default reasoning in all aspects of their work, both in generating and confirming theories and in applying those theories to particular events.[14] Scientists begin with empirical observations about objects or events in the world. They generate "data" by systematically classifying those objects or events into categories, using explicit measurement criteria whenever possible. Examples of measurement or classification variables are height, age, the concentration of hormone residue in meat, and whether a person has a malignant tumor. The classification or measurement criteria must be as transparent and explicit as possible, so that numerous researchers can be trained to gather data in consistent ways, and future studies can produce data compatible with past studies. Nevertheless, uncertainty about measurement data is a fact of scientific life – such uncertainty includes both whether there is human or instrument error in particular data

---

13  For discussions of the logic of default reasoning, see Henry E. Kyburg, Jr., and Choh Man Teng, *Uncertain Inference* (Cambridge, UK: Cambridge University Press, 2001); John L. Pollock, *Nomic Probability and the Foundations of Induction* (New York: Oxford University Press, 1990); Henry Prakken, *Logical Tools for Modelling Legal Argument* (Dordrecht: Kluwer, 1997); Stephen Toulmin et al., *An Introduction to Reasoning* (New York: Macmillan, 2nd ed., 1984); Douglas N. Walton, *Argument Schemes for Presumptive Reasoning* (Mahwah, NJ: Lawrence Erlbaum Associates, 1996); Douglas Walton, *Legal Argumentation and Evidence* (University Park, PA: Pennsylvania State University Press, 2002).

14  Vern R. Walker, "Restoring the Individual Plaintiff to Tort Law by Rejecting 'Junk Logic' about Specific Causation," *Alabama Law Review* 56, no. 2 (2004): 381, 386–452; Vern R. Walker, "Theories of Uncertainty: Explaining the Possible Sources of Error in Inferences," *Cardozo Law Review* 22, no. 5–6 (2001): 1523, 1543–59.

entries and whether the measurement processes themselves are sufficiently reliable and valid, given the kinds of conclusions that scientists wish to draw.

Moreover, scientists usually gather their data only from samples of objects or events, not from the entire population that they wish to study. Examples of samples are the meat products actually tested for hormone residues, the people who are the subjects in a cancer study, and the events included in a study's time frame. There is always uncertainty about whether the sample used to provide the data is adequately representative of the population about which scientists want to draw conclusions. First, an available sample might be systematically unrepresentative or biased. For example, for certain variables, older voters might not be representative of the general voting population, laboratory rats might not be representative of humans, and adults might not be representative of children. Second, even if a sample is randomly drawn from the target population, a researcher might draw an unrepresentative sample merely by chance. As explained by Professor David Adelman in Chapter 9 of this book, scientists employ various tests of statistical significance in order to characterize and reduce the uncertainty created by random sampling. It is reasonable to rely on conclusions about populations only if both measurement uncertainty and sampling uncertainty are within acceptable bounds.

Whenever scientific research reaches conclusions based on measurements of samples, generalizations are at the heart of scientific reasoning. A "generalization" is an assertion that a proposition is true of only a portion of a group, but not the entire group. Examples are propositions about "most" people, "a few" people, "5 percent of" American males, and "14 percent of" the products tested. A generalization is also a probabilistic assertion – it asserts only that the proposition has some degree of plausibility or some specified likelihood of being true. For example, a generalization might assert that a proposition is "probably true," or is "unlikely to be true," or has "a 0.25 probability of being true." Scientists engage in default reasoning when they couch their conclusions or their supporting reasoning in generalizations.

Often, both the conclusion and the reasoning contain generalizations. For example, if a scientist concludes that eating hormone residues in meat products *probably* causes cancer *in a small percentage of* consumers who eat such products, then the evidence might include an epidemiological study that the scientist believes has acceptable measurement and sampling uncertainty. This latter belief may be supported by the generalizations that 99 percent of the laboratory measurements of hormone residues in the study are *probably* within 3 percent of the true values for the products tested (measurement validity), and that 95 percent of the samples drawn in the way they were drawn for this study *probably* have a mean residue concentration that is within 5 percentage points of the actual mean concentration for meat products generally (sample representativeness). In other words, when we analyze how scientists normally reason, we find layers upon layers of generalizations.

In addition, conclusions about causation add a kind of uncertainty beyond measurement and sampling, and international trade disputes are focused on the harms that imported products can cause. The central issue in *EC – Hormones*, for example, was whether eating meat products from farm animals that had been treated with certain hormones for growth-promotion purposes could cause cancer in humans. As evidence of causation, it is not enough merely to observe that some percentage of people who eat beef containing hormone residues develop cancer. There is a substantial background rate of cancer in people and there are many possible causal factors. Scientific evidence to answer whether eating hormone-treated beef *increases* that baseline risk of cancer requires that studies be designed so that appropriate analyses of the data can discover statistical evidence of causation. There can be good-faith scientific debates about which methods to use to analyze the sample data, about the likelihood of confounding causal factors for which there are no data, and about the relative plausibility of the causal interpretations that are consistent with the data. In reaching any conclusion about causation, a scientist will rely on those generalizations that she or he considers best supported by the data, by current theories, and by general experience.

Finally, when scientists use causal theories to predict or explain specific events or cases, they encounter an additional layer of uncertainty. Examples include predicting the results of retesting a particular meat product, estimating the risk for an individual who has eaten some amount of hormone-treated beef, and explaining the probable causes of a particular case of cancer. Some scientists do not regard such predictions and explanations as scientific, whereas other scientists believe that a major task of science is to make progress on predicting when the next earthquake will occur or what its effects will be, as well as the likelihood that a disease will spread from a particular cattle herd.

How well scientists understand a particular case depends on how completely they understand the mechanisms causing the type of harm, and how adequately the available causal models match that particular case. For most kinds of controversial risks, there is such high variability from individual to individual that we may have only weak generalizations about small percentages of cases. And even when there is adequate evidence of causation in a (small) percentage of cases, it may be impossible to identify which particular cases are likely to be affected. Any predictions or explanations necessarily rest on a large number of generalizations.

When scientific research about risk involves significant uncertainty, any findings usually rest on many generalizations about what is likely to be true in some but not all cases. Any scientific conclusions are tentative and defeasible, and they rest on judgments about the acceptability of the uncertainty in the measurements and data, in the samples employed, in the causal models developed, and in the predictions and explanations of particular events. Science makes progress by engaging in default reasoning based on generalizations. The reasoning given for one generalization often employs more generalizations. Scientific reasoning is often saturated with uncertainty, and scientists can never make all of the generalizations explicit. Practicing scientists take most of their generalizations for granted and do not even try to make them explicit.

Principles of transparency require honesty in accurately representing the limitations of scientific research, and sets the goal of making explicit as much of the scientific reasoning as possible. Honesty about uncertainty, however, means frustration about achieving complete transparency. This outcome is especially true for findings about the kinds of risk that parties to WTO disputes litigate. When litigated disputes involve uncertainty about what risks a product poses, any scientific reasoning will be based on numerous default generalizations, and uncovering all of the inherent assumptions may be impossible. As we will see, the pursuit of complete transparency in scientific reasoning must be combined with honest reporting about when complete transparency is not possible.

## Default Reasoning in WTO Fact Finding: The *Japan – Apples* Case

Legal systems also rely heavily on default reasoning in their fact-finding processes. Legal fact finding is by nature practical. In every type of legal setting – whether judicial, administrative, or legislative, and whether national or international – the legitimacy of particular governmental actions usually depends upon findings that particular propositions are (probably) true. Such fact-finding processes have the objective of producing accurate findings warranted by the available evidence, but they balance that objective against such goals as ensuring due process and achieving administrative efficiency.[15]

For example, in emergency situations posing immediate threats to health, safety, or the environment, the law might authorize precautionary measures after an abbreviated fact-finding process or despite considerable uncertainty about the danger. If, however, the risk is remote in time, or the potential harm is minor or reversible, then the law might require more deliberate procedures or more certainty before authorizing any action, especially if the economic disruption due to the governmental action is certain and substantial. Such a mix of epistemic and nonepistemic objectives is also present in the fact finding involved in WTO disputes.

In 2003, the WTO Appellate Body decided the appeal of the trade dispute entitled "Japan – Measures Affecting the Importation of Apples" (the "*Japan – Apples*" case).[16] The dispute involved a complaint by the United States about several measures that Japan had imposed on apples imported from the United States. Japan defended its measures as protecting Japan against the entry of fire blight – a disease in which the bacterium *Erwinia amylovora* (*E. amylovora*) infects apple trees, destroying the fruit and potentially killing the plants.

The fire blight bacterium apparently had originated in North America, but had spread in the twentieth century across much of Europe and through the Mediterranean. An example of Japan's protective measures was its prohibition on all imported apples from the United States except those from orchards designated to be fire blight–free, which at that time were only in

---

[15] Vern R. Walker, "Epistemic and Non-epistemic Aspects of the Factfinding Process in Law," *APA Newsletter* 3, no. 1 (2003): 132, reprinted in *The Journal of Philosophy, Science and Law* 5 (May 2005) (available at http://www.psljournal.com/archives/all/walkerpaper.cfm).

[16] WTO Panel Report, Japan – Measures Affecting the Importation of Apples, WT/DS245/R (July 15, 2003) (available at http://docsonline.wto.org/DDFDocuments/t/WT/DS/245R.doc) (hereinafter Apples Panel Report); WTO Appellate Body Report, Japan – Measures Affecting the Importation of Apples, WT/DS245/AB/R (Nov. 26, 2003) (available at http://docsonline.wto.org/DDFDocuments/t/WT/DS/245ABR.doc) (hereinafter Apples Appellate Body Report).

the states of Washington and Oregon. The United States argued that this and other protective measures were inconsistent with Japan's obligations under the SPS Agreement.

As discussed previously, the SPS Agreement provides that any phytosanitary measure against imports must be based on "sufficient scientific evidence."[17] Because the United States was the complaining party, it bore the initial burden of proving that Japan's measures did not have sufficient scientific evidence.[18] By the time of the *Japan – Apples* case, several decisions by the Appellate Body had elaborated additional legal rules for how a party could prove that the available evidence is "sufficient."[19] The available evidence must be "scientific" in nature and "relevant" to the issue at hand, and it must have some "rational or objective relationship" to the particular measure under consideration.

The logic diagram shown in Figure 8.1 is one way of depicting these substantive rules. The arrows in the diagram represent logical implications. When an arrow connects two propositions, this means that if the proposition at the blunt end of the arrow is true, then the proposition at the pointed end of the arrow is also true. Because legal reasoning begins by knowing which conclusions are at issue in the case, we can place the proposition to be proved at the top, with implication arrows running upward to that proposition. An implication whose lower-level propositions are connected to the upper-level proposition by an "AND" represents an inference in which *all* of the lower-level propositions must be true in order for the upper-level proposition to be true.

[17] The entire SPS Article 2.2 reads:

Members [of the WTO] shall ensure that any sanitary or phytosanitary measure is applied only to the extent necessary to protect human, animal or plant life or health, is based on scientific principles and is not maintained without sufficient scientific evidence, except as provided for in paragraph 7 of Article 5 [which provides for provisional measures when available scientific evidence is insufficient and the member seeks to obtain additional information]. Vern R. Walker, "Keeping the WTO from Becoming the 'World Trans-Science Organization': Scientific Uncertainty, Science Policy, and Factfinding in the Growth Hormones Dispute," *Cornell International Law Journal* 31, no.2 (1998): 251, 255–77.

[18] Apples Appellate Body Report, para. 153.
[19] The caselaw is summarized in WTO Appellate Body Report, Japan – Measures Affecting Agricultural Products, WT/DS76/AB/R, paras. 72–84 (Feb. 22, 1999) (available at http://docsonline.wto.org/DDFDocuments/t/WT/DS/76ABR.DOC).

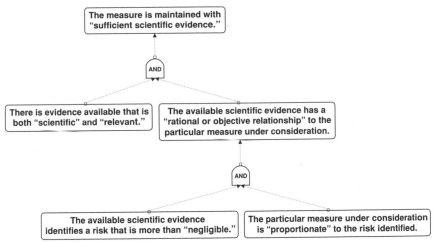

Figure 8.1. Implication Tree of the Legal Rules for "Sufficient Scientific Evidence"

Default-logic diagrams such as those in Figure 8.1 allow us to model the reasoning behind a finding, by tracing the reasoning through lower branches of the inverted implication tree. In each dispute decided by the WTO, new rules may be added to extend numerous branches. For example, with regard to proving whether any proffered evidence is "scientific," the *Japan – Apples* Panel adopted the rule that such evidence must be "gathered through scientific methods" or must be "scientifically produced," and it excluded from consideration what it called "insufficiently substantiated information" and any "non-demonstrated hypothesis."[20] Moreover, it added that evidence could be gathered using scientific methods, yet have various degrees of probative value in relation to possible findings. Although this line of new legal rules invites further development in later cases (which might adopt new rules for which methods are "scientific" or when a hypothesis is "sufficiently substantiated"), here we will follow the Panel's reasoning down the rightmost branch of reasoning in Figure 8.1.

With regard to proving whether there is a "rational or objective relationship" between the available scientific evidence and Japan's measures, the Panel found that from the standpoint of assessing risk, it is relevant to distinguish "mature, symptomless apples" from immature or

---

[20] Apples Panel Report, paras. 8.90–8.99.

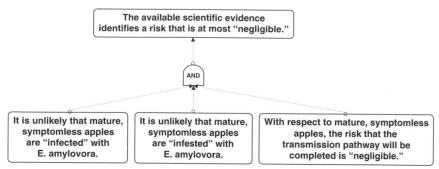

Figure 8.2. Logic Diagram of the Warrant for Finding a "Negligible" Risk from "Mature, Symptomless Apples"

identifiably infected apples.[21] As one branch of its inquiry, therefore, the Panel addressed whether mature, symptomless apples could cause the entry of fire blight into Japan. The Panel assessed the risk of this occurring, and "compared" that risk with Japan's measures. The Panel reasoned that in order to prove that there is a "rational or objective relationship" of the kind required by the SPS Agreement, one would have to prove two propositions: that the available scientific evidence identifies a risk that is more than "negligible," and that the measure must be "proportionate" to that risk. This reasoning is also represented in the diagram in Figure 8.1.

After reviewing the evidence and arguments in the *Japan – Apples* case, the Panel made a finding that there was *not* a "rational or objective relationship" between the available scientific evidence and Japan's measures, and gave two reasons for its conclusion. First, the Panel found that the risk of mature, symptomless apples introducing fire blight into Japan was in fact "negligible." Second, it found that Japan's measures were "clearly disproportionate" to the risk so identified.

Figure 8.2 diagrams the Panel's reasoning behind the first of these two findings – namely, its finding that the available scientific evidence identifies a risk that is at most "negligible."[22] First, the Panel found that mature applies are "unlikely" to be *infected* by fire blight if they do not show any

---

[21] The reasoning discussed in this paragraph and Figure 8.3 can be found in the Apples Appellate Body Report, paras. 159–60, 163–8, 243, and in the Apples Panel Report, paras. 8.89, 8.123–8.199, 8.224.

[22] The reasoning discussed in this paragraph and Figure 8.2 can be found in the Apples Panel Report, paras. 2.12–13, 8.123–39, 8.142, 8.147.

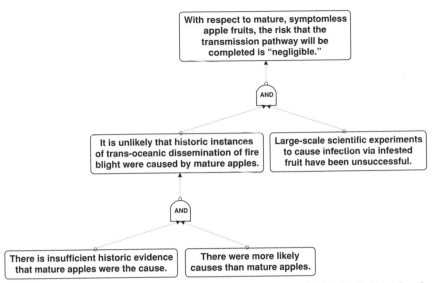

Figure 8.3. Logic Diagram of the Warrant for Finding a "Negligible" Risk of a Completed Transmission Pathway

symptoms. "Infection" is a pathogenic condition in the apple, as distinguished from "infestation," which is contamination that is not pathogenic. Second, with regard to possible *infestation*, the Panel found there was not "sufficient scientific evidence" that mature, symptomless apples either would contain populations of bacteria inside the fruit or are "likely" to carry on their outer surface populations of bacteria that are capable of transmitting *E. amylovora*. In concluding that bacteria populations on the surface of mature, symptomless apples are possible but "very rare," the Panel relied on the generalization that "the number of apples" contaminated with surface bacteria, even in severely blighted orchards, is "a very small percentage."

Third, because infestation on the surface of mature apples cannot be excluded as a possibility, the Panel assessed the evidence that the transmission pathway could be completed – namely, that such bacteria would survive through commercial handling, storage, and transportation, and that there would be a "vector" or means of contaminating a host plant in Japan.[23] Figure 8.3 models the Panel's reasoning in finding that the risk of a

---

[23] The reasoning discussed in this paragraph and Figure 8.3 can be found in the Apples Panel Report, paras. 4.63–81, 6.20–40, 6.50–71, 8.142–53.

completed pathway is "negligible." Even if past instances of trans-oceanic dissemination of fire blight could be documented, the Panel concluded that there is insufficient historic evidence that apple fruit was the cause, and it believed that alternative explanations are more probable. Moreover, large-scale scientific experiments to cause infection via surface and calyx-infested fruits had all been unsuccessful, and the Panel believed that, given the complexity of the transmission process feared by Japan, "it may be very difficult to experimentally replicate all possible pathways and combinations of circumstances and thus exclude categorically all possibilities of transmission." Therefore, the Panel found the risk of a completed transmission to be "negligible," agreeing with the opinions of those experts who considered any such risk to be "unlikely," "very remote," "insignificant," "extremely low," or "extremely unlikely." At bottom, therefore, the Panel's findings rested on generalizations about infection, infestation, and completed pathways, as well as generalizations about the uncertainties inherent in the evidence.

## The Role of Scientists in Creating New Legal Reasoning

This brief examination of one narrow chain of reasoning in the *Japan – Apples* case illustrates several important characteristics of legal fact finding. First, the default-logic model shows the continuity of reasoning from the authoritative, rule-based inferences in the upper levels of the implication tree to the case-specific, generalization-based inferences in the lower levels of the tree. The implications in the upper levels of the tree (which model the legal rules) are triggered directly by the implications in the lowest levels of the tree (which model the generalizations about the evidence). The ultimate conclusion at the top is warranted by a structured combination of legal rules and factual generalizations. The chain of reasoning as a whole constitutes default reasoning because it is practical, dynamic, defeasible, but presumptively valid.

Second, the default-logic model shows how the law evolves over time by extending the branches of the tree downward. While the SPS Agreement itself provides the rules represented in the very top levels, the subsequent caselaw of the fact-finding panels and the Appellate Body can add new legal rules that interpret and extend those upper levels. As the fact-finding panels explain their reasoning and their assessment of the evidence in particular cases, they elaborate new levels of reasoning. The documented reasoning of the panels can then generate new legal rules (which would be reviewed by the Appellate Body if challenged), as well as new patterns of reasoning for later panels to use in assessing the probative value of evidence. A default-logic model capturing the changes in reasoning from case to case would show a single implication tree that is expanding downward and branching outward.

The capacity for extending the tree is provided in part by the uncertainties inherent in scientific reasoning about risk. As discussed previously, the default reasoning in the face of these uncertainties will be based on numerous generalizations. The reasoning about which generalizations to apply and about how to apply them will lead in turn to more generalizations. The reasoning in support of any finding is therefore complex, and often unstated. As principles of transparency operate to make explicit more of the implicit reasoning, and as fact-finding panels articulate additional layers of their reasoning, the implication tree expands downward.

Third, the model for the *Japan – Apples* reasoning suggests one mechanism by which new legal rules evolve. After the Appellate Body adds a new legal rule, fact-finding panels try to apply that new rule transparently to the evidence in new cases. When a panel articulates its reasoning under the new rule and the Appellate Body upholds that reasoning, this creates new lines of reasoning that panels are likely to follow in subsequent cases. Even if a panel does not declare a new rule of law as such, the panel's reasoning becomes a new "soft rule" because subsequent panels will think it unlikely that the Appellate Body will reverse a finding based on such reasoning. In some future case, the Appellate Body might even adopt such a pattern of reasoning itself, turning it into a new legal rule to be applied in all cases. Declaring a new legal rule is obviously not essential, however, if a reasoning pattern is de facto recognized as acceptable.

Through this dynamic process, for example, new legal rules (whether "hard" or "soft") may evolve in the future for proving that evidence is truly "scientific" or that an identified risk is merely "negligible." As mentioned earlier, the caselaw already requires finding that a risk is more than a "theoretical uncertainty."[24] The *Japan – Apples* Panel recited a variety of possible interpretations that some future panel might adopt in deciding

---

[24]  Apples Panel Report, para. 8.144; Salmon Appellate Body Report, para. 125.

what constitutes a "negligible" risk – including the quantitative criterion of "a likelihood of between zero and one in one million."[25] When fact-finding panels adopt the reasoning of testifying experts whom they consider credible, the panels transform the generalizations of those experts into "soft" legal rules of reasoning, and perhaps eventually into "hard" rules of law. In effect, the scientists testifying before the panels are in a privileged position of influence, because their personal reasoning may gradually evolve into new legal rules under the SPS Agreement.

## Transforming Science into Law

Within the expanding branches of the tree, there is a dynamic between rule-based reasoning and generalization-based reasoning that can have a politicizing effect on science. As we follow the reasoning down any particular branch of the tree, we reach some propositional node where rule-based reasoning ends and generalization-based reasoning begins. To state this point differently, and at some risk of oversimplification, there is a place in every branch of reasoning where authoritative law ends and scientific proof begins. One thesis of this chapter is that the pursuit of transparency and the rule of law creates a steady downward "pressure" at this interface between law and science – a steady pressure to convert more of the scientific, generalization-based reasoning into legal, rule-based reasoning. Moreover, when scientists become involved in legal fact finding, they have an incentive to transform the role of science into a more regulatory function. Scientists who wish to influence the fact finding may convert mere generalizations about uncertainty into authoritative rules about "correct" scientific method. When that fact finding happens to be about risk, a rule-oriented scientific "establishment" may overlook dangers to society that are very real, but unknown or poorly understood. In addition, the economic and political importance of what is at stake in international trade disputes ensures that scientific uncertainties will provide contentious political battlegrounds. This section of the chapter discusses the logic underlying these various developments.

[25] Apples Panel Report, paras. 8.144, 8.149.

## Transforming Scientific Generalizations into Legal Rules

From the perspective of transparency and the rule of law, rule-based reasoning has several desirable characteristics that generalization-based reasoning lacks, and these differences create a legal preference for rules over generalizations. First, rule-based inferences are more transparent than generalization-based inferences because rules apply universally. A rule applies in every situation where the triggering conditions are true. Rule-based reasoning is transparent because any refusal to follow the rule once it is triggered should be warranted by another rule that recognizes an explicit exception. The rule identifying the exception is also transparent, applying universally in all situations that satisfy its exceptional conditions. The warrant provided by universal rules is still defeasible, but the conditions of defeat are transparent and explicit. Rule-based reasoning is therefore "objective" in the sense that the criteria driving the fact finding are available for scrutiny by all interested parties. Figure 8.1 diagrams several rules that are transparent and universally applicable in SPS Agreement cases.

In contrast to rules, generalizations accurately describe less than all the cases to which they refer. For example, in Figures 8.2 and 8.3, the generalizations about what is "unlikely" do not claim to describe accurately every situation. It may be true that mature, symptomless apples are unlikely to be infested with E. amylovora, but this proposition is consistent with the proposition that a particular apple or shipment is infested with the bacteria. While a generalization claims that it will be accurate in some portion of the reference cases, it also implies that there may be cases where it is *not* accurate. The *Japan – Apples* Panel recognized that mature, symptomless apples have in fact been infested with E. amylovora from time to time.

Moreover, a generalization itself does not usually provide the criteria for deciding precisely *when* it is accurate, nor does it explain *why* it is accurate in some cases but not others. Variability among cases usually implies that there are explanatory factors that are unknown or unstated, but which would provide more accurate or complete explanations if they were taken into account. The generalization that most mature, symptomless apples are probably not infested does not itself disclose when or why the occasional infestation occurs, or how it can be detected. Reasoning that rests on mere generalizations acknowledges that the scientific evidence relevant to the finding is not completely transparent.

Second, rule-based inferences generate more consistency in application than generalization-based inferences do. When universal rules of inference warrant the conclusions, then fact finders will reach the same conclusions in all cases with similar evidence. The rule structure increases the likelihood that fact finders will analyze similar evidence similarly. Generalization-based inferences, however, invite subjective judgment, and increase the likelihood that different fact finders will reach different conclusions on very similar evidence. When a particular fact finder decides to rest the ultimate finding on a generalization that "probably, most mature, symptomless apples are not infested," that fact finder is making a judgment that he or she finds the inherent uncertainties acceptable. Another fact finder might insist on more quantitative evidence to explain the word "most," or more convincing evidence than the word "probably" implies. Generalization-based reasoning therefore makes subjective judgments seem inevitable and reasonable, to an extent that legal rules do not. Generalizations suggest that transparent reasoning must end somewhere, and that subjective judgment must take over.

Third, rule-based reasoning is more efficient than generalization-based reasoning. Authoritative rules of law determine which evidence is relevant and irrelevant to the fact-finding process. Fact finders are obligated to ignore any irrelevant considerations, which not only slow down the fact-finding process, but can contaminate it by masking subjective bias or a hidden agenda. The confined process of inquiry produced by legal rules is far more efficient than the open-ended exploration in which scientists normally engage. Working scientists form hypotheses in order to design their studies, but basically conduct their research by following the evidence wherever it leads. For scientists, it might be the anomaly or the small percentage of cases *not* covered by a generalization that points the way to the next scientific discovery. Or it might be a rethinking of old evidence that allows a new theory to emerge. By contrast, the closed-ended efficiency of legal reasoning tends to assume that we can know at the outset which evidence is relevant and which concepts to use in our reasoning.

In a legal context, therefore, the values of transparency, consistency, and efficiency point in the same direction: toward an increase in rule-based reasoning and a decrease in generalization-based reasoning. For reasons of principle (transparency and consistency) as well as practicality (efficient fact finding), legal practitioners prefer rule-based reasoning over generalization-based reasoning, to the extent that rule-based reasoning is achievable. The less transparent, more subjective, and less efficient reasoning based on mere generalizations is tolerated, to the extent necessary, but it is not the legal ideal. The legal mind prefers universal rules when it can get them.

This preference for rule-based reasoning over generalization-based reasoning creates a tendency for the legal fact-finding process to transform generalizations into rules. This natural tendency can easily operate through the mechanism previously discussed: Individual scientists testify before fact-finding panels about their scientific reasoning, fact-finding panels adopt some of that reasoning as their own, some of that reasoning becomes "soft rules" as the Appellate Body defers to it and later panels follow it, and some generalizations are explicitly converted into default rules of law. Perhaps the WTO has little need for an explicit rule of law about "mature, symptomless apples," but the reasoning patterns diagrammed in Figures 3 and 4 might make very useful rules if they are reformulated as rules about "apparently unaffected products." Once we focus on similarities and use them to classify cases together, we tend to produce legal rules for deciding these cases transparently and consistently.

## Transforming Scientists into Regulators

This tendency to transform generalizations into rules also transforms the role that scientists play within a legal context. The area of risk regulation in international trade illustrates this transformation in role. Oddly enough, this change in role for scientists is mediated by an insistence on all sides that there should be a clear separation between legal, policy-driven reasoning and scientific, evidence-driven reasoning. To understand this change in role, therefore, it is first necessary to understand this insistence on a distinction between law and science.

Despite the tendency to create more legal rules, there is also a strong incentive for the political decision makers who create the initial legal rules (for example, those who negotiated the high-level rules in the SPS Agreement), as well as for the legal decision makers who elaborate the midlevel rules (such as the members the fact-finding panels and of the Appellate

Body), to insist that there is a "bright-line," fixed boundary between rule-based reasoning and generalization-based reasoning, between policy-driven laws and evidence-driven science. It is to their advantage to assert that scientists must independently determine "the facts" at the bottom of the chain of reasoning before legal decision makers can decide what management actions to take in response to those facts. We can appreciate this incentive by imagining a hypothetical scenario stemming from the *Japan – Apples* decision. If, as a result of the decision, Japan removes its protective measures on imported apples and then fire blight enters Japan by means of contaminated apples, the WTO would prefer to lay responsibility for this adverse outcome on scientists, who perhaps underestimated the likelihood of latent infestation in mature fruit or overlooked a pathway of transmission. To anyone who assumes that there is a clear, fixed boundary between political decision making and scientific fact-finding, such an explanation might even appear to be the only reasonable one. Thus, political risk managers can appear reasonable while blaming the scientific risk assessors for undesirable outcomes.

On the other hand, many scientists also insist that there is a bright, fixed line between legal policy and science. They do so in the hope of keeping politics out of science. Scientific reasoning about uncertain risks makes an inviting target for political manipulation. To the extent that there is uncertainty about how to conceptualize a problem, or about the validity of measurements, or about sample representativeness, or about how to model causal relationships, then good science keeps an open mind. It may be necessary to engage in default reasoning in order to extend scientific knowledge, but careful scientists are very candid about the inherent uncertainties. Indeed, the generalization-based reasoning of science is less transparent, more subjective, and less efficient than rule-based legal reasoning precisely because scientists refuse to oversimplify the phenomenon being studied, or to overstate their knowledge about that phenomenon. But the recognized need for professional judgments by individual scientists also makes those judgments and scientists inviting targets for those who want to exert political influence.

If there is a domain of science that is separate and distinct from that of law and politics, however, then perhaps science can better resist political pressure and keep legal decision makers from influencing the scientific portion of fact finding. The European Union has gone so far, in the area of food safety, as to establish the European Food Safety Authority (EFSA) as a separate governmental agency to conduct scientific risk assessment. EFSA is expected to perform risk assessments independently, and the European Commission would then base its management decisions on the findings of those risk assessments.[26] Part of the motivation behind the establishment of EFSA was the public desire for sound, independent science – a desire heightened by the scares involving Bovine Spongiform Encephalopathy (BSE) in 1996 and dioxin-contaminated animal feed in 1999.[27]

Politicians, other legal decision makers, and many scientists, therefore, have a common goal of distinguishing legal reasoning from scientific reasoning. In terms of the default-logic model of fact finding, the upper levels of an implication tree, representing legal rules, are distinguishable from the lower levels, consisting of generalizations. As long as scientists can make their reasoning transparent and as rule-governed as possible, then such reasoning should satisfy legal ideals without the encroachment of the legal or political establishment. The regulatory approach of the United States Environmental Protection Agency (EPA) provides an example of a sustained effort to transform scientific reasoning into legal rules, explicitly and transparently.

EPA recognizes that within a scientific risk assessment, there are numerous places where reasoning must rest upon inadequate scientific evidence. For example, it may be uncertain whether a particular animal species is a good predictive model for humans, whether a dose-response curve extrapolated below the range of the observational data is accurate, or whether a particular margin of safety is likely to protect sensitive subpopulations (such as children or the elderly). In the absence of complete scientific evidence, decisions are necessary about how to assess the risks despite gaps

[26] European Parliament and Council Regulation 178/2002/EC, preamble paras. 33–66, arts. 22–3, 2002 OJ L31/1 (laying down the general principles and requirements of food law, establishing the European Food Safety Authority, and laying down procedures in matters of food safety); Health and Consumer Protection Directorate-General, "European Food Safety Authority (EFSA) – Introduction, European Food Safety Authority" (available at http://europa.eu.int/comm/food/efsa_en.htm); European Food Safety Authority, "EFSA Science, European Food Safety Authority" (available at http://www.efsa.eu.int/science/catindex_en.html).

[27] Raymond O'Rourke, *European Food Law* (Bembridge, UK: Palladian Law, 2nd ed., 2001), 7–8, 167–8, 216–28.

in scientific knowledge. For guidance in conducting risk assessments, EPA therefore adopts what it calls "science policies" or "default options," also sometimes called "inference guidelines."[28] Science policies establish the rules of default reasoning that risk assessment scientists are supposed to use. Such science policies create presumptions for fact finding, which are subject to defeat if there is sufficient evidence to overcome the presumption. By establishing authoritative default rules, science policies produce risk assessments that are more transparent, more consistent, and more predictable than would be the case if such decisions were left to individual scientists to decide on a case-by-case basis.

On the other hand, EPA recognizes that evaluating the "weight of the evidence" requires scientific judgment.[29] Integrating a multitude of evidence into a single judgment involves reasoning that is difficult to explain and not fully transparent.[30] The open-ended and not-completely-transparent nature of generalization-based reasoning is in conflict with the ideals of transparency and the rule of law.

Interestingly, emphasizing the nonrule nature of scientific reasoning can also be useful in shielding the agency's fact finding from attack, especially upon judicial review.[31] EPA can insist on deference to its expert judgment about when uncertainties are within acceptable bounds. So while the agency tries to satisfy the legal principles of transparency and the rule

---

[28] U.S. Environmental Protection Agency, "Guidelines for Carcinogen Risk Assessment," (2005): appendix A (available at http://www.epa.gov/iris/cancer032505.pdf); U.S. Environmental Protection Agency, Science Policy Council, "Guidance for Risk Characterization," (1995) (available at http://www.epa.gov/osa/spc/htm/rcguide.htm); National Research Council, *Risk Assessment in the Federal Government: Managing the Process* (Washington, DC: National Academy Press, 1983) 51–85; National Research Council, *Science and Judgment in Risk Assessment* (Washington, DC: National Academy Press, 1994), 85–105; Walker, "Keeping the WTO from Becoming the 'World Trans-Science Organization'," 256–72.

[29] National Research Council, *Science and Judgment*, 126–31; U.S. Environmental Protection Agency, "Guidelines for Carcinogen Risk Assessment," 1–11 to 1–12, 2–49 to 2–58.

[30] National Research Council, *Understanding Risk: Informing Decisions in a Democratic Society* (Washington, DC: National Academy Press, 1996), 37–72; Vern R. Walker, "The Myth of Science as a 'Neutral Arbiter' for Triggering Precautions," *Boston College International and Comparative Law Review* 26, no. 2 (2003): 197; David Winickoff et al., "Adjudicating the GM Food Wars: Science, Risk, and Democracy in World Trade Law," *Yale Journal of International Law* 30, no. 1 (2005): 81, 93–9.

[31] *Environmental Defense v. U.S. Environmental Protection Agency*, 369 F.3d 193 (2d Cir. 2004); *International Fabricare Institute v. U.S. Environmental Protection Agency*, 972 F.2d 384 (D.C. Cir. 1992).

of law, it also tries to shield its reasoning from external attack by its critics. As a result, the implication trees under the different statutes that EPA
administers exhibit different degrees of elaboration, as the agency mixes
administrative rule making and science-policy development (on the one
hand) with case-by-case fact finding (on the other hand).

The agency's attempt to manage the interface between rule-based reasoning and generalization-based reasoning leads to a hybrid role for science
within regulation – a role that many call "regulatory science."[32] The
agency's regulatory programs also illustrate the inherent tension between
rules and generalizations, the legal tendency to turn generalizations into
rules, and the resulting tendency to turn scientists into regulators.

## Transforming Science into Politics

The WTO fact-finding panels and the Appellate Body, however, do not
have an institution like EPA to manage the interface between rules and
generalizations. EPA has the statutory authority, resources, and expertise to
conduct both risk assessment and risk management in well-defined areas,
such as hazardous substances or pesticide products. The WTO disputes
involve disparate products and risks, and panels are appointed to conduct
the fact finding case by case. This institutional design might increase the
probability that science will be politicized.

Scientists who influence fact finding using generalization-based reasoning wield significant power, whether in adopting generalizations as default
rules or in subjectively applying generalizations to evidence in particular cases. Because scientific reasoning plays such an important role in
WTO fact finding, and as political decision makers and scientists alike
insist on a boundary between science (risk assessment) and political decision making (risk management), it becomes increasingly important to
those interested in the outcomes to have the "right scientists" conducting the scientific reasoning. It is important to appoint scientists with the
"right instincts" to sit on governmental advisory panels, to conduct the risk

---

[32] Wendy Wagner and David Michaels, "Equal Treatment for Regulatory Science: Extending the
Controls Governing the Quality of Public Research to Private Research," *American Journal of
Law and Medicine* 30, nos. 2–3 (2004): 11

assessments within administrative agencies, and to establish the default rules for such risk assessments. The uncertainties inherent in default reasoning make it rational to fight for the power to make the appointment decisions. Even if the scientific reasoning occurs in an institutional setting that is separate and independent from management decision making, this does not save it from the logic behind the politics of appointment. It becomes reasonable to reach even into those institutions of science that appear to be the most independent of politics – institutions such as university research centers, scientific journals, and prestigious scientific committees that can articulate and influence the very canons of sound scientific reasoning.

It is the logic of generalization-based reasoning itself that creates the opportunity and incentive for political influence. The analysis based on default logic shows that the problem lies not merely with individual scientists, but rather with scientific reasoning itself, and therefore with science itself. And that logic virtually ensures politicization.

The strategy of choice for those who happen not to possess the power of appointment at a particular time is usually to insist upon more transparency and more adherence to the rule of law. Parties adversely affected by the outcome of legal fact finding tend to attack the reasoning leading to that outcome. Opposing parties produce conflicting evidence and additional theories, fact finders provide more reasons for their findings, and appellate bodies convert more of those reasons into "soft" or even "hard" legal rules. This is the very dynamic, however, that pushes rule-based reasoning deeper into scientific reasoning, which turns scientists into regulators, and which in turn leads to more political influence over scientific institutions.

The advent of WTO fact finding in the last decade promises to globalize that chain of transformations. Even the short series of dispute settlement decisions under the SPS Agreement, culminating in the *Japan – Apples* case, shows the tendency to transform open-ended, scientific generalizations about risk into rules for identifying "non-theoretical" risks on the basis of evidence that is methodologically "scientific." When the causal situation is not well understood, however, as with genetically modified organisms (GMOs) or BSE, do scientists really understand the risks and uncertainties well enough to make findings that are transparently warranted? Even for the relatively well-understood risks of fire blight in apples, the Panel's reasoning in finding that the risk is "negligible" that apple fruit will serve as a pathway for the entry of fire blight into Japan may appear to be too political to be reassuring, at least to the Japanese. If the ideal is to make the scientific reasoning completely transparent, then the price of doing so may be to make that reasoning more rule-based, to transform the role of scientists from advisors about uncertainty to regulators of default reasoning, and to politicize scientific reasoning.

## Conclusion

This chapter argues that default reasoning combines law and science in legal fact finding, but that the ideals of transparency and the rule of law tend to transform scientific reasoning into legal reasoning. Scientists involved in legal fact finding have an incentive to turn the open-ended, generalization-based reasoning of science into the closed-ended, rule-based reasoning of law. Moreover, the fact-finding process itself provides a structure that can transform generalizations into rules, scientific reasoning into legal reasoning, research scientists into regulatory scientists, and scientific institutions into political institutions. If it is the logical nature of default reasoning that makes these transformations possible, does it also make them inevitable? Merely insisting on a bright, fixed boundary between those who make legal decisions and those who conduct scientific reasoning seems unlikely to solve the problem, because it is the logical nature of fact finding itself that underlies these transformations.

The place to begin the rescue of science is with the transparency principles that are part of the framework for this book. As applied to governmental fact finding, they require the fact finder to make clear to all interested parties the evidence relevant to a finding of fact, the fact finder's evaluation of that evidence, and the reasoning connecting the evidence to the finding. But the transparency principles also emphasize the need for honesty in representing that reasoning accurately, and in reporting the limitations of the evidence. The principles balance the ideal of complete transparency against the ideal of honest reporting. Legal rules may be more transparent than generalizations, but generalizations are often more faithful to the underlying uncertainties. Regulators should report all of the default patterns of reasoning upon which they rely, to the extent that they can do so. But they should also resist turning generalizations into rules if this means misrepresenting the underlying uncertainties. In the bottom levels of the implication tree, generalizations honestly reflect the default reasoning about uncertainty.

Protecting the integrity of science means openly preserving its anti-authoritarian dimension – that is, openly reporting the methods, reasoning, and logic, so that all interested parties can judge for themselves the reasonableness of the conclusions. Although uncertainty creates a target of opportunity for those who wish to politicize regulatory science, adherence to the transparency principles and honest reporting of reasoning provide the best protections against distortion and manipulation. And when governmental fact finding is about the risk of harm, such as in international trade disputes, it is particularly important to rescue science from politics, and to do so in ways that respect not only the laws of nations, but also the laws of logic.

# 9

# Two Models for Scientific Transparency in Environmental Law

David E. Adelman, Ph.D., J.D.

## Transparency in Science and in Law

Maximizing the transparency of scientific determinations is critically important to the disciplines that inform environmental policy. Environmental issues are riven by disputes over the use of quantitative methods and by uncertainty about risk. Despite the obvious limits of science, or perhaps because of them, agency officials and political actors who use science often fail to represent scientific uncertainty accurately, and instead overstate the role that science played in supporting particular findings to elevate the outcomes to which they are predisposed. As a result, science without transparency risks devolving into consequentialist science.

Chemical risk assessment provided the impetus for much of the debate over how science is used in a regulatory context. Objections to chemical risk assessment methods stem from the high uncertainties in risk estimates that exist at the low exposure levels relevant to regulatory standards. The controversy is also driven by the potential consequences of inaction – failures to protect workers against asbestos exposures, for example, may result in 250,000 additional cancers in the United States.[1] These uncertainties require scientists to make difficult judgments, including critically important decisions to rely on highly simplified models to obtain the quantitative results needed to derive regulatory standards.

The vulnerability of scientific judgment to political pressure is evident in the high-profile controversies surrounding the Bush Administration's stacking of scientific advisory committees in agencies throughout

---

[1] Julian Peto, "Cancer Epidemiology in the Last Century and the Next Decade," *Nature* 411, no. 6835 (2002): 393.

the federal government.[2] It is also illustrated by the Klamath Basin water conflict that Professor Holly Doremus discusses in Chapter 7 of this book. In that example, the limited data available to regulators failed to provide "substantial scientific support" for any position, whether in favor of protecting the fisheries or supporting the agricultural interests. As Professor Doremus notes, the data could be interpreted in a variety of ways because the basic ecology of the system was poorly understood and the existing data were subject to a number of confounding factors that could not be eliminated. When empirical support is inconclusive in this manner, political or ideological commitments far too often fill the void and distort the limited good science that exists. Adding irony to bias, scientific "truth" is frequently called forth to justify such blatantly political decisions, reinforcing further the capture of science by politics.

The susceptibility of science to political influence has deep theoretical roots. No real-world scientific theory – particularly where knowledge is limited – ever lacks contrary or equivocal data. Scientific support is therefore a matter of degree. Moreover, developing a coherent interpretation of necessarily inconclusive data is further complicated by the fact that competing theories often will be consistent with different types of data (for example, in vitro experiments, animal testing, epidemiological studies). In such cases, both the incommensurability and limited amount of empirical support preclude a purely objective approach, and force scientists to make judgments based on broad scientific principles that are almost always debatable. It is these fundamental limits that make transparency essential to ensuring that policy makers use science wisely.

Transparency itself has multiple meanings and attributes. Defined simply, transparency requires disclosure of a decision maker's reasoning and the empirical bases for it. Ensuring transparency in a legal context typically involves requiring decision makers to adhere to certain procedural requirements, such as those found in the Administrative Procedure Act. Among other requirements, agencies must create a publicly accessible administrative record that contains all of the evidence on which an agency relies to support a regulatory decision. Under judicial review, transparency is closely linked to standards that gauge whether the justifications for a regulatory decision are reasonable, the most common being the "rational

[2] Donald Kennedy, "An Epidemic of Politics," *Science* 299, no. 5607 (2003): 625.

basis" standard. Importantly, legal procedures designed to maintain transparency do not prescribe how the analysis should be conducted; instead, they emphasize direct, unmediated access to information and opportunity for public comment.

Scientific transparency both resembles and deviates from its legal counterpart. In the scientific context, transparency has two primary elements: open access to experimental data and accurate representation of and inference from experimental findings. The principle of open access to underlying data clearly parallels the basic principle of public access and openness in law. The second principle is qualitatively different because it implicates the manner in which a scientific analysis is undertaken. In other words, unlike law, scientific method and transparency are inextricably linked together.

Statistical methods are the touchstone of this second element of scientific transparency. They provide the analytical framework for accurately representing experimental findings and for formal scientific inference. Although it is rarely recognized, two radically different models of statistical analysis exist: frequentist hypothesis testing and Bayesian probability estimates. A principal difference between the two approaches is the contrasting ways in which they structure scientific inference and judgment. The procedurally oriented frequentist approach uses objective testing methods that separate judgments from standardized methods for rigorously testing hypotheses.[3] Bayesians reject an objectivist approach. Bayesian methods integrate scientific judgments, which must be quantified, directly into its probability estimates pursuant to several basic logical principles.[4]

The close ties between statistics, whether frequentist or Bayesian, and scientific transparency expose an essential difference between science and law. While transparency in law has practical limitations, such as time and resources, full disclosure is achievable in theory if not in practice. The constraints on scientific transparency, however, are often rooted in the underlying science and statistical methods. These technical obstacles cannot necessarily be circumvented and thus place absolute limits on scientific transparency. Further, the interplay between statistical methods and substantive science – statistical methods will not be equally effective in all

[3] Deborah G. Mayo, *Error and the Growth of Experimental Knowledge* (Chicago: University of Chicago Press, 1996), 10.
[4] Ian Hacking, *An Introduction to Probability and Inductive Logic* (Cambridge, UK: Cambridge University Press, 2001), 172.

areas of science – is incompatible with a uniform set of rules for ensuring scientific transparency.

This story does have a silver lining. Standard statistical methods impose a consistent order on scientific analyses. I will argue that statistical frameworks should be exploited in a regulatory context by directing legal procedures for enhancing transparency at the key decision points of frequentist and Bayesian analyses. The virtue of this strategy is that it reduces reliance on scientists and judges to separate policy from science and to distinguish the important decisions from the tangential.

This chapter begins with an explanation of frequentist and Bayesian methodologies and the critical role they play in promoting scientific transparency, accuracy, and good judgment. The chapter then turns to a discussion of the practical limitations of both theories, including the interpretive challenges that impede transparency and the tensions that exist between our principles of transparency and the methodological constraints present in the environmental sciences. The chapter concludes by considering how legal procedures and statistical methods can be effectively integrated to enhance transparency in regulatory decision making, paying particular attention to the relative merits of frequentist and Bayesian methods in data-poor environments common to most environmental policy making.

## Bayesian and Frequentist Methods of Scientific Inference

Frequentist methods have traditionally dominated scientific testing because of their long-accepted objectivity and relative simplicity. Bayesian methods, however, are gaining acceptance because they are easier to interpret and potentially more flexible. Prominent environmental scientists, for example, have urged the adoption of Bayesian methods because they believe that the quantitative estimates they generate are easier for policy makers to understand.[5] Bayesian methods are nevertheless the subject of heated debate within the scientific community. Most prominently, critics worry that Bayesian estimates will obscure the solid science that does exist, as they combine objective data and often contentious subjective judgments into a single quantitative estimate. The discussion that follows is intended

---

[5]  Stephen H. Schneider, "What Is 'Dangerous' Climate Change?" *Nature* 411, no. 6833 (2001): 18.

to enable the reader to understand the basic elements of Bayesian and frequentist statistics necessary to appreciate the significance of this debate.

Bayesian and frequentist methods are best understood through an example. The likelihood that global warming of 5 degrees Celsius will occur in the next decade is a fitting example. Beginning with the Bayesians, they would input quantitative information – both data and expert judgments – into the theorem first derived by Reverend Thomas Bayes, "Bayes' theorem," to derive inductively the probability that a 5-degree increase in global temperature will occur during this time period (that is, it is 60 percent likely). A frequentist, by contrast, would start with a "null hypothesis" that global warming will not occur and would then conduct experiments to test whether this null hypothesis is consistent with the collected data. If the experimental data are inconsistent with this null hypothesis, the result is characterized as "statistically significant."

Unlike Bayesian estimates, frequentist methods do not quantify directly the likelihood of global warming; rather, they provide a means for stringently testing (that is, falsifying) hypotheses about it. For frequentists, scientific judgments are based on whether a hypothesis withstands rigorous statistical testing. The more rigorous and extensive the testing, the greater a scientist's confidence in her hypothesis.

This example exposes two critical differences between Bayesian and frequentist methods. Bayesian methods require experts to make initial probability estimates for each hypothesis being tested. This collection of probability estimates is referred to as a "prior distribution," and it is input directly into Bayes' theorem at the beginning of the analysis.[6] In the process, Bayesian methods seamlessly mix judgment and data together. Frequentist methods, by contrast, separate scientific judgment and fact to maintain their objectivity. This objectivity has a significant cost – frequentist methods do not generate direct probability estimates for test hypotheses. Once a frequentist analysis is completed, scientists must still weigh the available quantitative and qualitative evidence to judge the ultimate validity of their test

---

[6] The simplest prior distributions have two competing hypotheses (for example, a chemical is or is not toxic). A prior distribution for such a case would consist of two probability estimates, one for each hypothesis. A scientist with, for example, reliable anecdotal information about a chemical's toxicity might start a Bayesian analysis with the following prior distribution: a probability of 0.6 for the hypothesis that the chemical is toxic, and a probability of 0.3 for the hypothesis that the chemical is not toxic. Much more complex prior distributions are, of course, also common.

hypotheses. In other words, where Bayesians sacrifice objectivity for simple probability estimates, frequentists sacrifice interpretive ease to preserve the objectivity of their methods.

Frequentist and Bayesian methods also ascribe different meanings to probability. Frequentists define probability *objectively* as the "long-run frequencies" in a system. The frequency, for example, that samples from a river exceed a regulatory limit is representative of this interpretation. The great innovation of frequentist significance testing is that it maintains this objectivity by assessing the likelihood that a test hypothesis predicts the collected data, not the probability that a test hypothesis is true given the existing data. This strategy avoids the problem of having to rule out other competing hypotheses, which is no small matter in environmental science, where information is often limited.

Bayesians define probability as the level of confidence an individual has about an event or thing based on their *subjective* judgment (that is, based on extensive, or even minimal, experience or experimental work) and the available data. Bayesian methods, for instance, may be used to combine expert judgment and observational data to determine the "conditional probability" that air emissions from a power plant are harmful to human health.[7] Because of this subjectivity, Bayesian probabilities may differ from person to person – even if they utilize the same data. Scientists using identical monitoring data, for example, could derive very different Bayesian estimates for the probability that air-pollution levels in a city will exceed a regulatory standard.

The preceding discussion has described the general characteristics of Bayesian and frequentist methods. The two sections that follow discuss the details of how they are used for scientific inference.

## Frequentist Significance Testing

The frequentist definition of probability is central to understanding traditional statistical significance testing. Frequentists define probability as the "long-run frequency" or propensity of a population, system, or thing. The

---

[7] "Conditional probability" signifies that the probability estimate is conditioned on (that is, based on or relative to) an initial judgment about the system being studied and the available data. In essence, Bayesians begin with a quantitative estimate of the probabilities of the competing hypothesis, the prior distribution, and use experimental data to refine the starting predictions.

long-run frequency of a fair coin turning up heads, for example, converges to one-half as the number of coin flips increases. Scientists thus conduct repeated measurements to obtain an accurate measure of such long-run frequencies. Statistical significance testing assesses the correspondence of statistical samples (that is, experimental data) with a hypothesis about the true long-run frequency being measured.

Testing a pesticide's toxicity provides a relatively straightforward example of significance testing. Frequentists utilize the following conventions for hypothesis testing: (1) a "null" hypothesis, which assumes the pesticide is harmless (no effect exists); (2) a "conjecture," which assumes the pesticide has a discernable toxic effect (a nonzero effect exists). In this scheme, the null hypothesis incorporates the standard "bell-shaped curve" for random variation as a model of the population (that is, a human population insensitive to pesticide exposure) that the experiment is sampling. The experimental data are then compared against this population model to determine whether the null-hypothesis model should be rejected.

Significance testing leads to a counterintuitive result: The probability calculated is *not* the probability that the pesticide is harmful, but rather the probability of obtaining the experimental data assuming the null hypothesis is true. Under a standard analysis, the incidents of harm observed experimentally are counted. The null-hypothesis model is then used to estimate the probability that harm would occur at the experimentally observed frequency, presuming that the pesticide has no effect. If the null-hypothesis model predicts that the experimentally observed frequency is very unlikely, the result is deemed "statistically significant," and it is reasonable for a scientist to reject the null hypothesis. As discussed previously, frequentist statistical testing does not directly estimate the probability that the pesticide is harmful; it instead uses two measures of the null-hypothesis model's error rates: significance and, to a much lesser extent, power.

The principle that underlies this approach is simple: "[T]here should be very little chance of mistakenly rejecting a true hypothesis . . . [and] a good chance of rejecting false hypotheses."[8] By convention, the significance of a test is defined as the probability of rejecting the null hypothesis when it is true, and the power of a test is defined as the probability of rejecting the null

---

[8]   Ian Hacking, *The Logic of Statistical Inference* (Cambridge, UK: Cambridge University Press, 1965), 92.

hypothesis when it is false. Following the preceding principle, experiments should have low significance (a low chance of rejecting the null hypothesis when it is true) and high power (a high probability of rejecting the null hypothesis when it is false). Unfortunately, the simple elegance of this principle is marred by reality. Two critical obstacles get in the way: First, it is often difficult to formulate an appropriate measure for power.[9] Second, a trade-off exists between minimizing significance and maximizing power – for a given study size, it is mathematically impossible to minimize them simultaneously.

Statisticians have responded to these constraints by focusing on statistical significance – hence the term "significance testing" – and only secondarily on statistical power. Stated simply, a "significance test determines whether an observed result is so unlikely to have occurred by chance alone that it is reasonable to attribute the result to something else."[10] In the pesticide example, a finding of statistical significance enables one to infer that the pesticide has nonzero toxicity. Importantly, significance tests do *not* give an estimate of the magnitude of an effect (that is, the potency of the pesticide); such an estimate, as we shall see, requires a separate analysis altogether.

Significance tests are characterized by their "p-value," such that a p-value of 0.01 (1 percent) means that the probability of obtaining the observed data if the null hypothesis were true is 1 percent or, more simply, that the experiment is significant at the 1 percent level. The most common scientific convention (it cannot be objectively derived) for statistical significance is 5 percent, or 95 percent when expressed as a "confidence level" for a specific interval around the mean,[11] meaning that if an experimental p-value is less than 0.05, the result is deemed statistically significant.

---

[9] If we return to the pesticide example, delimiting the potential alternative hypotheses is far from straightforward. The alternative to "harmless" is not "harmful," it is actually a host of alternatives hypotheses (and degrees of potency) that entail some kind of harmful interaction.

[10] David Kaye, "Is Proof of Statistical Significance Relevant?" *Washington Law Review* 61, no. 4 (1986): 1333.

[11] To make things more confusing, scientists often use "confidence intervals," which I will refer to here as "confidence levels." Formally, a confidence level of 95 percent indicates that there is a 95 percent chance that the mean value of a new sample of experimental data would fall within the specific interval delineated (for example, an interval of plus or minus 3 percent around the calculated mean). Stated more simply, the confidence level is typically the complement of the standard for statistical significance that applies to an experiment. Accordingly, if an experiment is required to meet a 5 percent significance level to establish statistical significance, the confidence limit will typically be 95 percent.

## Bayesian Statistical Inference

Bayesian statistics presumes that scientific data should be incorporated into decision making pursuant to the logic of Bayes' theorem. This approach to statistical inference is novel because it can be applied even when one begins with little or even no empirical information. Once again, consider the pesticide example: if I have several competing hypotheses about the toxicity of a chemical (e.g., the chemical is benign, the chemical is harmful only at high doses, or the chemical is harmful at any level of exposure) but no starting data exist, Thomas Bayes established a method for inductively incorporating new information and inferring which of the competing hypotheses is most probable.

Bayes' theorem states that the probability of a hypothesis $H$, such as it will rain today, conditioned on an event $E$, such as news of diminishing barometric pressure, $P(H/E)$, is simply the probability of $H$ prior to the new information, $P(H)$, multiplied by the "likelihood" of observing $E$ if $H$ is true, $P(E/H)$, which, simplifying greatly, gives $P(H/E) = P(H)^*P(E/H)$.[12]

A crucial aspect of Bayesian methods is the initial scientific judgment from which the analysis starts. This judgment reflects a scientist's understanding of the system being studied and, as discussed earlier, must be reduced to a prior distribution. Where a prior distribution is well circumscribed by existing scientific knowledge, judgments about it will likely be relatively consistent and uncontested. In practice, environmental scientists will often differ substantially in their judgments about the appropriate prior distribution for a system.[13]

A Bayesian analysis of contaminant levels in a river provides a fairly realistic example of Bayesian methods and highlights the importance of the starting prior distribution. Assume that a river is found to have been contaminated with copper from an industrial plant and that ten water samples have been collected from the river. Assume further that an analysis of the ten samples reveals that the mean (that is, average) concentration of copper for the ten samples is 50.6 micrograms/liter ($\mu$g/l) and that the variance in

---

[12] More formally, the probability of A occurring conditioned on the occurrence of B, – that is, $P(A/B)$ – is defined to be $P(A\&B)/P(B)$. Combining the relevant equations, Bayes' theorem has the following general form: $P(H_j/E) = P(H_j)P(E/H_j)/[\sum P(H_i)P(E/H_i)]$, for hypotheses $H_1, H_2, \ldots, H_k$, where $P(H_i) > 0$ for each $i$ and $P(E) > 0$.

[13] Mayo, 75–7, 119–20.

the copper concentrations across the ten samples is 25.0 $\mu g/l$.[14] Bayesian methods can be used to determine whether the mean concentration of copper in the river is likely to exceed a federal regulatory standard of, for example, 46 $\mu g/l$.

To begin the analysis, the scientist, whom we will assume is an employee of the plant, would specify a prior distribution delineating the probabilities of a continuous range of mean copper concentrations in the river. To simplify the calculation, we will assume that the scientist judges that the prior distribution, $P(H)$ in our previous discussion, is a normal distribution (that is, a traditional bell-shaped distribution for random variation) with a variance of 4 $\mu g/l$ centered around a mean copper concentration of 20 $\mu g/l$. In this case, the relatively low estimate and narrow spread of values reflect the scientist's presumed bias toward the interests of his employer. The scientist would use Bayes' theorem to combine the sample data with his prior distribution, which here results in an estimated most probable mean concentration of copper in the river of 36.1 $\mu g/l$.[15] This most probable level clearly falls below the regulatory standard of 46 $\mu g/l$.[16]

It is notable that combining the scientist's prior distribution with the observed copper concentrations through Bayes' theorem dramatically reduces the estimated mean concentration of copper in the river relative to the measured levels. In effect, the scientist's low-ball prior distribution offsets the sampled levels that exceed the regulatory limit. Moreover, if another scientist, perhaps from an environmental group, were to start with a prior distribution much closer to the mean of the measured values, the two estimates would not converge even with a significant increase in the quantity of data – implying that the end results are strongly determined by the scientists' initial prior distributions rather than collected data.[17]

---

[14] Brian Dennis, "Statistics and the Scientific Method in Ecology," in *The Nature of Scientific Evidence: Statistical, Philosophical, and Empirical Considerations*, ed. M. L. Taper and S. R. Lele (Chicago: University of Chicago Press, 2004), 333–4.

[15] Ibid., 342–3.

[16] The prior distribution in this case is continuous across a range of potential contaminant levels, such that each contaminant level encompassed by the normal distribution constitutes a hypothesis for the likely concentration of copper in the river and is given a discrete probability. While mathematically more complex than a discrete set of concentrations, the basic logic for applying Bayes' theorem is the same. More complex functions than a normal distribution can also be used.

[17] Dennis, 350.

The water-sampling example demonstrates that where a disparity exists between a scientist's prior distribution and observed values, which may occur where data are of poor or unknown quality (such as in the Klamath Basin conflict), the prior distribution will dominate the final result if data are limited. These constraints markedly qualify the power of Bayesian analysis to provide probability estimates that reflect a scientific consensus and highlight their subjectivity.

## Practical Limitations of Frequentist and Bayesian Methods

The contrasting attributes of frequentist and Bayesian methods underscore the significant trade-offs that must be weighed when selecting between them. The defining virtue of frequentist statistics is the objectivity of its methods, whereas the strength of the Bayesian approach is the intuitive simplicity of its probability estimates and its analytical flexibility. In both cases, the function of statistics bears important similarities to the role of procedure in law.[18] Most important in this respect are the frameworks that the two statistical models provide for promoting the consistency and accuracy of scientific determinations. Analogous to legal procedure, assessing the relative merits of frequentist and Bayesian methods revolves around their ability to maintain the accuracy, credibility, and transparency of scientific judgments. The following subsections explore in detail the differences and trade-offs between the two statistical models.

### Functional Constraints of Frequentist Methods

Frequentist methods require extensive data and carefully structured studies. Because of this, in the absence of adequate data, frequentist methods will be ineffectual for testing health or environmental effects because it will be impossible to reject no-effect null hypotheses. While these requirements ensure that testing is rigorous, they are often ill-suited to important areas of environmental science, such as ecology and toxicology. As Aaron Ellison has explained:

> From an ecological perspective, there are many difficulties with [frequentism]. Within experiments, true randomization is difficult,

[18] David E. Adelman, "Scientific Activism and Restraint: The Interplay of Statistics, Judgment, and Procedure in Environmental Law," *Notre Dame Law Review* 79, no. 2 (2004): 501–2.

replication is often small, misidentified, or by virtue of circumstance, nonexistent. Ecological experiments rarely are repeated independently. No two organisms are exactly alike, and consequently they are unlikely to respond to our treatment in exactly the same way. Evolution virtually guarantees that even if they were alike today, their offspring will be measurably different. Thus, the idea that there is a true, fixed value [i.e., long-run frequency] for any ecologically meaningful statistical parameter is a Platonic phantom.[19]

Similar concerns have been raised about the limits of epidemiological methods in environmental toxicology, such as the difficulties inherent in defining an appropriate sample and control group, that also derive from the requirements of frequentist methods.[20]

These problems pose critical dilemmas for how frequentist methods are applied and interpreted. The rigor of frequentist methods, which is central to its objectivity, places on scientific work significant constraints that are arguably unrealistic in many fields of environmental science given the difficulty of gathering uniform and adequately numerous data. For an increasing number of environmental scientists, these restrictions are more trouble than they are worth and are thus being viewed as impediments to scientific work.

The functional limitations of frequentist methods are compounded by their interpretive obscurity. Recall that the objectivity of frequentist methods derives from significance tests quantifying how likely a test hypothesis is to predict the observed data, as opposed to estimating how well the observed data support a test hypothesis. As a consequence, the scientific convention that requires confidence levels to be 95 percent (that is, statistical significance at the 5 percent level) is not a *direct* standard of persuasion that is based on the degree to which evidence supports a hypothesis. Interpreting frequentist confidence or significance levels as quantifying the degree of support for a hypothesis is equivalent to concluding that where $A$ implies $B$, it necessarily follows that $B$ implies $A$. Yet, many lawyers, judges, and policy makers fail to appreciate this distinction, leading to confusion that impedes scientists' efforts to convey accurately the implications of experimental data used in regulatory decisions.

---

[19] Aaron M. Ellison, "An Introduction to Bayesian Inference for Ecological Research and Environmental Decision-Making," *Ecological Applications* 6, no. 4 (1996): 1037.

[20] Gary Taubes, "Epidemiology Faces Its Limits," *Science* 269, no. 5221 (1995): 164–5.

The indirect nature of frequentist significance tests limits their role in regulatory decision making. For regulatory decisions, scientists must undertake a qualitative assessment of how well each experiment was designed and implemented.[21] Accordingly, while statistical significance serves an important purpose, its role in rigorously testing hypotheses is less relevant or meaningful for the final process of regulatory standard setting.

Consider an example in which the results of two experiments on a chemical's toxicity both satisfy a 95 percent confidence level, but their estimates of its toxicity differ markedly. Assume further that one of the experiments involved dosing rats under controlled conditions, while the other was a human epidemiological study for which exposure levels could not be controlled stringently. These experimental differences are critical because the data are not directly comparable. Statistical significance will be irrelevant to how a scientist weighs the credibility of the two studies and integrates their results to estimate the chemical's toxicity.

This simplified example is directly applicable to the Environmental Protection Agency's (EPA's) process for setting chemical toxicity levels under its Integrated Risk Information System (IRIS) program. IRIS toxicological reviews are designed to generate a consensus opinion on the potency of the toxic chemicals that EPA regulates. The IRIS process assesses all of the available toxicological studies performed on a chemical. When integrating the available data to arrive at a consensus opinion, scientists consider a variety of experimental factors, such as whether the data are derived from animal or human studies, the degree to which the conditions for the experiments were controlled, and any confounding exposures that could bias the results. Statistical significance is independent of these considerations – even poorly crafted experiments can generate statistically significant results. In the end, judgments on the value of specific data "count most, not some meeting of, or failure to meet, an arbitrary level of statistical 'significance.'"[22]

Some scientists believe that it is absurd to presume that policy makers have the expertise necessary to interpret frequentist statistics.[23] Among other things, they fear that a "95 percent confidence level" will mislead lay decision makers into placing undue reliance on a specific finding. For

[21] Randall Collins, "Statistics versus Words," *Sociological Theory* 2, no. 2 (1984): 336–7.
[22] Ibid., 337.
[23] Schneider, 18–19.

example, a frequentist working on global climate change research would be limited to supplying policy makers with statistically significant results on one or more scenarios for global warming, each of which would be supported by a variety of experimental and observational data. If he or she followed the frequentist precept of letting the data tell the story, the scientist would not identify the scenarios he or she believes are the most probable, which, as in the preceding IRIS example, entails a qualitative assessment of the validity of the existing studies (for example, the degree to which the experimental findings can be generalized, the influence of simplifying assumptions, and the limits of specific experimental instruments or methods). Instead, the scientist would leave that ultimate judgment to the policy maker.

These criticisms are valid, but they can be taken too far. Frequentist statistics both enhance transparency, by separating statistical analysis from judgment, and compromise it, by making statistical estimates more subject to misinterpretation. To take full advantage of the transparency that such methods afford, lay recipients of statistical analyses must become better educated about the limits of frequentist methods. Until this occurs, policy makers and other lay people will continue to misapprehend the significance of experimental findings that are essential to understanding what is actually occurring in the environment.

## Subjective Bias in Bayesian Analysis

Bayesian methods generate direct estimates of the probability that a hypothesis is true. However, as the river example demonstrated, the judgments of the scientist conducting the analysis can heavily influence these estimates. Bayesians claim that it is better "to put more trust in the probability estimates of [environmental scientists] – however subjective – than those of the myriad special interests that have been encouraged to make their own [predictions]."[24] Presumably, part of the rationale for this belief is that Bayesian estimates can be subject to detailed analysis and questioning by policy makers and other scientists. It is also driven by the view that Bayesian estimates are superior because they are simpler to understand and do not require policy makers to interpret the data de novo.

[24] Ibid., 19.

This interpretive ease is bought at a significant price – objective results.[25] Consider again the scenario involving emissions from an industrial plant into a river. In analyzing the risks, a scientist from an environmental organization would adopt a precautionary approach incorporating assumptions that are very protective of human health and natural resources. For example, the scientist might assume that the contaminants do not biodegrade rapidly, that they are not sequestered, and that river flow dynamics cause them to concentrate in certain areas. By contrast, an industry scientist would presumably start with a very different, less-protective set of assumptions that would lead to much lower estimates of the concentrations of the contaminants. As the river example illustrated, the differences in their respective perspectives will cause the two scientists to arrive at divergent Bayesian probability estimates, although their results will both be cloaked in the unassailable mantle of statistical proof.

Bayesians have a simple response to such concerns: Scientists' prior distributions are irrelevant because Bayesian analyses will converge to the most probable hypothesis irrespective of these initial judgments. Bayesians in essence claim that given sufficient data, Bayes' theorem ultimately produces objective results that are independent of the initial probability estimates for each hypothesis being tested. It achieves this objectivity by causing expert opinion to converge as more data are collected, meaning at some point Bayesian assessments of any group of experts would derive the same most-probable hypothesis. Thus, an environmentalist and industry scientist may start with divergent estimates of contaminant levels, but once sufficient data are collected, their estimates will converge to the same value. These claims raise an obvious question, namely, *how rapidly* do Bayesian analyses cause the opinions of scientists to converge? If a large amount of data is required and it must be assembled by expensive sampling in the field, convergence may be foreclosed as a practical matter.

Bayesian methods estimate the probabilities for each hypothesis under consideration in an experiment or series of experiments. The number of hypotheses in a Bayesian analysis can vary from as few as two – a chemical has a certain property or not – to a continuous range of hypotheses about the magnitude of a property, such as hypotheses about the concentration of a pollutant in a river. While this process is relatively straightforward for

[25] Dennis, 356.

simple experimental systems, such as a series of coin-flipping experiments, it becomes much more variable and complex for nonuniform experimental information.[26] Most experimental data are not uniformly equivalent and thus cannot be easily run through Bayes' theorem like a sequence of experiments involving coin flips, which are simply reported as either heads or tails.

In chemical risk assessment, like many other areas of environmental science, all of the available experimental studies must be evaluated, but few (if any) of them will have been conducted under identical conditions. These differences preclude data from distinct experiments being quantitatively intertranslatable and instead require scientists to judge how data from each experiment will be weighted and integrated into a Bayesian analysis. This interpretive step in a Bayesian analysis and the interdependence of how experimental data are viewed collectively make it impossible to predict when Bayesian convergence of opinion will occur.

## The Interplay of Science and Statistics

Science is not monolithic, and environmental science, which is based on relatively new fields of inquiry, is especially diverse. This diversity must be considered when evaluating the relative merits of Bayesian and frequentist methods with respect to transparency.[27] For example, some areas of environmental science involve collecting large quantities of data under carefully controlled conditions (such as toxicological animal testing), other areas have access to vast quantities of data but under relatively uncontrolled conditions (for example, retrospective epidemiological studies), and still others control experiments at a level of precision once thought unattainable and require relatively few data (as in certain areas of chemistry).

The data demands of a frequentist approach inhibit its effective use by policy makers and can impede public understanding of experimental results. In particular, too much is often read into findings deemed to be statistically significant. On the other hand, the contentious politics, theoretical

---

[26] John Earman, *Bayes or Bust?: A Critical Examination of Bayesian Confirmation Theory* (New York: Bradford Books, 1992), 148–9.

[27] Aaron M. Ellison, "Commentary," in *The Nature of Scientific Evidence: Statistical, Philosophical, and Empirical Considerations*, ed. M. L. Taper and S. R. Lele (Chicago: University of Chicago Press, 2004), 364–6; Charles E. McCulloch, "Commentary," in ibid., 361–2.

uncertainties, and limited data found in environmental science all suggest that the Bayesian mixing of judgment and data could add fuel to existing disputes by obscuring the solid data and theories that do exist. Trade-offs must be made between interpretive transparency and analytical flexibility. Ecological studies, for example, that are less amenable to frequentist analyses (because ecological systems are unavoidably dynamic) could be conducted using Bayesian methods. Scientists could then be required to explain the rationale for their choice of prior distribution. Climate change estimates may be candidates for Bayesian methods for the same reasons. Indeed, institutional developments in climate change science policy at the Intergovernment Panel on Climate Change provide an interesting model that integrates elaborate procedures and sophisticated statistical methods into the scientific consensus process.[28]

As a general rule, frequentist methods will be better suited to areas of science in which scientists are less mathematically sophisticated, as they are relatively easy to apply. The objectivity of frequentist methods also makes them well suited to fields for which divisive disciplinary controversies are common. More technically, frequentist methods are most powerful in disciplines for which large-scale controlled experimental testing dominate. By contrast, Bayesian methods, because of their greater complexity, will be preferred where scientists are comfortable with challenging mathematical methods. Similarly, the interpretive ease of Bayesian analysis will provide the greatest benefits at the least cost where disciplinary consensus is attainable because the consensus will counterbalance the subjective nature of Bayesian methods. Finally, Bayesian methods have unique capacities where observational studies dominate or, as in the case of ecological science, statistical long-run frequencies are elusive. These observations are obviously generalizations that must be reexamined in particular contexts.

## Integrating Scientific and Legal Transparency

Legal mechanisms should take greater advantage of the well-defined decision points in frequentist and Bayesian methods to maximize transparency. Too often, lawyers fail to consider adequately whether legal procedures enhance or detract from the transparency of scientific methods. This

[28] Adelman, 570–89.

blindness is reflected in the current regulatory policies that ignore these opportunities. Yet, by considering how statistical and legal mechanisms can work together, lawyers, scientists, and policy makers stand to gain added flexibility that will enable them to develop more refined legal procedures that complement the available scientific methods. Legal procedures must also be attuned to the differences between Bayesian and frequentist methods. Indeed, attention to these differences will become ever more important as environmental scientists increasingly resort to Bayesian methods.

Optimizing legal procedures in this manner will require lawyers and scientists to consider the relative strengths of frequentist and Bayesian methods as they apply to specific scientific problems that arise in a regulatory context. For example, ecological studies that can benefit from Bayesian methods should be subjected to additional procedural requirements. At minimum, legal procedures should require that scientists explain the rationale for their choice of prior distribution, describe how experimental data were weighted in the analysis, and calculate Bayesian probabilities under a range of starting assumptions (that is, use a variety of prior distributions). Where frequentist methods are used, legal procedures should, consistent with well-established policies, require scientists to account for the divergence of experiments from prescribed frequentist methods (such as confounding factors and systematic biases), to explain how different studies factored into their final (that is, post-statistics) analysis, and to describe how quantitative estimates were derived.

The water-sampling example discussed earlier illustrates how legal procedures and scientific methods can be effectively integrated. Recall that the scientist in the water-sampling example was an employee of the polluting plant and started with a prior distribution strongly favoring the interests of his or her employer. Requiring scientists to explain the reasoning behind their prior distribution and to conduct the analysis using a variety of prior distributions (such as a Monte Carlo method) will temper, if not neutralize, such scientists' biased or self-interested claims. It would also provide a range of estimates and a gauge of the relative importance of a scientist's prior distribution to the final estimate. Further, in more realistic cases where multiple experimental studies are at issue, the effect of adding new data to the statistical estimate should be evaluated iteratively. While these procedures would not dispel the deeper methodological concerns some scientists have about Bayesian statistics, they will provide an effective framework for maximizing transparency when they are used.

The Klamath Basin water controversy offers a more complex example of how this approach could be applied. The data in this case were equivocal for several reasons: (1) A reliable benchmark (control) for the endangered fish did not exist; (2) little was understood about the life cycle of the fish and whether it was particularly vulnerable at certain stages of its development; (3) the data suggested a positive correlation between species abundance and water level, but the year of highest larval abundance occurred during the driest year; and (4) sampling errors of species abundance were known to be high.

Frequentist statistics are unlikely to be of much use under these circumstances because the data are poorly controlled and the small number of data all but foreclose a finding of statistical significance. The binary nature of frequentist statistics – either data are statistically significant or not – precludes them from providing a basis upon which to assess the relative support for competing theories when there are so few data; their primary function is setting a conservative threshold for whether to accept the data at all.

Bayesian methods have the capacity to discriminate between opposing theories even where data are very limited. However, as you might expect, the fewer the data, the greater the influence of the initial scientific judgment (that is, prior distribution) in Bayesian estimates – even the most sophisticated statistical methods cannot turn leaden data into gold. Accepting the versatility of Bayesian methods also creates the risk that policy makers and stakeholders will take the estimates too literally. To compensate for this tendency, it will be essential that policy makers balance the potential for people to read too much into numerical estimates– a tendency that Bayesian methods are liable to encourage – against the perils of inchoate (and potentially biased) scientific judgment, which a Bayesian framework supplemented by complementary legal procedures has the potential to counteract.

Particularly where the science is relatively underdeveloped, as in the Klamath example, transparency will be a matter of degree. Lawyers know all too well that there is significant virtue in simply having a consistent (ideally simple) analytical framework for decision making. Legal rules routinely sacrifice accuracy and fairness for analytical simplicity and ease of implementation. Bayesian methods offer analogous benefits, particularly its logical consistency and the intuitive accessibility of its estimates, that should not be blithely dismissed because the methods incorporate subjective judgments. After all, subjective judgments will be unavoidable when data are deficient, and the primary question will be how to make such judgments as fair-minded and transparent as possible.

## Toward Real Reform

Deciding between frequentist and Bayesian methods should rest on two central factors: objectivity and technical constraints. Where technical constraints – including marginal or difficult-to-replicate data – are not limiting factors, frequentist methods should be utilized in conjunction with legal procedures that require a detailed discussion of empirical results. In a world in which agency science is vulnerable to manipulation and challenges to credibility, objectively verifiable results are of paramount importance. Consequently, although frequentist statistics do not provide direct probability estimates, this limitation is more than offset by the objectivity and rigor of the methods. Careful explanation of experimental results is a fundamental principle of science. However, in the regulatory context, this principle is often honored in the breach, making it necessary to adopt legal requirements for disclosure.

Bayesian analysis will be the better approach where technical constraints limit the available empirical support. Bayesian methods provide a rigorous analytical framework by, among other things, requiring scientists to make their initial views explicit upfront in a prior distribution. While the process of translating scientific judgments into prior distributions is likely to be opaque to most lay people and the analysis itself highly abstract, biased analyses can be exposed. The legal procedures recommended in this chapter are designed to provide the context and benchmarks necessary to make Bayesian analyses transparent to policy makers and stakeholders. Further, concerns that Bayesian methods do not adhere to proper scientific methods are much less central to regulatory decision making than to basic science. Regulatory decisions typically cannot wait for scientists to collect the often extensive new data required or to produce new theoretical insights, as failures to act have their own unintended or irreversible consequences. What they most need is an efficient and consistent method for analyzing the science that is available at the time. In a technically constrained, data-poor context, the analytical power and logical consistency of Bayesian methods will frequently make them the least-worst option.

I have argued that the impact of our clean science principles can be enhanced by directing legal procedures at critical scientific judgments built into the basic structure of broadly applicable statistical methods. This approach is already evident in the ways that frequentist methods have informed regulatory procedures. Using Bayesian methods and legal procedures in tandem to structure expert judgment stands to expand and strengthen the options available for improving transparency. Moreover, by linking law and science in this manner, this strategy will promote a fuller appreciation among policy makers of the limits of scientific methods and will demonstrate to scientists that legal procedures can complement, rather than frustrate, science in a regulatory context. Both stand to improve how science is used in environmental policy making.

## PART
# III

# A PUBLIC INFRASTRUCTURE FOR SCIENCE

In this final part, we consider the appropriate role for government in ensuring both the validity and support of science used for regulation. The principles stress that peer review and support of research should be balanced and prioritized, giving greatest attention to scientific research that promises the greatest public benefit and is in the greatest need of government oversight.

## Peer Review

The first, important area of government oversight of regulatory science – peer review – requires the assembly of balanced panels and careful attention to preventing unwarranted intrusions into research through politicized review. The applicable principles state:

- In appropriate circumstances, peer review is an important step in the process of scientific discovery, but peer review should never be used to censor scientific research.
- Legitimate scientific peer review does not encompass processes that enable outside stakeholders to pressure scientists to change their views in light of an anticipated policy outcome.
- Peer review should be done by a balanced group of peer reviewers who have no present or past conflicts of interest likely to affect their review and who specialize in the area. Peer reviewers should disclose the limits of their expertise in assessing the research.

- Entities that select peer reviewers should disclose any financial conflicts of interest and affiliations or perspectives that may influence their choice of reviewers. The selection of reviewers must never be politicized.

Despite widespread consensus among scientists, these basic commitments have been violated in a number of ways over the last decade. Senior officials in both the executive and legislative branches have proposed peer review policies for regulatory science that are so antithetical to sound peer review that large segments of the scientific community have registered their opposition. Two authors explore these developments from a scientific and a legal perspective.

In the first chapter in this final part, Dr. Michaels discusses the history of peer review practices in the scientific community and contrasts this more collaborative process with recent proposals for use of peer review to improve the quality of regulatory science. Rather than providing constructive criticism of research, several recent proposals to expand regulatory peer review establish a binary, yes-or-no evaluation of scientific research with limited opportunities for correction. Moreover, the importance of identifying reviewers who represent the full range of views is sometimes discounted in these proposals, further undermining the promise of a fair review. These weaknesses in the design of regulatory peer review processes present dangerous opportunities for government officials to misuse peer review by assembling review panels that are not only imbalanced, but imbalanced in ways that produce a desired political outcome. They also present the worrisome possibility of censoring quality research. Dr. Michaels explains the outcome of the heated debate provoked by the Office of Management and Budget's (OMB) recent peer review proposal and cautions that we must keep a careful eye on further incursions of this nature.

Professor Shapiro approaches the same issues from a legal perspective, explaining how trends that promote imbalanced, even biased, peer review violate basic principles of administrative decision making. Professor Shapiro recognizes that there are important benefits to regulatory peer review, but suggests that some of the proposals to expand its scope are disingenuous because they have the effect of delaying protective regulation by providing self-interested participants with additional opportunities to impose their own policy references through the guise of scientific review.

Shapiro suggests several reforms to the legal system that would combat these trends, modeling his proposals on the basic tenets of the Federal Advisory Committee Act, which attempts to limit such abuses by requiring peer review processes to be open and balanced.

## Funding

The second set of principles addresses the need to build a more stable public infrastructure for basic and applied research that informs regulation. These principles underscore the fundamental role of government support in generating scientific knowledge, particularly for applied questions that involve research on pollution and other health and environmental harms created by the private sector:

- Government support of research is essential to produce discoveries that benefit the public good.
- Much research that benefits the public good does not generate private compensation for its production. Generous public funding of research is essential for advancements in scientific knowledge, especially in areas where there are no private benefits to be gained from the discoveries.
- All research produced or used by the government should be subject to basic quality assurance/quality control checks, especially if that research is not published or disseminated widely within the scientific community.
- Public research monies should be allocated in ways that are disinterested and do not reflect a stake in the outcome of the research.

A long history of funding shortfalls in federal support of environmental research, coupled with inadequate incentives for the production of such research by the private sector, leaves significant gaps in the scientific information available to regulators and the scientific community. Until these problems are addressed, regulatory science will continue to be underproduced. In his closing chapter, Professor John Applegate discusses these disappointing funding shortfalls and explains why the legal system has failed to inspire the private sector to provide compensating investments in such research. Until the imperative for government support of research is acknowledged and priorities are identified for research needs, environmental science will be stuck in a holding pattern, producing only small and disconnected pockets of basic and applied research. Unjustified attacks on high-quality regulatory science, as documented elsewhere in this book, serve only to exacerbate such problems. To reform this state of affairs, Professor Applegate develops threshold principles for determining when the private sector should address research needs and when government investment and supervision are crucial.

# 10

# Politicizing Peer Review: The Scientific Perspective

David Michaels, Ph.D.

## The Role of Peer Review

Peer review, or independent review by experts, is an important but limited mechanism for quality control within the scientific enterprise. While it has many manifestations, peer review generally involves a review of materials by experts who are thought to have adequate knowledge and technical expertise to judge the material's quality, while being sufficiently impartial and disinterested to provide judgment free of conflict of interest.[1]

Peer review plays an important role in the production and shaping of the scientific knowledge that is the product of the current scientific enterprise. This enterprise is one in which, at least in theory, scientists are constantly evaluating and building upon each other's works through a continual system of experimentation, publication, dissemination, replication, and further experimentation. Peer review may be performed in at least two aspects of this process: in the decision-making processes of agencies and institutions that provide financial support for scientific research, and in the editorial prepublication assessment of manuscripts submitted to scientific journals (often called "refereeing"). There is significant competition both for space in prestigious journals and limited research funds, and peer review plays a pivotal role in allocation of both of these highly valued resources.

Beyond these two models of peer review, in recent years there has been a growing interest in a new, distinct function for peer review: an evaluation of analytical and synthetic documents prepared by governmental agencies,

---

[1] U.S. General Accounting Office, *Federal Research: Peer Review Practices at Federal Science Agencies Vary* (Washington, DC: Government Printing Office, 1999) (available at http://www.gao.gov/archive/1999/rc99099.pdf).

often in support of regulatory programs. This is being driven in part by opponents of the environmental and public health protections that require significant corporate expenditures or even limit production of particularly toxic materials. These increasingly fervent calls for peer review in regulatory science were evidently heard in the White House, which, in the later part President George W. Bush's first term, began an effort to require peer review of most reports and documents produced by federal agencies.

The official adoption of uniform peer review requirements by all federal agencies is a mechanism by which corporate interests can question the science underlying not just regulation but virtually any "information" disseminated by federal agencies. This development has the potential to impede the implementation of programs that protect public health and the environment. While peer review will no doubt be useful in some cases, it is increasingly being invoked in a way that is likely to magnify the ability of parties with a financial interest in the outcome to intervene successfully in the process, to the detriment of the public good. Further, when peer review of regulatory documents is applied in a way that impedes the dissemination of study results, it becomes a tool for stifling rather than improving science.

To provide a context for discussion of peer review of regulatory science, this chapter first examines very briefly the historical development of peer review and then reviews the function of peer review of editorial and program evaluation. Following these explanations, the chapter focuses on the debate over the application of peer review to regulatory science, with particular attention to the Bush Administration's imposition of a federal government–wide mandatory peer review program in 2005. My goal is to present a scientist's perspective on these developments, while Professor Sidney Shapiro presents the legal perspective in the next chapter.

## A Brief History of Peer Review

The antecedents of prepublication editorial peer review appear to date from the middle of the seventeenth century, with the publication of the journal *Philosophical Transactions*. The initial authorization for its publication, by the Council of the Royal Society of London, included the order that it be "first reviewed by some members" of the Council.[2] A century later,

---

[2]  Harriet A. Zuckerman and Robert K. Merton, "Patterns of Evaluation in Science: Institutionalization, Structure and Functions of the Referee System," *Minerva* 9, no. 1 (1971): 68–9.

*Philosophical Transactions* became the official publication of the Royal Society; it is the oldest scientific journal in continuous publication.[3] In 1752, the Society established a "Committee on Papers," to review all articles considered for publication.[4] For centuries, such prepublication review appears to have been the exception rather than the rule in scientific publishing. While casual refereeing of individual journal submissions occurred in the nineteenth and early-twentieth century, the widespread acceptance of editorial peer review as an integral part of development of scientific knowledge is a relatively new development, starting in the middle of the twentieth century.

A review of this history by John Burham, a professor of history and psychiatry at Ohio State University, suggests that the institutionalization of peer review practices by editors was not initially the result of a generalized recognition of the intrinsic value of this mechanism. Rather, the imposition of peer review was a reflection of the needs of editors, scientists, or physicians themselves "either to handle new problems in the numbers of articles submitted or to meet the demands for expert authority and objectivity in an increasingly specialized world."[5] As a result, the institutionalization of editorial peer review occurred in an idiosyncratic and haphazard manner, without the recognition of a single predominant model.

Editorial peer review appears to have developed independently of peer review procedures used to determine funding allocations. In the United States, the use of a formal peer review procedure to consider applications for support of research began in the early part of the twentieth century; by 1937 it was already established in the authorizing legislation of the National Cancer Institute. The diffusion and acceptance of peer review for funding, in contrast to that of editorial peer review, reflected a shared recognition of the value of this process within the scientific community.[6]

Peer review, as a process fundamental to the functioning of the scientific enterprise, is often the subject of superlative description. In an oft-cited

[3] For a brief history of the Royal Society, see the Royal Society, "Brief History of the Society," the Royal Society, http://www.royalsoc.ac.uk/page.asp?id=2176.

[4] David A. Kronick, "Peer Review in 18th-Century Scientific Journalism," *Journal of the American Medical Association* 263, no. 10 (1990): 1321.

[5] John C. Burnham, "The Evolution of Editorial Peer Review," *Journal of the American Medical Association* 263, no. 10 (1990): 1323.

[6] Ibid., 1328.

1971 paper, Harriet Zuckerman and Robert Merton asserted that despite its flaws,

> ...the system of monitoring scientific work before it enters into the archives of science means that much of the time scientists can build upon the work of others with a degree of warranted confidence. It is in this sense that the structure of authority in science, in which the referee system occupies a central place, provides an institutional basis for the comparative reliability and cumulation of knowledge.[7]

More recently, two editors of the *New England Journal of Medicine* called peer review "indispensable for the progress of biomedical science."[8] The Royal Society, Britain's national academy of sciences, opined that "peer review is to the running of the scientific enterprise what democracy is to the running of the country."[9]

## Refereeing or Editorial Peer Review

### Framework for the Peer Review Process

Perhaps the best-known type of scientific peer review is prepublication assessment by independent experts of manuscripts describing scientific research. This editorial peer review plays an important role in determining and shaping what many scientific journals publish. Generally, authors submit papers for consideration by editors or editorial boards, who send the manuscripts to other scientists, often called referees, who provide feedback and advice to the editors and the manuscripts' authors. Editors usually ask the referees to evaluate a paper's quality in terms of its reliability, originality, relevance, and appropriateness to the journal.[10] The editors may use that information to request that the authors modify (and, they hope, improve) the original paper, and to decide whether to publish the revised paper. The publication decision generally rests solely in the hands of the editor or editorial board, who retains discretion to accept or reject the advice of the

[7] Zuckerman and Merton, 99–100.
[8] Jerome P. Kassirer and Edward W. Campion, "Peer Review: Crude and Understudied, But Indispensable," *Journal of the American Medical Association* 272, no. 2 (1994): 96–7.
[9] The Royal Society, "Brief History of the Society."
[10] Sandra Goldbeck-Wood, "Evidence on Peer Review: Scientific Quality Control or Smoke-screen?" *British Medical Journal* 318, no. 7175 (1999): 44.

independent referees. Editors of scientific journals have traditionally been able to shape the specific rules and applications of the peer review system and use this manuscript management system to fit their needs. As a result, there is much heterogeneity in the charges given to reviewers.[11]

There is also variation in the use of anonymity in the peer review process. Some journals employ a system in which the reviewers know the names and affiliations of the authors; other journals blind the referees to the identity of the authors, although it is sometimes possible for knowledgeable reviewers to guess the identity of one or more authors of a paper from reading the material under review. For the most part, only the journal editors know the identity of the referees, although a list of all reviewers is often published annually, to thank the reviewers who are not otherwise remunerated for their work. The anonymity of the reviewers presumably allows them to provide critical feedback without risking the personal or professional wrath of the authors being critiqued. However, there are little hard data on the value of anonymity in peer review, and there appears to be growing interest in altering or abandoning it.[12]

## Limitations of Editorial Peer Review

The limitations to peer review as a mechanism for quality control are widely recognized within the scientific community. Among those most critical of the peer review system are editors of the leading biomedical journals, scientists who are intimately involved in its use.[13] Richard Smith, the editor of the *British Medical Journal*, has written:

> The problem with peer review is that we have good evidence on its deficiencies and poor evidence on its benefits. We know that it is expensive, slow, prone to bias, open to abuse, possibly anti-innovatory, and unable to detect fraud. We also know that the published papers that emerge from the process are often grossly deficient.[14]

[11] Stephen Lock, *A Difficult Balance: Editorial Peer Review in Medicine* (London: Nuffield Provincial Hospitals Trust, 1985).
[12] Richard Smith, "Opening Up *BMJ* Peer Review," *British Medical Journal* 318, no. 7175 (1999): 4–5.
[13] Kassirer and Campion; Lock.
[14] Robin Smith, "Peer Review: Reform or Revolution," *British Medical Journal* 315, no. 7111 (1997): 759.

Perhaps the most widely recognized failing of peer review is its inability to ensure the identification of high-quality work. The list of important scientific papers that were initially rejected by peer-reviewed journals goes back at least as far as the editor of *Philosophical Transaction*'s 1796 rejection of Edward Jenner's report of the first vaccination against smallpox.[15]

Nor is peer review a tool for ensuring honesty or for detecting fraud in science. In submitting a manuscript for consideration for publication, authors assert, either implicitly or, with increasing frequency, explicitly through signed testaments, that they have personally conducted the work (that is, the experiment or analysis) presented in the article. For the most part, referees do not request additional material, examining only the manuscript that is provided by the authors; the system operates on an assumption of honesty and trust. It is widely understood among scientists that peer review is not a defense against data fabrication, since a scientist intent on fraud would likely be able to falsify results in a way undetectable to a manuscript's reader.[16] Peer review is also not particularly effective in identifying poor laboratory practices, or mistakes in computation associated with incorrect results.

Bias and conflict of interest among reviewers may be problematic in editorial peer review. In theory, conflicts of interest can be overcome in pre-publication peer review since final publication decisions generally rest with the editor. Many journals, especially in the biomedical sciences, require referees to provide conflict-of-interest disclosures.[17] In selecting papers to publish, editors are therefore able to evaluate and discount the views of referees who have conflicts that are reflected in their commentary.

Referee bias is a more subtle and difficult issue to resolve. In those systems in which the authors of a manuscript are identified, academic status, scientific discipline, institution, gender, or other characteristics of

---

[15] Joshua S. Gans and George B. Shepherd, "How Are the Mighty Fallen: Rejected Classic Articles by Leading Economists," *Journal of Economic Perspectives* 8, no. 1 (1994): 165–79; Lock, 2.

[16] It appears that in most cases in which fraud is actually detected, the detection occurs after publication. At that point, the article is generally retracted, either by the author or the editors.

[17] Frank Davidoff et al, "Sponsorship, Authorship and Accountability," *Journal of the American Medical Association* 286, no. 10 (2001): 1232–3; Drummond Rennie et al., "Conflicts of Interest in the Publication of Science," *Journal of the American Medical Association* 266, no. 2 (1991): 266–7.

the author or authors may influence referees, consciously or not.[18] Editors may or may not be able to discern such bias and it is generally not easily identified.

Although editorial peer review holds an important position in the system of production of scientific knowledge, there is a dearth of empirical research of its impact on the quality of scientific research. One recent review of peer review as practiced by biomedical journals found little agreement about how to measure either its effects or processes.[19] A second review could identify only a few well-designed studies, and the results of these were for the most part ambiguous or inconclusive, leading the authors to conclude that "editorial peer review, although widely used, is largely untested and its effects uncertain."[20]

While peer review has been blamed for the increased probability that studies with positive results will be published, this problem does not appear to be a result of inequities in the peer review process itself. Authors and sponsors may be more likely to submit positive studies for publication.[21] Moreover, recent analyses actually found no difference in the time to publication between positive and negative studies: This also suggests that the peer review process may not be imposing added impediments to the publication of negative studies.[22]

## Research Evaluation or Peer Review for Funding Allocations

Peer review is widely used in evaluating the progress and performance of research programs, particularly those operated or funded by federal

---

[18] Lock, 26–9.

[19] Tom Jefferson et al., "Measuring the Quality of Editorial Peer Review," *Journal of the American Medical Association* 287, no. 21 (2002): 2786–90.

[20] Tom Jefferson et al., "Effects of Editorial Peer Review: A Systematic Review," *Journal of the American Medical Association* 287, no. 21 (2002): 2784.

[21] Philippa J. Easterbrook et al., "Publication Bias in Clinical Research," *Lancet* 337, no. 8746 (1991): 867–72; Anastasia L. Misakian and Lisa A. Bero, "Publication Bias and Research on Passive Smoking: Comparison of Published and Unpublished Studies," *Journal of the American Medical Association* 280, no. 3 (1998): 250–253; Jerome M. Stern and R. John Simes, "Publication Bias: Evidence of Delayed Publication in a Cohort Study of Clinical Research Projects," *British Medical Journal* 315, no. 7109 (1997): 640–5.

[22] Carin M. Olson et al., "Publication Bias in Editorial Decision Making," *Journal of the American Medical Association* 287, no. 21 (2002): 2825–8.

agencies. In a review of the peer review practices at federal science agencies, the U.S. General Accounting Office (now called the Government Accountability Office) found that while there is no uniform federal peer review policy or even definition, the agencies sampled all used some type of program evaluation process involving assessment by independent experts.[23] The science community generally supports this approach. In 1999, for example, the Committee on Science, Engineering, and Public Policy, a collaborative effort of the National Academy of Sciences, the National Academy of Engineering, and the Institute of Medicine, recommended that "Federal agencies should use expert review to assess the quality of research they support, the relevance of that research to their mission, and the leadership of the research."[24]

Most government agencies also employ some type of peer review structures to assist in funding decisions.[25] Grant-making peer review is similar to editorial peer review in how its resources are allocated. In both cases, scientists are competing for scarce resources – pages in a scientific journal or funds from an agency. Yet the two processes also differ in several key respects.

For the most part, the identities of researchers are known to the reviewers, while reviewer identities are not (although membership on a federal review panel is public information). Peer reviews of funding applications rarely have the iterative quality of editorial peer review, in which authors are offered and re-offered the opportunity to refine their manuscript until a point at which the paper is either accepted for publication rejected, or withdrawn. In reviewing funding proposals, competing applications are evaluated and scored, with the superior proposals generally being selected for funding by the sponsoring agencies. In contrast to the ultimate power of editors to accept or reject the advice of editorial peer reviewers, agency funders have little discretion to diverge from the rankings of the evaluators.

Given the explicit financial implications of decisions by research reviewers, it is widely understood that conflict of interest concerns must be addressed in the choice of reviewers. In the review of competitive funding

[23] U.S. General Accounting Office, *Federal Research*.
[24] Committee on Science, Engineering, and Public Policy (COSEPUP), *Evaluating Federal Research Programs: Research and the Government Performance and Results Act* (Washington, DC: National Academy Press, 2000).
[25] U.S. General Accounting Office, *Federal Research*.

applications, at least as practiced by the U.S. National Institutes of Health, members of review panels with financial, institutional, or personal conflicts of interest are generally barred from reviewing individual proposals.[26]

## Peer Review of Regulatory Science

### The Rise of Policy-Based Peer Review

The application of peer review to the science involved in regulatory decision making is a relatively new and controversial phenomenon. As regulatory agencies are called upon to make decisions and issue rules on the basis of increasingly complex science, they have developed quality assurance programs that share characteristics with the two types of peer review previously described. Given the scientific community's traditional reliance on peer review in determining which studies are published in scientific journals and which research proposals are supported by funding agencies, the application of some form of peer review to regulatory science seems reasonable at first glance. Shouldn't the scientists' own system be employed to distinguish good science from bad science in the regulatory context? This argument has been raised with some frequency over the last few decades, especially in Congress, where critics of the regulatory system regularly introduce legislation requiring use of peer review in agency science.

In her seminal work *The Fifth Branch: Science Advisors as Policymakers*, Professor Sheila Jasanoff recounts examples from the 1970s in which government agencies issued alarming warnings regarding the potential impacts of environmental exposures, including nitrites in food, the dioxin-contaminated herbicide 2,4,5-T, and Love Canal. Critics of government's regulatory decisions disputed the agencies' analyses, disparaging the scientific competence and performance of the agencies. Since then, according to Jasanoff, the call for peer review is a refrain heard often from corporate interests that feel that regulatory policy makers have not adequately separated "good" science from "bad" science, and that policy makers have exercised their sizable regulatory discretion to formulate science policies

---

[26] National Institutes of Health, "Review Procedures for Scientific Review Group Meetings" (available at http://www.csr.nih.gov/guidelines/proc.pdf).

that do not adhere to the standards used by the scientific community to evaluate evidence.[27]

Two political scientists, Stuart Shapiro and David Guston, describe regulatory peer review as an administrative procedure used by the president to exert political control over the burgeoning expert bureaucracy. This exercise of power occurs primarily as an executive branch initiative because congressional supporters of "regulatory reform" have been largely unsuccessful in passing legislation to alter the basic functioning of the regulatory agencies.[28]

As Professor Jasanoff has noted, regulatory science has many characteristics that are different from those of "investigator-initiated" or "curiosity-driven" science, which is judged in peer review systems (both editorial and resource-allocation) for its originality and significance. In contrast, regulatory science is rarely innovative; although it may involve generation of new knowledge, it is generally designed to answer questions specific to regulatory requirements. Jasanoff further distinguishes science used in the policy process from research science:

> The efficacy of regulatory science depends in part on its capacity to provide timely answers to pressing policy questions or, put differently, to produce "serviceable truths." Research science operates under no comparable time pressures; in principle, it can wait indefinitely to produce results. Accordingly, the meanings of reliability and "doing well" are legitimately different for regulatory and research science. The reliability of regulatory science cannot and should not necessarily be measured according to the same criteria as the reliability of research science. Correspondingly, the procedures used to ensure reliability may reasonably differ from the one scientific context to the other.[29]

Unless peer review is structured in a manner that recognizes the context in which regulatory science is used, it can become unnecessary and

---

[27] Sheila Jasanoff, *The Fifth Branch: Science Advisers as Policymakers* (Cambridge, MA: Harvard University Press, 1990).

[28] David H. Guston and Stuart Shapiro, "Procedural Control of the Bureaucracy, Peer Review, and Epistemic Drift" (paper presented at the annual meeting for the Association of Public Policy Analysis and Management, Atlanta, GA, October 29, 2004), 24 (available at http://papers.ssrn.com/sol3/papers.cfm?abstract_id=631161).

[29] Comment on Office of Management and Budget (OMB) Proposed Bulletin on Peer Review and Information Quality from Sheila Jasanoff, Harvard University, to Mabel Echols, OMB Peer Review 2 (December 16, 2003) (available at http://www.whitehouse.gov/omb/inforeg/2003iq/159.pdf).

cumbersome, and thus undermine agency functioning. In a comment on a Bush Administration government-wide peer review proposal discussed later in this chapter, Shapiro and Guston explain:

> Any individual peer reviewer will have the potential power to derail a rule-making effort by providing a negative peer review. This is not the case in academic peer review, where editors and program managers are free to ignore negative reviews of articles or proposals. The context of regulatory peer review is very different however. It is very easy to envision a court using a negative peer review as evidence that an agency was arbitrary and capricious in promulgating a regulation. It is also very easy to envision political actors hostile to a regulation using a negative peer review to attempt to derail regulatory initiatives for purely political reasons.

> And such negative peer reviews need not (and indeed are likely not to) come from peer reviewers with particular anti-regulatory agendas.... [D]isagreement in the sciences is common. Disagreement in economics is rampant. It is unlikely that very many analyses that agencies submit for regulatory peer review will result in unanimous endorsement. Such a lack of consensus, which is useful in the academic setting may provide a deathblow for regulatory efforts in the policymaking setting. This may be true even for regulations with large net benefits.[30]

In summary, independent review by experts of the documents and reports used in regulatory science shares some characteristics with but is also quite different from the peer review processes used for editorial decision making or research or program funding. Although peer review of regulatory science can help improve the quality of these documents, it can also be applied in a way that is antithetical to the outcome for which it is being invoked: to utilize the best available science to protect the public good.

## Peer Review at the Environmental Protection Agency

The Environmental Protection Agency (EPA) has regulatory needs that require research involving an extraordinarily wide range of scientific and

---

[30] Comments on the Office of Management and Budget's Proposed Bulletin on Peer Review and Information Quality from Stuart Shapiro and David Guston, Rutgers University, to Mabel Echols, OMB Peer Review 3 (December 12, 2003) (available at http://www.whitehouse.gov/omb/inforeg/2003iq/87.pdf).

technological disciplines, and it has become the federal regulatory agency with the most well-known engagement in the peer review process. The EPA is charged with developing environmental safeguards in areas in which there is much uncertainty and disagreement, often relying on complex mathematical models that may predict risk, exposure, emissions, and costs. The variables involved in the design and use of these models are often the subjects of great debate.

Since the regulatory and financial implications of EPA's research are so huge, it is not surprising that heated disputes have erupted over the nature and quality of EPA science. Polluters and producers of hazardous products have often expressed their displeasure at various EPA activities (that is, regulations and the risk assessments upon which they are based), claiming that the science at EPA was biased or otherwise questionable. In many instances, these parties have called for peer review, or better peer review, of the EPA documents in question.

In responding to these concerns, both the EPA and the National Academy of Sciences (NAS) have convened several groups of experts to evaluate the quality of science at the Agency. Congress first mandated peer review at EPA through the 1978 authorization of the Science Advisory Board, whose mandate is to review "the quality and relevance of the scientific and technical information being used or proposed as the basis for Agency regulations."[31] In 1992, the EPA appointed a committee of independent academic scientists, who issued the report *Safeguarding the Future: Credible Science, Credible Decisions*. After reviewing the production and evaluation of science at the EPA, these observers recommended that:

Quality assurance and peer review should be applied to the planning and results of all scientific and technical efforts to obtain data used for guidance and decisions at EPA, including such efforts in the program and regional offices. Such a requirement is essential if EPA is to be perceived as a credible, unbiased source of environmental and health information, both in the United States and throughout the world.[32]

[31] U.S. Environmental Protection Agency, "EPA Science Advisory Board," U.S. Environmental Protection Agency, http://www.epa.gov/sab.
[32] U.S. Environmental Protection Agency. *Safeguarding the Future: Credible Science, Credible Decisions: The Report of the Expert Panel on the Role of Science at EPA* (Washington, DC: U.S..Environmental Protection Agency, 1992).

Since the first Bush Administration, EPA policy has required that major scientific and technical work products related to agency decisions should be peer-reviewed, with independent or external peer review required for those documents supporting the most important decisions. In 1998, Carol Browner, EPA Administrator under President Clinton, issued a detailed handbook (revised and reissued in 2000) to ensure uniform implementation of the peer review policy.[33] As specified in the procedures outlined in the EPA handbook, only a relatively small portion of all documents that the agency produces are peer-reviewed. This policy was reviewed by an NAS panel, which, in its report *Strengthening Science at the U.S. Environmental Protection Agency*, congratulated EPA on its peer review practices.[34]

According to this policy, EPA scientific and technical work products that are considered candidates for peer review are those that are used to support a regulatory program or policy position and that meet certain additional criteria, the first of which is that the work product "establishes a significant precedent, model, or methodology." This policy recognizes that many of the studies and reviews used to support regulatory activity are not novel, but rather summaries and recapitulations of work that has already been subjected to other quality assurance processes and therefore does not require additional review.[35]

## Peer Review in the Second Bush Administration: Code Red in the Science Community

The deliberative process through which the EPA developed and implemented this program stands in stark contrast to an effort by the White House Office of Management and Budget (OMB) in the later part of the first term of President George W. Bush to compel all federal agencies to subject a tremendous proportion of their reports and documents to peer review. While similar in some ways to the EPA peer review system, this

---

[33] U.S. Environmental Protection Agency, Science Policy Council, *Peer Review Handbook* (Washington, DC: U.S. Environmental Protection Agency, 1998); U.S. Environmental Protection Agency, Office of Science Policy, *Science Policy Council Handbook: Peer Review* (Washington, DC: U.S. Environmental Protection Agency, 2nd ed., 2000).

[34] National Research Council, *Strengthening Science at the U.S. Environmental Protection Agency* (Washington, DC: National Academy Press, 2000), 19.

[35] U.S. Environmental Protection Agency, *Science Policy Council Handbook*, 26–7.

initiative was far more sweeping, requiring that a huge quantity of federal "information" – including reports, pamphlets, web pages, perhaps even statements by federal officials – be subject to new levels of review before dissemination. The proposal went through two public comment periods, in which many individuals and organizations in the scientific as well as business communities voiced their opinions on the matter. The final formal policy was issued in December 2004.

OMB's "Peer Review and Information Quality" guidance for agencies was first proposed in August 2003.[36] The proposal was overtly aimed at what some critics of federal regulatory authority call "regulation by information." In explaining the proposal, Dr. John Graham, director of OMB's Office of Information and Regulatory Affairs (OIRA) and the signatory of the peer review proposal, asserted "that release of governmental information that has important impacts on the private sector, is in itself in some ways, a form of regulation."[37]

Under the initial proposal, all covered information issued by an agency would undergo some form of peer review; covered information that might influence a major regulation, or that could have a "substantial impact" on public policies or private sector decisions with a possible impact of more than $100 million annually, would be put through a cumbersome process during which experts independent of the agency review the information. The proposal required that agency-generated information undergo multiple time-consuming reviews before release. Moreover, the information (reports, web pages, and so on) would first have to be published in draft form and disseminated for public comment, after which it would be sent to a peer review panel, along with the public comments. The agency would then issue a formal response to the peer reviewers' comments before the information could be redisseminated.[38] It was reasonable to conclude that application of this process could delay dissemination of information important in protecting that public's health and environment.

---

[36] Proposed Bulletin on Peer Review and Information Quality. 68 Fed. Reg. 54,023–54,029 (Sept. 15, 2003).
[37] John Graham, Statement at the Workshop on Peer Review Standards for Regulatory Science and Technical Information, Hosted by the National Academies, the National Research Council, Global and Policy Affairs Division, Science, Technology, and Law Program, Nov. 18, 2003, 16 (available at http://www7.nationalacademies.org/stl/1Peer_Review_Transcript.pdf).
[38] Proposed Bulletin on Peer Review and Information Quality. 68 Fed. Reg. 54,023–54,029 (Sept. 15, 2003).

One particularly troubling aspect of OMB's plan was the notably unbalanced or asymmetrical conflict-of-interest provision. Applying the untested hypothesis that financial support from an agency compromises the independent judgment of academic scientists, the proposal barred all scientists with a financial tie to an agency from participating in the review of agency documents. Because the proposal would exclude those scientists whose research is funded by the agency involved, many of the nation's leading academic experts could not be utilized. At the same time, the proposal did not equally preclude industry-employed scientists from appointment to the panels.[39]

Certain categories of information were exempt from the proposal's requirements, including documents relating to national defense or foreign affairs. All permits and licenses were also exempted so that, for example, peer review was not required of studies submitted by a manufacturer to demonstrate the safety of a new pesticide. In all, this suggested that OMB had targeted agencies with missions to protect the public's safety, health, and environment.

Interestingly, the initial attempt by OMB in August 2003 to impose governmentwide peer review requirements was met with opposition not only from the environmental and public interest communities but also from an unexpected source: institutions and organizations representing mainstream science. Much of this opposition solidified at a November 2003 workshop convened at OMB's request by the NAS Science, Technology, and Law program. The workshop began with an address by Dr. Graham, who explained that the proposal was a "major priority" for the Bush Administration, asserting that peer review would improve the quality of regulations and information.[40]

In response, speaker after speaker, all invited as experts in regulatory sciences by the NAS, warned that the OMB proposal would lead to increased costs and delays in disseminating information to the public and in promulgating health, safety, environmental, and other regulations, while potentially damaging the existing system of peer review. Many of the speakers challenged OMB to identify a single report or regulation that would have

---

[39] Ibid., 54,027–54,028; Anthony Robbins, "Science for Special Interests," *Boston Globe*, Dec. 7, 2003, Op-Ed sec.

[40] Graham, 16.

been improved had the proposed peer review system been in place. Following the NAS meeting, the American Association of Medical Colleges, representing the nation's schools of medicine, and the Federation of American Societies for Experimental Biology, a federation of twenty-two scientific societies, sent a scathing letter of opposition to the White House, as did the Council on Government Relations, representing more than 150 leading U.S. research universities. Both the American Association for the Advancement of Sciences[41] (AAAS) and the American Public Health Association[42] passed resolutions at their annual meetings opposing the peer review guidelines. This response by the scientific community was surprising to many. Traditionally, the organizations that represent mainstream scientists and their research institutions have focused their Washington political efforts on research funding, avoiding involvement in policy fights that might be perceived as partisan.

The widespread opposition among mainstream scientists can be seen in a powerful editorial that Donald Kennedy wrote in *Science* magazine. Dr. Kennedy, who also wrote the prologue to this book, is a giant in the scientific community, having held major posts in academia (president of Stanford University) and government (commissioner of the Food and Drug Administration), before becoming editor of *Science*, the AAAS's weekly journal. In the editorial, Dr. Kennedy remarked that calling OMB's proposed process peer review "seems strange to us here."[43]

Perhaps most notable reaction, however, was the harsh language used by Bruce Alberts, at the time president of NAS. As the nation's preeminent scientific organization, the NAS chooses its battles carefully and rarely joins the open opposition to major White House initiatives. Dr. Alberts described OMB's peer review model as "highly prescriptive," and warned Dr. Graham that "if enacted in its present form [the model] is likely to be counterproductive." It is possible that the NAS's response was prompted by concern that this new approach could require government-sponsored NAS

---

[41] American Association for the Advancement of Science, AAAS Resolution: On the OMB Proposed Peer Review Bulletin, American Association for the Advancement of Science, http://archives.aaas.org/docs/resolutions.php?doc_id=434.

[42] American Public Health Association, "Late Breaker Resolution: Threats to Public Health Science," American Public Health Association, http://www.apha.org/legislative/policy/2003/LB-03-01.pdf.

[43] Donald Kennedy, "Disclosure and Disinterest," *Science* 303, no. 5654 (2004): 15.

reports to undergo additional agency-administered peer review, a requirement that would undermine the NAS's position as the final authority on the interpretation of science.

From the tone of the comments by scientists at the meeting and subsequently, it seems that the proposal evoked an almost visceral response among scientists whose work is used by regulatory agencies. The White House was providing an opportunity for interests who are discomforted by the results of these scientists' studies to "stack the deck" in order to disparage or diminish the importance of their work. This concern was also evident in Dr. Kennedy's *Science* editorial, which expressed that the proposed system would contribute to the erosion of public trust in the work of scientists.[44]

In contrast, the proposal had the strong support of most of the major trade associations – the U.S. Chamber of Commerce, the National Association of Manufacturers, the American Chemistry Council – plus a host of minor ones (such as the California Avocado Commission, the Council of Industrial Boiler Owners, and the National Funeral Directors Association). Many of these groups wanted the proposal to go even further, eliminating any connection with traditional scientific peer review.[45]

These arguments seem to prove that the trade associations do not actually desire high-quality peer review (after all, NAS reports are peer-reviewed by some of the country's leading scientists), but rather seek to delay or prevent dissemination of information about which they disagree. Given this objective, it is logical that they should discard peer review in which journal editors, rather than the White House, select the peers.

Not all trade associations supported White House control of agency peer review systems. The comments filed by the drug industry suggest it is clearly comfortable (perhaps too comfortable) with its regulators at the FDA. Criticizing OMB with unusually direct language, the Pharmaceutical Research and Manufacturers of America asserted that the proposed requirements "would contribute little value and would add to the time and expense of a gatekeeper function that has historically been criticized for obstruction and delay."[46]

---

[44] Ibid.
[45] Office of Management and Budget. 2003 Public Comments on Peer Review. Available at http://www.whitehouse.gov/omb/inforeg/2003iq/iq_list.html. Access verified May 26, 2005.
[46] Comments on Proposed Bulletin on Peer Review and Information Quality from Erika King, Assistant General Counsel, Pharmaceutical Manufacturers of America, to Margo Schwab,

In a victory for the science community, the final version of the peer review requirements, issued in December 2004, was significantly modified to address several of the community's concerns. Perhaps the most significant revision involved the conflict-of-interest provisions, which now allow scientists who have grant funding from agencies to participate in peer review panels. OMB has also deferred to the NAS in several areas; NAS panel reports are now presumed not to require additional peer review, and OMB requires agencies to adopt the NAS policy for dealing with conflict of interest in the selection of nongovernment employee members of peer review committees.[47]

While other modifications make the peer review requirements somewhat less onerous for agencies (for example, the level that triggers the most cumbersome and time-consuming level of peer review was raised from $100 million to $500 million), the fundamental issue raised by scientists at the initial NAS workshop remained: OMB failed to establish the need for a single governmentwide peer review policy. The final bulletin provides little evidence with which to question the initial conclusion of many observers: that the new requirements are a poorly camouflaged attempt to introduce delays into already slow regulatory processes, and further hamper government activities aimed at protecting the public health and environment.[48]

## Conclusion

Over the last few decades, polluters and manufacturers of other dangerous materials have increasingly adopted the strategy of manufacturing uncertainty in the face of proposed government action. In virtually every instance in which a federal regulatory agency proposes protecting the public's health by reducing the allowable exposure to a toxic product, the

Office of Management and Budget, Office of Information and Regulatory Affairs (Dec. 15, 2003) (available at http://www.whitehouse.gov/omb/inforeg/2003iq/118.pdf).

[47] Memorandum from Joshua B. Bolten, Director, Office of Management and Budget, to the Heads of Executive Departments and Agencies, "Issuance of OMB's 'Final Information Quality Bulletin for Peer Review' (Dec. 16, 2004) (available at http://www.whitehouse.gov/omb/memoranda/fy2005/m05-03.pdf).

[48] OMB Watch, "OMB Watch Analysis on Final Peer Review Bulletin," OMB Watch, http://www.ombwatch.org/article/articleview/2594/1/232?TopicID=3.

regulated industry hires scientists to dispute the science on which the proposal is based.[49]

New mandates for peer review in regulatory science appear to be an additional component in the strategy that enables producers of hazardous products and pollution to delay formal regulation, and avoid compensating their victims. While independent review by impartial experts may help improve the quality of regulatory science, the improvident imposition of ill-fitting peer review structures and approaches might needlessly impede the work of government agencies and delay programs needed to protect the public's health and environment. In contrast to refereeing and program evaluation, regulatory peer review is invoked not to assist in the allocation of scarce resources but primarily as a procedural mechanism to control information dissemination. As a result, it seems likely that the newly implemented federal peer review requirements, while less onerous than those originally proposed, will provide new and convenient opportunities for special interests to promote an antiregulatory agenda.

[49] David Michaels, "Doubt Is Their Product," *Scientific American* 292, no. 6 (2005): 96–101; David Michaels and Celeste Monforton, "Manufacturing Uncertainty: Contested Science and the Protection of the Public's Health and Environment," *American Journal of Public Health* (forthcoming).

# Politicizing Peer Review: The Legal Perspective

Sidney Shapiro, J.D.

## The Role of Peer Review in the Crusade for "Sound" Science

Because the public at large strongly supports a prominent government role in protecting health and safety, opponents of regulation have tried to put a more acceptable face on their efforts by cloaking their opposition as a demand for "sound science." As professors Thomas McGarity and Donald Hornstein have explained in Chapters 1 and 5 of this book, rather than dispute the public policies behind protective regulation of people and the environment, the "sound-science" campaign attempts to convince the public that strong regulation lacks an acceptable scientific rationale. This approach gives regulatory opponents the advantage of casting themselves as favoring regulatory protection in general, but allows them to combat specific regulations on the grounds that such measures are based on poor – or "junk" – science.

The "sound-science" campaign seeks to blur the crucial distinction between incomplete data and poor-quality data. For example, an excellent study of the adverse health effects caused by heightened blood lead levels can be incomplete with respect to the hazards of heightened levels of lead in the air if the rates of transfer between airborne lead and blood lead are poorly understood. Regulatory opponents seek to convince the public that the absence of knowledge about air-to-blood transfer rates means that the scientific evidence about the hazards of lead to human health is of poor quality.

Since the 1970s, however, regulatory legislation has committed the country to protect the public and the environment based on the best available evidence.[1] In other words, Congress authorized regulators to act on basis of incomplete but reliable scientific information. In fact, one of the most successful protective actions ever taken was EPA's 1973 decision to phase out the lead content in gasoline, despite our incomplete understanding of air-to-blood transfer rates.

Despite their sound-science rhetoric, regulated entities and other regulatory critics oppose the preventive tilt of existing legislation. They prefer that the government wait until it obtains more evidence concerning potential risks before acting. While this argument may be plausible from a policy perspective, it has nothing to do with the quality or completeness of science.

Moreover, there is little or no evidence that agency regulations are actually based on poor science. In seeking to justify the peer review requirements described by Professor David Michaels in Chapter 10, the Office of Management and Budget (OMB) offered no evidence of regulations that had been based on "poor science." Indeed, if the claims of the sound-science campaign were true, the courts would have remanded the regulations because the promulgating agency had failed to respond adequately to comments filed by regulatory opponents pointing out the errors in the agency's scientific analysis. As Professor Wendy Wagner observes concerning EPA:

> After more than thirty years of vigorous public health and safety regulation, it seems almost inevitable that an agency would have relied upon a scientific study that ultimately proved unreliable. Yet, despite the thousands of public health and safety regulations promulgated annually, there are surprisingly few examples of EPA using unreliable science or using science inappropriately to support a final regulation . . . , virtually all of which are contested.[2]

The overuse of independent peer review supports the sound-science campaign in several ways. It suggests that existing efforts to vet science are insufficient, and that agency scientists are incompetent to give sound advice to administrators about the quality of the scientific information

[1]  Sidney A. Shapiro and Robert L. Glicksman, *Risk Regulation at Risk: Restoring a Pragmatic Approach* (Stanford, CA: Stanford University Press, 2003), 33–5.

[2]  Wendy E. Wagner, "The 'Bad Science' Fiction: Reclaiming the Debate over the Role of Science in Public Health and Environmental Regulation," *Law and Contemporary Problems* 66, no. 4 (2003): 63.

available to an agency. In turn, both of these inferences support a further inference that prior regulations were based on poor science, which is the sine qua non of the sound-science campaign.

This chapter provides a legal perspective on the use of peer review to politicize science and delay regulation for reasons that have very little to do with legitimate concerns about scientific quality. It explains why the recent OMB proposal was misguided, given the elaborate checks and balances on excessive regulation already incorporated by law in the regulatory process. In light of these protections, the chapter suggests the appropriate role and possible limitations on peer review and proposes legal reforms that would prevent its systematic abuse by opponents of regulation.

## The Downsides of Regulatory Peer Review

As Professor Michaels has explained, the OMB guidelines, as proposed – and, to a certain extent, as promulgated – require regulatory agencies to have independent scientists conduct peer review of most of the scientific information used or disseminated by the government.[3] The requirement of independent peer review applies both to scientific information that the government uses to justify regulation and information that is the basis of government reports and websites. As Professor Michaels also noted, the idea that government should obtain such peer review may appear to be an appropriate reform. After all, peer review has long been an important element in the development and verification of information in science. Professor Michaels has explained the distinctions between how peer review is used and implemented in the scientific and regulatory arenas, and questions its utility in improving the performance of scientific research. An analysis of the law's approach to regulatory decision making leads to a similar conclusion: Peer review is a blunt and often destructive instrument for improving regulation and is redundant of existing legal procedures that ensure the wisdom of such policy making.

### Redundancy

As administrative law should teach us, a procedure may assist the government in making a more accurate or fair decision, but it also delays the

---

[3]  Final Information Quality Bulletin for Peer Review, 70 Fed. Reg. 2664 (Jan. 14, 2005).

government from fulfilling its affirmative responsibility to protect people and the environment. As a result, the potential benefits of such a procedure – "fairness and accuracy" – need to be balanced against the "efficient disposition of agency business."[4] The use of peer review in science does not pose a similar trade-off because, if properly practiced, it does not delay or obstruct the continuation of valuable research.

Scientific researchers "on the whole, work within established scientific paradigms, subject to relatively well-negotiated prior understandings about what constitutes good research methodology," while regulatory science "is more often done at the margins of existing knowledge," where science and policy are difficult to distinguish and claims are backed by "few, if any facts" that cannot be contested or deconstructed.[5] Consequently, the interpretation of scientific information concerning human and environmental risks often requires making assumptions that have significant policy ramifications. This aspect of such evaluations creates a greater potential for politically motivated outcomes in regulatory science than in academic science.

According to the OMB directive, agencies must seek peer review of scientific information whenever the dissemination of such information "will have or does have a clear and substantial impact on public policies or private sector decisions."[6] Thus, just as an editor uses peer review to determine whether to publish a particular paper, OMB requires an agency administrator to use peer review to evaluate whether the agency should rely on scientific information in its possession. In fact, OMB cited the widespread use of peer review in the scientific community to justify this broad requirement.[7]

The use of peer review in the scientific context, however, does not justify the OMB requirement. In the publication context, peer review constitutes the primary means of vetting research that has been submitted for publication. In the regulatory context, the government has two other effective

---

[4] Roger C. Cramton, "A Comment on Trial-Type Hearings in Nuclear Power Plant Siting," *Virginia Law Review* 58, no. 4 (1972): 592.
[5] Shelia Jasanoff, *The Fifth Branch: Science Advisers as Policymakers* (Cambridge, MA: Harvard University Press, 1970), 79.
[6] Final Information Quality Bulletin for Peer Review, 2675.
[7] Proposed Bulletin on Peer Review and Information Quality, 68 Fed. Reg. 54,023, 54, 024 (Sept. 15, 2003).

methods for evaluating the scientific information before it: rule making and consultation of the government's own scientists. Unless these other means of review are somehow deficient, it is difficult to justify the time and expense that consultation of independent scientists entails.

The consultation of nongovernment scientists is unnecessary whenever government scientists are available to screen the information and the public can point out potential problems with the information in a rule-making process. In such instances, requiring peer review by independent scientists adds little to the regulatory process and imposes costs and delays that are not justified.

Further, well-established principles of administrative law require that before an agency can promulgate a regulation, it must utilize a notice and comment procedure that invites members of the public to comment on the merits of the proposal.[8] Since the lawyers for regulated entities have considerable experience and expertise in using the opportunity to comment to attack the science used by an agency, it is almost inconceivable that a regulatory agency would be unaware of weaknesses in the scientific evidence on which it is relying. To the extent that commentators have persuasive objections about the evidence, agencies know that they risk a judicial remand if they do not change a proposed regulation in light of valid objections. A court will remand a regulation to an agency if the agency has not responded adequately to such rule-making comments.[9]

The dissemination of scientific information can occur outside of the rule-making process, but peer review by independent scientists may not be necessary in this context either. An agency can rely on its own scientists to determine the validity of scientific information. Scientists on the staff of regulatory agencies provide an independent evaluation of research produced by outside scientists in the contexts of reports distributed on the Internet and decisions made during the rule-making process.

## Ossification

When OMB was developing its peer review guidelines, a number of organizations opposed the type of across-the-board peer review requirement that

---

[8] Administrative Procedure Act, 5 U.S.C. § 554 (2005).
[9] Alfred C. Aman, Jr., and William T. Mayton, *Administrative Law* (St. Paul, MN: West Group, 2nd ed. 2001), 54.

OMB eventually adopted. They instead recommended that peer review be reserved for novel, complex, or precedent-setting scientific issues. The commentators stressed that the routine use of peer review would likely add time and expense to the regulatory process without offsetting benefits. The American Bar Association, for example, told OMB, "Peer review is simply not the correction mechanism to address the significant use of routine, established, or accepted scientific information."[10]

Rather than limit the scope of its peer review requirements, OMB permitted agencies to choose less burdensome forms of peer review for routine types of scientific information as appropriate. OMB, for example, authorized agencies to obtain peer review by soliciting letters from outside experts where this method is sufficient to obtain the necessary peer review. Even minimal procedures, however, start to add cost and delay, particularly when they must be used over and over. In light of the tight budget situation in agencies, a universal peer review requirement will inevitably divert agencies from doing other things. Moreover, the rule-making process already proceeds at a glacial pace, with complicated regulations taking three to seven or eight years or more.[11] In fact, the rule-making process already takes so long that the literature routinely describes it as being "ossified."[12] Additional peer review, obviously, will further slow this process.

## The Upsides of Regulatory Peer Review

What, then, are the justifications for independent peer review in a regulatory context? Proponents of independent peer review cite three reasons for it. First, the rule-making process has defects that justify the use of peer review. Second, seeking the advice of nongovernmental scientists permits agencies to gain expertise that may be lacking in an agency. Finally, if an agency follows the advice of peer reviewers, peer review helps to support the legitimacy of the agency actions in the eyes of the White House, Congress,

---

[10] Letter from William Funk, American Bar Association, to Dr. Margaret Schwab, Office of Information and Regulatory Affairs 2 (Dec. 23, 2003).

[11] Thomas O. McGarity, "Some Thoughts on 'Deossifying' the Rulemaking Process," *Duke Law Journal* 41, no. 6 (1992): 1387–90.

[12] William S. Jordan, III, "Ossification Revisited: Does Arbitrary and Capricious Review Significantly Interfere with Agency Ability to Achieve Regulatory Goals through Informal Rulemaking?" *Northwestern Law Review* 94, no. 2 (2000): 393.

the courts, and the public. All of these justifications have merit, but as the following analysis reveals, they do not justify the use of peer review every time the government uses scientific information for any significant purpose.

## Rule-Making Limitations

Although rule making normally subjects an agency's scientific information to careful scrutiny by interested parties, agencies receive adversarial, not neutral, scientific input. Sophisticated parties will consult scientists when they comment on proposed rules, but this scientific input is filtered through the lawyers representing those parties. Scientists who are not in the employ of regulated entities or interest groups are unlikely to file comments as individuals.

Rule making has other limitations as well. Whereas regulated entities typically can afford to hire scientists to assist them in writing their comments, public interest groups, such as environmentalists and consumer advocates, may lack the resources to obtain similar scientific input. This disparity in resources means that the rule-making process may be dominated by industry comments, resulting in a one-sided attack on the agency's science.

In addition, it is more efficient for an agency to receive scientific input about the limitations of its evidence earlier in the process of the development of a rule. If there really are infirmities in the scientific evidence, an agency ideally would know about these defects before writing a proposed regulation. These arguments might justify a broad requirement of peer review, except for the fact that agencies have their own scientists. Since agencies can consult in-house experts, independent peer review is justified only if reliance on the agency's scientists is somehow inadequate to ensure the proper use of scientific information.

## Expertise

Reliance on agency scientists may be inadequate in two situations. First, the agency's scientists may be the source of the information that the agency is using, as for example when an agency makes a risk assessment that is based on the weight of the scientific evidence before it. Second, the agency's scientists may not have sufficient expertise to evaluate the work of other scientists.

When agency scientists have created the scientific information under review, an administrator has two ways in which to vet the information. A notice and comment process, despite its limitations, may be entirely sufficient to vet the work product of agency scientists if the work is within their expertise. Put another way, rule making may be adequate to vet such work unless it involves complex or unusual issues. An administrator can also seek public comment on information that will be used in a report or put on a website. Alternatively, the administrator can enlist independent scientists to undertake a peer review of the information.

The strongest potential justification for independent review is that an agency might benefit from additional scientific expertise. If agency scientists review information produced by other scientists, additional peer review appears unnecessary unless they do not have the level of scientific expertise necessary to evaluate the scientific information before the agency. Similarly, the agency may not wish to rely solely on a notice and comment process to vet scientific information produced by its own staff if their assessment involves issues that are sufficiently complicated or unusual that "catch-as-catch-can" notice and comment may be insufficient to help the agency understand and appreciate potential problems with the data.

## Legitimacy

A second justification for outside peer review is that it can add legitimacy to the agency's decision-making process. After peer review, agency administrators can cite the support of peer reviewers in justifying their reliance on the scientific information that they used. As noted earlier, however, there is an important trade-off between efficient disposition of agency business and the use of additional procedures to promote accuracy. This possible advantage raises the issue of whether it is advisable to have an across-the-board peer review.

The need for legitimacy is greatest when the government relies on scientific information that raises novel, complex, or precedent-setting issues. In such cases, the additional review should make the outcome more legitimate for both regulatory supporters and opponents. Although peer review will delay government action, the delay is justified because additional scientific review will likely lead to a more accurate evaluation of the scientific evidence. Moreover, the additional review should satisfy regulatory opponents that the government has made as accurate an evaluation of the scientific evidence as is possible.

This analysis suggests that the legitimacy justification for peer review is strongest when reliance on agency scientists and rule making may not provide an agency with sufficient assistance in evaluating scientific evidence. The justification therefore adds nothing to the prior reasons for peer review. The government should seek the advice of independent scientists when it is necessary because of the nature of the issues before the agency. This was the role for peer review before the OMB guidelines, and this is what OMB changed when it ordered agencies to engage in across-the-board peer review.

## The Politics of Peer Review

Agencies have scientists who can conduct their own peer review of scientific information originated by other scientists, and scientific information is subject to vetting in the rule-making process. The use of independent peer review is indicated when an agency is confronting novel, complex, or precedent-setting scientific issues, but it is difficult to justify when the agency seeks to resolve routine scientific issues because of the cost and delay involved. Since, however, the overuse of peer review slows down and complicates the regulatory process, it serves the political interests of opponents of government regulation. The overuse of peer review has another advantage for these interest groups: It reinforces their "sound-science" campaign.

The potential for overuse is not the only problem that arises concerning peer review in government regulation. Most agency officials understand that scientific advisors are only competent to address the purely scientific questions. But as long as the policy aspect of evaluating scientific information is not immediately apparent to the public, officials can use peer review as a shield from criticism for policy choices by maintaining that the decision was made in accordance with the neutral advice of independent scientists.[13] As Professor Holly Doremus explains in Chapter 7 of this book, scientists have their own reasons for going along with this "science

---

[13] Thomas O. McGarity and Sidney A. Shapiro, *Workers at Risk: The Failed Promise of the Occupational Safety and Health Administration* (Westport, CT: Praeger, 1993), 196.

charade,"[14] including the ability to influence policy decisions and protect their hegemony over scientific issues that are intertwined with policy issues.[15] Ultimately, the science charade harms the legitimacy of regulation by misleading members of the public, discouraging them from commenting on the policy issues, wasting scientific resources, and slowing the regulatory process.[16]

Besides hiding the policy components of a regulatory issue, regulatory officials may also seek to influence the outcome of peer review.[17] They can normally accomplish this persuasion by choosing scientific advisors whose past actions indicate that they will generally resolve mixed questions of science and policy in accordance with the administrator's preference. An administrator may take this action because he or she is acting at the behest of powerful political interest groups, because the person has a strong policy or ideological interest in the outcome, or both. Whatever the motivation, the administrator is better off if the public believes that the government was simply following the advice of independent scientists.

The potential for biased advice exists even if agency administrators do not seek to stack a committee to obtain a preordained result. Unless an agency carefully screens potential advisors for conflicts of interest, it can end up choosing persons who have a financial stake in the outcome of the regulatory issue being resolved. Furthermore, unless the agency solicits a range of viewpoints concerning issues about which reasonable scientists hold different positions, the agency may receive advice that is biased toward a particular outcome.

The antidote to all these unfortunate outcomes is to make the peer review process as transparent as possible. The ability of outside watchdog groups to probe the selection and mission of independent peer review panels is the best insurance that against their manipulation by special interests.

## The Value of Transparency

The Federal Advisory Committee Act (FACA)[18] is the primary law addressing the previous concerns. FACA was designed to make the wide range

---

[14] Wendy E. Wagner, "The Science Charade in Toxic Risk Regulation," *Columbia Law Review* 95, no. 7 (1995): 1613.

[15] Ibid., 1672–3.

[16] Ibid., 1719.

[17] McGarity and Shapiro, 196.

[18] Pub. L. No. 92–463, 86 Stat. 770 (1988) (codified at 5 U.S.C. app. II).

of opportunities for the government to obtain advice from outside experts operate in public by specifying that agencies not only announce their intent to appoint such panels but ensure that they are balanced across the interests that will be affected by the decisions under review. Unfortunately, court decisions and administrative practice have created a situation where it is relatively easy for agencies to create a peer review system that is not subject to FACA or to limit the disclosures the law requires even where it does apply. Congress should therefore amend FACA to ensure that it applies whenever an agency consults independent scientists and to ensure that agencies are subject to appropriate procedures.

## The Law's Intent

Congress passed FACA "in large part to promote good-government values such as openness, accountability, and balance of viewpoints."[19] The legislation seeks to accomplish these goals in two ways. First, it mandates open government. Agencies must keep minutes of peer review meetings, permit interested persons to attend meetings, allow them to appear before the committee or file statements, and make available to the public any records or documents made available to the committee. An agency, however, can withhold documents if they fall within one of the exceptions for public disclosure under the Freedom of Information Act (FOIA),[20] and it can close a meeting if it determines that one of the exceptions to the Sunshine Act applies,[21] but these exceptions apply only in narrow circumstances. Second, it requires agencies to seek diverse scientific viewpoints in order to minimize the potential for bias. According to regulations interpreting FACA, agencies must ensure that their advisory committees are "fairly balanced in [their] membership in terms of the points of view represented and the functions to be performed."[22]

---

[19]  Steven P. Croley, "Practical Guidance on the Applicability of the Federal Advisory Committee Act," *Administrative Law Journal of American University* 10, no. (1996): 111, 117.

[20]  5 U.S.C. app. II §10.

[21]  5 U.S.C. app. II §10(d).

[22]  41 C.F.R. §§ 102–3.30(c) (2003). The obligation of fair balance arises under §5(c) of FACA, although the requirement is somewhat convoluted. For an explanation, see Steven P. Croley and William F. Funk, "The Federal Advisory Committee Act and Good Government," *Yale Journal on Regulation* 14, no. 2 (1997): 451, 507.

## The Law's Limitations

Although FACA promotes good government values, it does not apply to two prominent forms of peer review. It does not apply when an agency consults with individuals who do not meet as a group, and it does not apply when an agency hires a private contractor to organize and conduct the peer review. Neither of these exceptions is justified.

According to the statutory language, FACA applies whenever there is a "committee, penal task force or similar group" that is "established or utilized" by an agency "in the interest of obtaining advice or recommendations" from persons outside of the federal government.[23] Congress assigned to the General Accounting Office (now the Government Accountability Office, or GAO) the responsibility to interpret this language, and a GAO regulation excludes instances where agencies consult individual scientists, because the consultation of individuals who do not meet as a group does not "establish" an advisory "committee."[24] Since the potential for misuse and abuse of the peer review process is not limited to advisory committees, an exception for individual consultation does not make sense.

Congress should also consider restricting the use of individual peer review. Under the current OMB procedures, agencies will favor individual consultations because they are easier to do and OMB requires peer review of most scientific information. If, however, independent peer review is used only for novel, complex, or precedent-setting issues, as recommended earlier, it is more feasible for Congress to require an agency to appoint a peer review committee. The advantage of requiring a committee is that members can challenge each other's evaluations and benefit from their mutual deliberations, which can make the meetings a "powerful shield against favoritism and animus."[25]

A second limitation on FACA's effectiveness was read into the statute by the courts. Although FACA applies whenever an agency "establishes" or "utilizes" an advisory panel of persons outside of the government, the courts have defined the words "establish" and "utilize" in a way that creates this loophole. According to the Supreme Court, an agency "establishes" an

---

[23]  5 U.S.C. app. II §3.
[24]  41 C.F.R. §§ 102–3.40(e) (2003).
[25]  Thomas O. McGarity, "Peer Review in Awarding Federal Grants in the Arts and Sciences," *High Technology Law Journal* 9, no. 1 (1994): 1, 64.

advisory panel only if it actually forms the panel, and an agency "utilizes" an advisory panel only if it is "so closely tied to an agency as to be amendable to 'strict management' by agency officials."[26] As interpreted by the appellate courts, an agency does not satisfy these tests even if it participates with the private contractor in forming the panel or if it has "significant influence" over the panel once it is formed.[27]

The Supreme Court justified its narrow interpretation of the word "utilize" on the ground that Congress could not have meant to "cover every formal and informal consultation between the President or an Executive agency and a group rendering advice."[28] There is an important difference, however, between the government seeking informal advice from an organization and officially hiring that organization to organize and implement a peer review process for the government. In the latter case, the government is making the group an official part of the government's deliberations. Thus, the input of the group has greater weight and legitimacy than it would have if the contacts were strictly informal.

Congress recognized the previous distinction when it amended FACA to apply to the National Academy of Sciences (NAS) and to the National Academy of Public Administration (NAPA) when they undertake peer review for the government. NAS and NAPA are subject to "open government" and "fair balance" provisions that are very similar to those that apply to agencies whenever either group "creates" an advisory committee "under an agreement with an agency."[29]

Congress should amend FACA to clarify that it applies to the consultation of individual scientific advisors and to private contractors who the government hires to organize and conduct a peer review. In addition to closing these loopholes, Congress should solve a second problem with FACA. One of the difficulties with the law is that an agency must seek a charter for each individual advisory committee that it forms.[30] Congress should eliminate this time-consuming process and make it easier for agencies to form advisory committees under FACA. These changes would ensure that the application of FACA to private contractors does not bog down the agency in paperwork.

[26] *Public Citizen v. Department of Justice*, 491 U.S. 440, 452, 456–8 (1989).
[27] *Washington Legal Found. v. U.S. Sentencing Comm'n*, 17 F.3d 1446, 1451 (D.C. Cir. 1994).
[28] 491 U.S. at 453.
[29] 5 U.S.C. app. II §15.
[30] 5 U.S.C. app. II §9(a)(1); Croley and Funk, 493–5.

## Inappropriate Anonymity

As noted, FACA requires, with some narrow exceptions, that advisory committees meet in public, make all of the information that the committee reviews available to the public, and permit members of the public to make presentations or submit statements to the committee. By comparison, the peer review process used by journal editors to review proposed submissions is conducted in secret, protecting both the identity of the scientist and peer reviewer. Moreover, some proponents of peer review argue that confidentiality is important to ensure a completely candid and useful exchange of views among the peer reviewers and between them and an agency. Neither the practice in science nor the need for candor, however, justifies keeping the peer review process secret.

As noted earlier, regulatory science is more susceptible to politicization. The public normally has a greater interest, and arguably a greater stake, in an agency's decision to promulgate a protective regulation or publish information about risks to people and the environment than in the gradual accumulation of scientific knowledge. In light of these two reasons, peer review should follow public policy process norms, not scientific process norms. Finally, it is likely that many members of the public will distrust a peer review process that operates behind a veil of secrecy. As Professor McGarity notes, "Open meetings allow outsiders to observe any overt bias in the decisionmaking process."[31] If one of the goals of using independent peer review is to increase public confidence in the information that the government uses and disseminates, closing the peer review meetings and hiding peer review documents will not serve this purpose.

The need for candor does not justify a secret peer review process either. EPA and the Food and Drug Administration (FDA) have a long-established and successful history of using peer review while complying with the open government provisions of FACA. In addition, the previous justifications for an open process seem to outweigh by far the disadvantage of any loss in candor. Finally, it is worth noting that the argument that secrecy is necessary for candor has been rejected by the courts as a common law privilege and as a First Amendment defense to an Equal Employment

---

[31] McGarity, "Peer Review," 64.

Opportunity Commission subpoena seeking tenure review materials by outside evaluators.[32]

While transparency is an important antidote to politicized peer review, even the most ideal approach to FACA would still leave the problem of panels that include scientists with conflicts of interest. To overcome this aspect of the politicization of peer review, normative rules are necessary.

## Eliminating Conflicts of Interest

The open government provisions of FACA permit the public to hold an agency more accountable for its use of peer review. The issue of accountability is important because of the potential for bias in the peer review process. Financial conflicts of interest are one potential source of such bias. Financial conflicts do not occur when agencies consult their own scientists because a criminal statute prohibits government employees from participating personally and substantially in any official capacity concerning any decision in which they have a financial interest.[33]

Under existing law, a person has prohibited financial interest "if there is a close causal link between any decision or action to be taken in the matter and any expected effect of the matter on the financial interest."[34] If an agency empanels an advisory committee under FACA, its members normally serve as special federal government employees, who are subject to the same prohibitions. These prohibitions, however, do not apply when agencies are not subject to FACA or when they do not hire peer reviewers as special government employees, providing yet another justification for strengthening FACA.

Federal law permits waiver of the financial conflict-of-interest rules in certain circumstances. Thus, a person can serve on an advisory committee that is subject to FACA if "the need for the individual's services outweighs the potential for a conflict of interest created by the financial interest involved."[35] There is no legal requirement, however, that the government give prompt public notice of such waivers. By comparison, Congress has required NAS and NAPA to give such notice when these organizations

---

[32] *University of Pennsylvania v. Equal Employment Opportunity Comm'n*, 493 U.S. 182 (1990).
[33] 18 U.S.C. § 209(a); 5 C.F.R. § 2625 (regulations implementing 18 U.S.C. § 209).
[34] 5 U.S.C. § 2625.402(b)(1).
[35] 18 U.S.C. § 208(b)(3).

undertake peer review under an agreement with the government. FACA permits these two organizations to waive an "unavoidable" conflict of interest, but the wavier must be "promptly and publicly disclosed."[36]

To permit effective monitoring of waivers, Congress should amend FACA to require agencies to disclose to the public the existence of a waiver, and explain the nature of the conflict of interest and the grounds for the waiver. This information should be available to the public at the time the waiver is made, as Congress has already required for NAS and NAPA.

## Balancing Bias

Besides a financial conflict of interest, a reviewer's bias may color the advice an agency receives. If an agency fails to seek a range of viewpoints among the scientists it consults, the advice that it receives may be skewed toward only one point of view. Moreover, unless an agency is required to seek a range of viewpoints, it may only seek one point of view in order to ensure that the advice it receives is consistent with its preferred outcome.

When FACA applies, an agency must ensure that an advisory committee is "fairly balanced . . . in terms of the points of view represented and the functions to be performed."[37] When FACA does not apply, agencies are free of this statutory requirement. Since, however, these exempt forms of peer review are subject to the same potential threat of bias, the balance requirement should apply to all forms of outside peer review.

The public must have some way to monitor how agencies implement the balance requirement in order to ensure that it is not honored in the breach. Congress should therefore require agencies to disclose the historical affiliations of peer reviewers (both agency- and industry-related) and the sources of funding that a scientist has received. As the GAO has observed, this approach gives the public information that can be used to evaluate the legitimacy of the advice being received because it indicates the degree of balance that the agency has obtained in its appointment of peer reviewers.[38]

---

[36] 5 U.S.C. app. II § 15(b)(1)(A).
[37] 41 C.F.R. §§ 102–3.30(c) (2003).
[38] U.S. General Accounting Office, *EPA's Science Advisory Board Panels: Improved Policies and Procedures Needed to Ensure Independence and Balance* (Washington, DC: Government Printing Office, 2001).

Requiring such disclosures might run afoul of protections provided to government consultants under the Privacy Act, but that Act permits individuals to waive any privacy protections that they might have.[39] Given the high potential for bias to infect peer review, it is entirely reasonable for an agency to require such waivers as a condition of serving as a peer reviewer. As the GAO recommended, Congress should require an agency to gather this information at the beginning of the peer review process when the agency can use the information to ensure that peer review is a balanced process. Finally, Congress must require an agency to disclose the information at the same time it is obtained to give the pubic an opportunity to object to the makeup of a committee if anyone so chooses.

## Conclusion

Because the government can rely on its own scientists and on rule-making participants to evaluate scientific information, the routine use of independent peer review is difficult to justify in light of the costs and delays that it involves. Interest groups concerned about regulatory decisions have ample opportunity to provide extensive comments on the science underlying a regulatory decision, and the courts provide an additional check on agency decisions that are not based on the best available science. The government can benefit from consultation with independent scientists when its other methods of vetting scientific information are inadequate to ensure proper evaluation of such information. When peer review is justified, it is important that the government be accountable for its use.

While peer review can assist the government in the resolution of complex, novel, or precedent-setting scientific issues, there is also a potential that peer review will be misused or abused. Administrators may refer inappropriate issues to a peer review committee or fail to screen potential advisors adequately for conflicts of interest or bias. From a legal perspective, the best antidote to this politicization is to strengthen FACA so that it provides more complete and adequate deterrence for these potential problems.

[39]  5 U.S.C. § 552a(b

# The Government Role in Scientific Research: Who Should Bridge the Data Gap in Chemical Regulation?

John S. Applegate, J.D.[1]

## Incentives and Disincentives

Regulation demands information, and regulatory systems create, deliberately or not, incentives and disincentives for generating the information they need. Effective regulatory systems are deliberately structured either to generate the information that they require or to require only the information that they can reliably generate. In this respect at least, federal environmental law and regulatory policy in the United States have failed spectacularly; it is universally acknowledged that, as the principles proposed in this book put it, "there are yawning gaps in the science available for regulation." Toxic chemicals, both those that are products and those that have become waste, pose particularly challenging regulatory problems, because much of the necessary information is complex, uncertain, and expensive to obtain. Ultimately, we cannot afford gross disparities between the demand for information and the supply of information that is generated by the marketplace and the existing regulatory system.

Most observers of chemical regulation (this author included) have concentrated on finding ways to encourage or to require industry to generate scientific information about toxic chemicals. There are, however, good reasons to think that a strong governmental role in generating chemical information is necessary to fill data gaps and to provide complete and unbiased research. Our principles incorporate that view, positing that government support of research is essential to produce discoveries that benefit the public good, especially because the scientists capable of producing the necessary

[1] I thank Dave Campbell and Joice Chang for research assistance.

data often cannot find private sector support for such research. Generous public funding of research is therefore an essential prerequisite for advancements in scientific knowledge. Of course, all research produced or used by the government should be subject to basic quality assurance/quality control checks, especially if that research is not published or disseminated widely within the scientific community.

This chapter provides a framework for deciding whether government or industry should generate the information necessary to produce effective chemical regulation. ("Government" and "industry" are, admittedly, simplifications, and their respective incentive structures are more complex than portrayed herein.) The chapter begins with a description of the chemical information problem and an analysis of its causes. It then considers the respective roles of industry and government in generating chemical information, and it recommends a general presumption in favor of industry. It discusses when government research is preferable to private sector research, and it concludes with a brief discussion of implementation issues.

## The Demand Side of Regulatory Information

### The Transcendence of Risk Assessment

It is neither accidental nor inevitable that information is such a serious problem for chemical regulation. As it has developed in the United States, the regulatory system for toxic chemicals and wastes requires an enormous amount of information, because regulators are constantly exhorted to base such requirements on the apparently precise (or "fine-tuned"[2]) measurement of risk, and in particular risk to human health. While the basic risk equation is simple – toxicity multiplied by exposure equals risk – its components are complex phenomena, and their precise measurement requires detailed knowledge of a chemical's biological effects, pathways through the environment, and routes of exposure to target species and organs.

The primacy of risk-based regulation results from the confluence of two trends that are in some tension with each other: a statutory commitment to preventive regulation and a demand for precise, quantitative justification of

[2] Howard Latin, "Ideal Versus Real Regulatory Efficiency: Implementation of Uniform Standards and 'Fine-Tuning' Regulatory Reforms," *Stanford Law Review* 37, no. 5 (1985): 1267.

regulatory actions that affect large segments of American industry.[3] The tort system (that is, private lawsuits to recover damages for personal injuries), which is the original, preregulatory way of handling harm from chemicals, fails to provide adequate environmental protection because its standard of individualized proof of causation is difficult or impossible to meet in cases of chemical exposure. Further, the tort system only compensates harm that has already occurred, and it does not prevent exposures. To remedy these limitations, preventive regulation controls chemical substances on the basis of predictions of the likelihood and severity of future harm or, in other words, on the basis of predicted risk.

Despite these precautionary goals, American chemical regulation consistently places the burden of proof on the government to demonstrate the existence and scale of the chemical's risk. Under most environmental statutes, before moving to restrict a chemical, a regulatory agency must be prepared to put forward a thoroughly documented, technically detailed, and quantitative case that governmental intervention is necessary to protect public health and the environment. Regulated industries give an obligatory nod in the direction of the uncertainties that inevitably attend preventive regulation. But regulators have a difficult time getting rules out of agencies over intense industry opposition, surviving review by a hostile Office of Management and Budget (OMB), and winning approval from skeptical courts. To make the required showing, agencies like the Environmental Protection Agency (EPA) turn to quantitative risk assessment to justify their decisions. Science and the apparent objectivity of quantified values have a cultural power ("allure," in Donald Hornstein's phrase[4]) that provides the agency with political cover for costly regulatory measures.

## The Size and Scope of the Regulatory Data Gap

In 1984, the National Academy of Sciences took a systematic look at the available data for toxicity testing, and found that only a very small minority of chemicals had adequate data even for the basic evaluation of acute and

[3] John S. Applegate, "Introduction," in *The International Library of Essays in Environmental Law: Environmental Risk*, ed. John S. Applegate (Aldershot, UK: Ashgate, 2004), xiii.
[4] Donald T. Hornstein, "Reclaiming Environmental Law: A Normative Critique of Comparative Risk Analysis," *Columbia Law Review* 92, no. 3 (1992): 562.

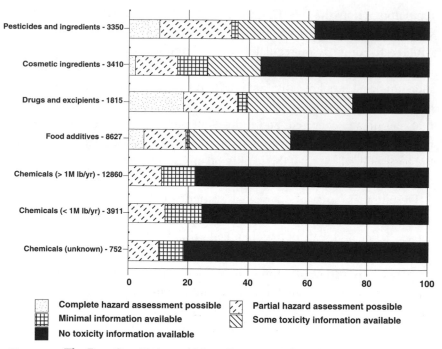

Figure 12.1. The Data Gap (Estimated Mean Percent in Selected Universe)

chronic hazards.[5] As the chart in Figure 12.1 shows, the data gap is pervasive across all categories of chemicals, but it is ameliorated in areas (drugs and pesticides) where industry bears the burden of demonstrating that its products are "safe" or at the very least will not present an unreasonable risk to public health or the environment.

More recent studies show that the situation is no better now than it was twenty years ago. EPA recently summed up the situation for high production volume (HPV) chemicals, the ones that ought to be *most* likely to have information generated about them: "Although HPV chemicals are produced or imported in large quantities in the United States, there is little or no publicly available information regarding the potential hazards associated with most HPV chemicals."[6] Environmental Defense (formerly

[5] National Research Council, *Toxicity Testing: Strategies to Determine Needs and Priorities* (Washington, DC: National Academy Press, 1984), 205.
[6] Data Collection and Development on High Production Volume (HPV) Chemicals, 65 Fed. Reg. 81686 (Dec. 26, 2000).

known as the Environmental Defense Fund) found that 70 percent of HPV chemicals lacked publicly available information to support a basic hazard assessment,[7] and a follow-up study by the chemical industry itself found a much lower but still significant number.[8] This yawning data gap is the dominant factor in any effort to improve chemical regulation.

## The Precautionary Principle and the Downsides of Precision

The obvious conclusion that we need to close or, more realistically, to bridge this data gap must be qualified in one important way: There is no inherent reason that we should value precision or pinpoint accuracy in the regulation of public health and the environment. Imposing such a stringent burden of proof on regulators is fruitless from a scientific perspective and inconsistent with the spirit and the letter of precautionary principle, as embodied in domestic and international environmental laws.

### Scientific Uncertainty

Measuring with precision the amount of a chemical that is likely to reach a person or organism and then determining with precision the long-term, low-dose health effects of such exposure are extraordinarily challenging undertakings.[9] Precise measurement of the first half of the risk equation

---

[7]  David Roe et al., *Toxic Ignorance: The Continuing Absence of Basic Health Testing for Top-Selling Chemicals in the United States.* Environmental Defense Fund, 1997 (available at http://www.environmentaldefense.org/documents/243_toxicignorance.pdf).

[8]  David Roe, "Toxic Chemical Control Policy: Three Unabsorbed Facts," *Environmental Law Reporter* 32, no. 2 (2002): 10232 (citing Chemical Manufacturers Association, *Public Availability of SIDS [Screening Information Data Set]-Related Testing Data for U.S. High Production Volume Chemicals* [1998]).

[9]  The process is authoritatively described in National Research Council, *Science and Judgment in Risk Assessment* (Washington, DC: National Academy Press, 1994); National Research Council, *Risk Assessment in the Federal Government: Managing the Process* (Washington, DC: National Academy Press, 1983); National Research Council, *Understanding Risk: Informing Decisions in a Democratic Society* (Washington, DC: National Academy Press, 1996); Presidential/Congressional Commission on Risk Assessment and Management, *Risk Assessment and Risk Management in Regulatory Decision-Making* (Washington, DC: Government Printing Office, 1997). Chemical testing needs and costs are described in John S. Applegate, "The Perils of Unreasonable Risk: Information, Regulatory Policy, and Toxic Substances Control," *Columbia Law Review* 91, no. 2 (1991): 261; Mary L. Lyndon, "Information Economics and Chemical Toxicity: Designing Laws to Produce and Use Data," *Michigan Law Review* 87, no. 7 (1989): 1795, 1812–13; Wendy E. Wagner, "Choosing Ignorance in the Manufacture of Toxic Products," *Cornell Law Review* 82, no. 4 (1997): 773, 784; Wendy E. Wagner, "Commons Ignorance: The Failure of Environmental Law to Produce Needed Information on Health

(exposure) requires tracing a chemical from release, through the environment, to an organism, and finally to the target organ or body system. The investigator must track minute amounts of chemicals through the external environments and internal pathways, which in turn requires the understanding of such diverse phenomena as atmospheric diffusion and wind currents, groundwater hydrogeology, respiration rates, and the pharmacokinetics of chemicals, to name a few. These are complex questions in themselves, and they often involve wide variations among environmental conditions and persons.

Evaluating the second half of the equation – the consequences of exposure – requires a detailed understanding of the toxicology of a chemical – what kinds of effects it has, at what dose, and over what period of time. Uncertainties invariably result from the difficulties of observing effects at low doses or in large populations. Additional uncertainty arises from the lack of understanding of the fundamental mechanisms of toxicity for certain diseases, notably cancer.

Thus, as discussed by Dr. Katherine Squibb in Chapter 2 of this book, some uncertainties can be resolved by greater investment in observation and experimentation, while others require greater investment in fundamental research. In both cases, the basic research is extremely expensive and laborious, a problem that is only compounded when effects on ecosystems (as opposed to humans only) are considered, as required by federal and state environmental laws.

### Legal Mandates

The precautionary principle – or, in lay terms, the idea that we should be "better safe than sorry" – has been widely adopted in both domestic and international environmental law. At the risk of oversimplifying, it requires that regulators use the best *available* scientific information in making decisions whether to regulate and it shifts some of the burden of proof onto the manufacturers of a chemical. The degree to which the precautionary principle uses risk assessment as part of its analysis varies among interpreters. The European Commission, for example, seeks to apply the principle

and the Environment," *Duke Law Journal* 53, no. 6 (2004): 1619, 1625–30; Wendy E. Wagner, "The Science Charade in Toxic Risk Regulation," *Columbia Law Review* 95, no. 7 (1995): 1613, 1688.

in a risk assessment framework, while environmentalists argue that the principle should replace risk analysis with hazard analysis, that is, looking only at the toxicity side of the risk equation.[10]

As Professor Howard Latin has forcefully argued, the demand for precision, which is almost always generated by regulated industry, is a mistaken – and often manipulative – transposition of the scientific paradigm of perpetual inquiry onto the legal-regulatory needs for real-world, real-time decision making.[11] In other words, demanding that we develop precise estimates of risk substantially undermines the goal of preventing harm, which is the centerpiece of modern public health and safety laws. The economists' concept of value of information – expressed by the question whether the cost of the acquisition of more information is worth the value it adds to a decision – underscores the point that precision should not be an ultimate, overriding goal.

Finally, it is important to recognize that reliance on risk-based regulation, with its attendant demand for large amounts of information, is itself a choice, and choice implies alternatives. Technology-based standards, which do not consider risk at all, have been highly effective and require far less information.[12] At the same time, however, technology-based approaches rely on prior identification of risk-producing chemicals or activities and do not themselves provide incentives for generating toxicity information; therefore, it is up to the legislature (as in the 1990 Clean Air Act Amendments[13]) or the agency (as in the Resource Conservation and Recovery Act)[14] to designate regulated chemicals on the basis of health concerns.

Regardless of these alternatives, American industry remains firmly committed to a precise, risk-based, agency-burdening regulatory system for chemicals, and it has been highly successful in maintaining this position by entrenching risk-based regulation in the relevant agencies and in

[10] John S. Applegate, "The Taming of the Precautionary Principle," *William and Mary Environmental Law and Policy Review* 27, no. 1 (2002): 13.
[11] Howard Latin, "Good Science, Bad Regulation, and Toxic Risk Assessment," *Yale Journal on Regulation* 5, no. 1 (1988): 89.
[12] Oliver A. Houck, "Tales from a Troubled Marriage: Science and Law in Environmental Policy," *Tulane Environmental Law Journal* 17, no. 1 (2003): 163, 172; Wendy E. Wagner, "The Triumph of Technology-Based Standards," *University of Illinois Law Review* 2000, no. 1 (2000): 83.
[13] 42 U.S.C. § 7412(b)(1).
[14] 42 U.S.C. § 6921(a).

| Demand | Supply |
|---|---|
| *Increases demand* | *Decreases supply* |
| Risk-based regulation | Declining public R&D funding |
| Aggressively skeptical judicial review | "Sound-science" demands |
| Scientific ("precision") paradigm | Data Quality Act |
| Burden of proof on government | Politicized peer review |
| OMB intervention | Legal incentives for ignorance |
| *Decreases demand* | *Increases supply* |
| Technology-based standards | Increased R&D funding |
| Putting burden of proof on polluters | Coherent, targeted R&D plans |
| Hazard-based regulation (Prop. 65) | Collections of data |
| Legislative listing of chemicals | Licensing |
| | Putting burden of proof on polluters |
| | Test rules and testing requirements |

Figure 12.2. Chemical Information Supply and Demand

Congress. There is, in consequence, little prospect of remedying the data gap by adjusting the demand side, so to speak, and so we must consider how to improve the supply side, or the production of information.

## The Supply Side of Regulatory Information

### A Ravenous System

By demanding precise answers to precise questions framed by industry (to paraphrase a particularly egregious case[15]), the present, risk-based mode of toxics regulation has created a system that is hungry – ravenous, really – for chemical information. Precautionary mandates in U.S. law have been successful to some extent in encouraging industry to undertake testing, but in many cases, the information is not just hard to get, it simply does not exist.[16] Figure 12.2 explains these competing pressures.

If we can liberate regulation from the insistent demands for precision, there is much that can be done to test chemicals, developing basic toxicity profiles and precursors or indicators of long-term, subtle toxic effects. This conclusion is evident from even a superficial analysis of the data gap studies cited earlier. Basic testing is available for far more chemicals than full chronic and cancer testing, for example, and EPA estimates that the price tag for the so-called Screening Information Data Set (SIDS) battery

[15] "To make precise estimates, precise data are required." *Gulf South Insulation v. Consumer Product Safety Comm'n*, 701 F.2d 1137, 1147 (5th Cir. 1983).
[16] Wagner, "Commons Ignorance," 1659–61.

of tests is a relatively modest $205,000.[17] The European Union's Registration, Evaluation, and Authorization of Chemicals, or REACH, proposal for chemical regulation reaches similar conclusions.[18] And the implementation of the burden-shifting Proposition 65 in California has demonstrated that acceptable standards can be set quickly when incentives for obstruction are removed.[19]

We have reached, then, the central question of this chapter: *Who* should provide the information that is needed to support the regulation of chemicals? There are several reasons to look first to industry for the generation of chemical information. However, there are also important limitations to consider in defining industry's role in generating chemical information, and they derive from the reasons for the data gap itself – market failure and regulatory failure. These limitations, and the related problem of reliability, suggest that certain kinds of chemical information are best obtained by the government from a nonindustry source, as discussed further in the following subsection.

## Industry's Supply-Side Role

As a normative matter, chemical information is essential both to the avoidance of harm from products, by identifying the potential harms and the means of preventing them, and to the justification and compensation of unavoidable harm, by identifying the potential victims and the extent of harms and benefits. Requiring industry to produce information is also

---

[17] Environmental Protection Agency, *Chemical Hazard Data Availability Study: What Do We Really Know about the Safety of High Production Volume Chemicals?* (Washington, DC: Government Printing Office, 1998); 11. Cumulatively, EPA found, this is a trivial portion of chemical industry revenues. These amounts could be reduced still further by advances in testing methods and the emerging field of toxicogenomics. The European Commission hopes to keep the cost of testing low with increased use of structure-activity relationships to predict toxicological effects. See Finn Pedersen et al., "Assessment of Additional Testing Needs under REACH: Effects of (Q)SARS, Risk Based Testing and Voluntary Industry Initiatives," (Sept. 2003) (available at http://www.jrc.cec.eu.int/more_information/download/summrepihcp.pdf).

[18] Commission of the European Communities, *Regulation of the European Parliament and of the Council Concerning the Registration, Evaluation, Authorisation and Restrictions of Chemicals (REACH), Establishing a European Chemicals Agency and Amending Directive 1999/45/EC and Regulation (EC) {on Persistent Organic Pollutants}*, (Oct. 29, 2003) (available at http://europa.eu.int/comm/enterprise/reach/docs/reach/eia-sec-2003_1171.pdf).

[19] Safe Drinking Water and Toxic Enforcement Act of 1986, Cal. Health & Safety Code §§ 25249.5–25249.13; Roe, "Toxic Chemical Control Policy," 10237.

appealing as a fair and logical outgrowth of the positions that industry has advocated. The industry public relations mantra "sound science" has been successful in producing the demand for ever more data to support regulation,[20] and a highly professionalized and largely industry-supported risk industry[21] has created an increasingly rococo structure of risk analytical tools on which regulation is to be based. Taking the advocates of "sound science" at their word, if they want the information so much, then they should provide it.

The sheer breadth of the data gap suggests that government alone cannot bridge it. Research spending, and indeed environmental protection generally, is a small part of an already small discretionary part of the federal budget. In a period of high deficits, high defense spending, and low taxes, the likelihood that environmental expenditures will rise considerably is very low, indeed. The chemical industry, on the other hand, is a $450 billion per year enterprise,[22] with ample resources for advertising, lobbying, and investment in new products – as well as a wide range of research activities.[23] If substantial new resources are going to be developed for chemical information, industry is a more likely source than government.

All of these justifications support a general presumption in favor of private over public provision of goods and services in market (capitalist) economies. The private approach is all the more compelling for chemical information because it relates to the safety of a privately produced good – one naturally sees the information and the product as part and parcel of each other. Moreover, by internalizing[24] the costs of a chemical's health and environmental

---

[20] Thomas O. McGarity, "Our Science Is Sound Science and Their Science is Junk Science: Science-Based Strategies for Avoiding Accountability and Responsibility for Risk-Producing Products and Activities," *University of Kansas Law Review* 52 (2004): 897.

[21] Society of Toxicology, "Career Resources: Where Do Toxicologists Work," Society of Toxicology, http://209.183.221.234/AI/CRAD/careerguide.asp.

[22] American Chemistry Council, "About Us," American Chemistry Council, http://www.americanchemistry.com.

[23] Rena I. Steinzor, "Toward Better Bubbles and Future Lives: A Progressive Response to the Conservative Agenda for Reforming Environmental Law," *Environmental Law Reporter* 32, no. 12 (2002): 11421, 11431; U.S. Public Interest Research Group, "Chemical Facilities Owned by 'Dangerous Dozen' Endanger Millions of Americans," U.S. Public Interest Research Group, http://uspirg.org/uspirgnewsroom.asp?id2=13533&id3=USPIRGnewsroom&; Wagner, "Choosing Ignorance," 813–14.

[24] Internalizing costs means charging them to the entity that generates them (in this case, the chemical manufacturer) so that the costs will be a factor in the manufacturer's decisions about the chemical.

consequences and of generating information, industry is encouraged to engage in efficient cost avoidance by producing safer products or by giving appropriate warnings, or both. Industry will also have an incentive to make the most efficient use of testing resources, and it can spread the costs of testing (through the price charged) to those who use the products, creating incentives among consumers to purchase only the most beneficial ones.

Industry testing can also be more effective in protecting health and safety by generating information at the beginning of the product development process. At an early stage, industry can anticipate and prevent harm from exposure to the general public. Industry-generated, chemical-specific information is potentially of higher quality, too, because manufacturers are considerably more familiar with their products and uses than are government regulators. In addition, as Professor Daniel Esty points out, "Competition and decentralization of the data gathering, information generation, and analytic processes may produce better results."[25]

## Engineering Incentives and Disincentives

The reasons for preferring industry generation of chemical information do not, however, tell us why the data gap persists. There is a broad consensus that the main answer is the incentives and disincentives caused both by market failure and by regulatory intervention.

### Market Failure

Market forces, operating in the context of the tort system, create strong *dis*incentives to produce information about the toxic effects of chemicals. Such information has liability, regulatory, and other economically negative consequences, but remaining in ignorance has almost none.[26] The problem is exacerbated by the special nature of toxic substances. Ordinarily, products with undesirable characteristics will not long survive in the market, because their characteristics become well known – for example, a car that disintegrates on impact. Either consumers will no longer buy it, or

---

[25] Daniel C. Esty, "Environmental Protection in the Information Age," *New York University Law Review* 79, no. 1 (2004): 115, 199–200.

[26] Esty, 198–209; Lyndon, 1813; Wagner, "Choosing Ignorance," 774–6, 784–5; Wagner, "Commons Ignorance," 1633–59.

the tort system will attach financial consequences (liability) to its sale. The "relative invisibility of chemicals"[27] – their pervasive presence in the environment, the adverse health effects they cause at extremely low (that is, unnoticeable) doses, the long latency and nonsignature nature of those health effects, and the diffuseness and rarity of such illnesses – preclude this simple feedback loop. Because it is extremely difficult to trace health effects to their toxic sources through ordinary observation, information is also subject to the free rider problem.[28] It is not only costly to generate such data, but the data can then be used as effectively by the firm that sponsored the study as by its competitors. All of these factors sharply reduce the market incentive to generate chemical information.

### Regulatory Failure

If the reason for the data gap is market failure, then government could try to repair the market. The current regulatory system, however, fails to bridge the data gap because, fundamentally, the burden of proving unsafety remains on the government, creating additional incentives for industry to generate as little information as possible and to challenge the few studies that exist.[29] Indeed, industry research is often designed to create uncertainty, rather than concentrate efforts on new information,[30] or to focus on relatively unimportant research that tends to exonerate chemicals. As an example of the latter, a recent study of EPA's Integrated Risk Information System (IRIS) database, the most prominent worldwide source of toxic chemical profiles, demonstrates that industry efforts have concentrated on pharmacokinetic modeling.[31] The goal of such modeling is to predict how toxic chemicals travel through the human body, thereby estimating the actual dose, and hence calculated risk, more precisely. These models can be

---

[27] Lyndon, 1796.

[28] A "free rider" makes use of another person's investment. Suppose Manufacturer A's research shows that Chemical X causes cancer. If Manufacturer B can use that information to avoid producing and incurring liability for X, without B having to invest in the research, then B is a free rider.

[29] Wendy E. Wagner, "The 'Bad Science' Fiction: Reclaiming the Debate over the Role of Science in Public Health and Environmental Regulation," *Law and Contemporary Problems* 66, no. 4 (2003): 63, 92–3; Wagner, "Commons Ignorance," 1649–59, 1711–17.

[30] Thomas O. McGarity, "MTBE: A Precautionary Tale," *Harvard Environmental Law Review* 28, no. 2 (2004): 281; David Michaels, "Doubt Is Their Product," *Scientific American* 292, no. 6 (2005): 96–101.

[31] Katherine Baer and Matt Shudtz, Center for Progressive Reform, "Data Gaps White Paper," available at www.progressivereform.org.

controversial because they are very hard to validate. And they do nothing about the fundamental issue of missing basic toxicity (such as SIDS) data.

Even without restricting industry's penchant for focusing its resources on creating doubt,[32] however, government can impose incentive mechanisms that do not directly demand chemical information, but rather provide industry with good reasons to generate information on its own. The most powerful incentive is a permit or licensing system, because a licensing scheme requires information *before* a return on investment can be realized. Licenses and permits also typically shift the burden of proving safety to the proponent of the chemical.

The effect of licensing on the production of information is dramatic. In its 1984 study, the National Academy of Sciences found that the amount of toxicity information for pesticides and drugs, the two chemical groups subject to licensing, was much higher for these than for other categories.[33] California's burden-shifting Proposition 65 has had the similar effect of encouraging manufacturers to come forward with chemical information.[34] Despite the demonstrated efficacy of such approaches, licensing and burden shifting remain rare in U.S. environmental law, with the result that "testing is simply not required for most chemicals."[35]

Several existing federal environmental laws that do not themselves require licensing do, however, grant affirmative authority to federal agencies to require the generation of information. Some of these provisions simply require reporting of known data, such as chemical spills, releases to the environment, or injury reports.[36] Other provisions require the collection and dissemination of new information – for example, the Toxic Release Inventory (TRI).[37]

The most aggressive authority, and the one most directly aimed at generating chemical information, is the rare requirement to undertake new testing. For pesticides, this testing is part of the licensing scheme and is known

---

[32] Michaels, "Doubt Is Their Product."

[33] Applegate, "The Perils of Unreasonable Risk," 309.

[34] David Roe, "Barking up the Right Tree: Recent Progress in Focusing the Toxics Issue," *Columbia Journal of Environmental Law* 13, no. 2 (1988): 275, 277–8; David Roe, "Toxic Chemical Control Policy: Three Unabsorbed Facts," *Environmental Law Reporter* 32, no. 2 (2002): 10,232, 10,235.

[35] Wagner, "Choosing Ignorance," 787.

[36] Comprehensive Environmental Response, Compensation, and Liability Act, 42 U.S.C. § 9603; Toxic Substances Control Act, 15 U.S.C. § 2607.

[37] Emergency Planning and Community Right-to-Know Act, 42 U.S.C. § 11023.

as a "data call-in."[38] The Toxic Substances Control Act (TSCA), however, hedges a similar requirement with procedures and prerequisite factual findings that have prevented the statute from becoming a meaningful source of information.[39] Even if EPA had the political will to impose such test rules more often, the resources required to justify such rules would be prohibitive. TSCA, indeed, is a veritable menu of information-generation techniques; however, for a variety of reasons, including a crushing burden of proof on governmental action, such as the heavy burden of proof imposed on government action, it has been a conspicuous underachiever among environmental laws.

## The Government's Supply-Side Role

### Quality and Credibility

Together, the market and regulatory failures suggest that industry will not produce chemical information at all or, more accurately, in the quantities needed to operate an effective risk-based regulatory system in which the burden of proof is on government. These failures do not, however, address the question of quality and credibility. Quality is particularly important in the area of chemical information, because it often requires the exercise of scientific judgment, and "interest groups have an incentive to withhold information that is inconsistent with their position and to present incomplete or biased information that supports their views."[40] Credibility is also essential, because chemical information supports public decisions about public health. Citizens will not widely accept these decisions if they do not trust the underlying science.

Quality and credibility are not theoretical concerns. Industry has a long and dismal history of suppressing negative health information about its products. As Professor Thomas McGarity and Dr. Squibb discuss in

---

[38] Federal Insecticide, Fungicide, and Rodenticide Act, 7 U.S.C. § 136a(c)(2)(B).

[39] Toxic Substances Control Act, 15 U.S.C. § 2603; McGarity, "MTBE," 297–301; Applegate, "The Perils of Unreasonable Risk," 312–16 (citing R. Noll and B. M. Owen, *The Political Economy of Regulation* [1983], p. 63).

[40] Robert R. Kuehn, "Suppression of Environmental Science," *American Journal of Law and Medicine* 30, nos. 2–3 (2004): 333; Barry Meier, "Contracts Keep Drug Research Out of Reach," *New York Times*, Nov. 29, 2004, sec. A.

Chapters 1 and 2 of this book, from asbestos to lead to tobacco, a number of industries have built up a record of secrecy, suppression, disinformation, and attacks on reputable scientists, which continues to this day.[41] The especially dramatic story of the pesticide atrazine, told by Dr. Squibb, and industry's dogged resistance to complete testing of MTBE, explained by Professor McGarity,[42] counsel caution in accepting industry data. Even beyond deliberate behavior, a study in the *New England Journal of Medicine* showed statistically significant differences of opinion on the safety of a particular drug between scientists who were funded by industry and those who were not.[43]

These concerns do not apply equally to all chemical testing and research. Industry, as we have seen, is well suited to undertake the battery of basic toxicity testing of individual chemicals that is necessary to fill the data gap, and there are strong reasons for looking first to industry to do so. Existing regulatory provisions that create incentives or impose requirements for generating information should therefore continue to receive serious attention and be strengthened at every opportunity. However, the pattern of market and regulatory failure and the history of unreliable information impose significant limitations on the potential of industry-generated information.

We therefore turn to government's role in bridging the gap in chemical information. The circumstances under which government should itself produce chemical information are related, but not identical to, the reasons for the existence of the data gap. Government should play the primary role in generating information in three overlapping situations: when there is structural or systematic market failure, when government is in a position to generate the information, and when industry's credibility gap is particularly acute.

## Specific Chemical Categories

Markets and the characteristics of toxic chemicals are such that it may not be either equitable or politically feasible to require industry to produce

[41] McGarity, "MTBE," 297–305, 318–21.
[42] Houck, "Tales from a Troubled Marriage," 173 (citing Howard T. Stelfox et al., "Conflict of Intent in the Debate over Calcium-Channel Antagonists," *New England Journal of Medicine* 338, no. 2 (1998): 101.
[43] Pat Phibbs, "EPA May Allow Nonagency Scientists to Use Its Specialized Facilities," *Environment Reporter* 35, no. 24 (2004): 1269.

some kinds of information in sufficient quantities, necessitating intervention by a collective entity like the government. Information that is not associated with any particular product, service, or activity is not subject to the cost-internalizing mechanisms of the market and traditional liability rules. Direct requirements to undertake such research are conceivable; however, any such requirement is likely to be resisted as arbitrary and unfair when there is no strong nexus between the information and the entity required to undertake the research.

Foundational information such as the development of basic frameworks and methods (for example, quantitative risk assessment or geographic information systems [GIS]) provides insights across a range of chemicals and so cannot meaningfully be connected to a particular chemical product. Indeed, foundational information is most useful if it is widely disseminated, and so *least* linked to particular profit centers. Fundamental research, as in basic toxicology or physiology, poses the same difficulty, as do issues like long-term management of hazardous waste sites, which retain their hazardous character long after the disposers have left the scene. One particularly promising avenue of basic research is the improvement of test methods. Better and cheaper tests – perhaps utilizing insights from the emerging field of toxicogenomics – is exactly the kind of basic research that would support and encourage data generation in the private sector.

Finally, some chemical information requires extremely large resources for specialized equipment or for wide-ranging research. For example, detecting very subtle harms or harms from very low exposures to chemicals requires both sophisticated hardware and surveys of large populations. Similarly, research with a long development period, such as finding alternatives or ways to reduce the use of existing chemicals, may or may not be motivated by market-based incentives. While industry's resources are, in aggregate, far larger than those realistically available to the government, industry suffers from the familiar difficulty (transaction costs) of assembling those resources and concentrating them on a single project. Thus, EPA has recently proposed making available to nongovernment scientists several of the specialized facilities at its laboratories, such as pilot plants for drinking water and a ship that studies water quality in the Great Lakes,[44] that few single enterprises or products could support.

[44] Esty, 156–61.

## Government's Comparative Advantage

Government is uniquely positioned to produce the kinds of information that involve collection, interaction, and dissemination of data from many sources.[45] Only government has the resources to reach out broadly and gather information with no economic return, or the ability to apply coercive power to obtain data that are not already in the public domain. Some information is useful only in such massive quantities that government is the only realistic source. No single nongovernmental entity could have raised the billions of dollars that the Human Genome Project required, and yet the project generated invaluable information for countless uses, including public health and environmental protection.[46]

Even simple compilations of data are useful because they improve access to information the way that a library does, and because they permit new insights, like finding toxic hot spots or data gaps. TOXNET, a "cluster of databases on toxicology, hazardous chemicals, and related areas" that is, appropriately enough, a project of the National Library of Medicine,[47] and inventories such as the Comprehensive Environmental Response, Compensation, and Liability Information System (CERCLIS),[48] which contains potential Superfund sites, provide such access. The National Library of Medicine's TOXMAP takes a further step to permit the viewer to map TRI facilities using GIS technology, integrating not only different sources but different types of information.[49]

"Coordination and combination are key productive functions" for compilations of information,[50] and TRI data allow EPA to make generalizations about the effectiveness (or ineffectiveness) of its programs.[51] Similarly,

[45] U.S. Department of Energy, "Human Genome Project Information," U.S. Department of Energy, http://www.ornl.gov/sci/techresources/Human_Genome/home.shtml.

[46] Specialized Information Services, "TOXNET," National Library of Medicine, http://toxnet.nlm.nih.gov/.

[47] U.S. Environmental Protection Agency, "Superfund Information Systems," U.S. Environmental Protection Agency, http://www.epa.gov/superfund/sites/siteinfo.htm.

[48] Specialized Information Services, "TOXMAP," National Library of Medicine, http://toxmap.nlm.nih.gov/toxmap/main/index.jsp.

[49] Lyndon, 1850.

[50] U.S. Environmental Protection Agency, "Summary of Key Findings of EPA Toxics Release Inventory for 2002," reprinted in *Environment Reporter* 35, no. 26 (2004): 1390.

[51] Heinz Center, *The State of the Nation's Ecosystems* (Cambridge, UK: Cambridge University Press, 2002); U.S. Environmental Protection Agency, *Draft Report on the Environment 2003* (Washington. DC: Government Printing Office, 2003).

collections of data that produce information about "indicators" (such as levels of air quality or amounts of marine vegetation) regarding the state of the environment[52] bring together data across environmental media.

More broadly, government is in a unique position to set – and then pursue – a coherent research agenda based on a wide-ranging analysis of gaps, needs, and statutory mandates. Compilations can identify inconsistencies and gaps, which are a kind of information in themselves. Discrepancies help researchers to understand what precisely is known and not known in the evaluation of chemicals. EPA's research programs for HPV and for persistent, bioaccumulative, and toxic (PBT) chemicals[53] target chemicals of particular concern for information collection and analysis.

One of the most important ways that government can integrate data is to provide uniform standards and formats for it.[54] It is frequently difficult to compare across databases and other sources, but by establishing protocols and standards, government can allow the compilation and cross-referencing of information in ways that dramatically increase its utility. A recent Government Accountability Office study recommended that Congress designate a "lead organization to coordinate the collection of water quality data to ensure better information for water management decisions."[55] Currently, these data are held by many federal agencies, in addition to states and private organizations. Without coordination, even heavy expenditures on monitoring are of limited utility.

Finally, government is well suited to disseminate information, because it is a focal point to which people and institutions naturally turn for information, including collections and interpretations of information. Dissemination of information serves several purposes. EPA offers educational information in booklets and on the web concerning radon, lead, and asbestos for buyers and sellers of homes. More aggressively, the disclosure of information can itself be a form of regulation. By publishing TRI data, EPA makes it possible for individuals and groups to analyze and evaluate the information. Such national public interest organizations as Environmental Defense, for instance, use TRI and other publicly available data to

---

[52] U.S. Environmental Protection Agency, "Persistent Bioaccumulative and Toxic (PBT) Chemical Program" (available at http://www.epa.gov/pbt/).

[53] Wagner, "Commons Ignorance," 1739–40.

[54] General Accounting Office, *Watershed Management: Better Coordination of Data Collection Efforts Needed to Support Key Decisions* (Washington, DC: Government Printing Office, 2004).

[55] Environmental Defense, "Scorecard," Environmental Defense, http://www.scorecard.org/.

support a website – the Environmental Scorecard[56] – that allows individuals to access data about their communities, particular companies, or particular chemicals.

Perhaps the most dramatic example of information as regulation is California's Proposition 65, which requires the labeling of products containing more than certain amounts of chemicals "known [by the state of California] to 'cause cancer' or to 'cause reproductive toxicity,'" and to make public announcements of such releases. Observers have credited TRI and Proposition 65 with motivating significant decreases in emissions of these chemicals and of their presence in products in California and elsewhere, as indeed was intended.[57]

## The Credibility Gap

Credibility is a particular issue for chemical information because analysis of such data often requires a high degree of interpretation, inference, and judgment. Such analyses provide ample opportunities for incompleteness, bias in judgment, delay, and even invalid scientific procedures. The TRI, for example, has been sharply criticized for simply presenting estimates of discharges submitted by industry, which may underestimate actual pollution in the ambient environment.

Government can help to close the credibility gap (and in that sense generate credible information) in several ways. Most obviously, government can take a supervisory role to ensure the quality and integrity of the chemical information used in regulation, to the extent possible. Government can establish quality assurance and quality control policies and practices, it can certify laboratories and researchers, and it can set down standards for peer review. EPA already publishes hundreds of test methods for dozens of characteristics of chemicals and environmental media.[58] Of course, private

56  Roe, "Toxic Chemical Control Policy," 10235–7.
57  U.S. Environmental Protection Agency, "Information Services: Index to Test Methods," U.S. Environmental Protection Agency, http://www.epa.gov/epahome/index/.
58  Commission of the European Communities, *Regulation of the European Parliament and of the Council Concerning the Registration, Evaluation, Authorisation and Restrictions of Chemicals (REACH), Establishing a European Chemicals Agency and Amending Directive 1999/45/EC and Regulation (EC) {on Persistent Organic Pollutants}* (Oct. 29, 2003) (available at http://europa.eu.int/comm/enterprise/reach/docs/reach/eia-sec-2003_1171.pdf).; Commission of the European Communities, *White Paper: Strategy for a Future Chemicals Policy* (February 27, 2001) (available at http://europa.eu.int/comm/environment/chemicals/pdf/0188_en.pdf).

entities may undertake this regulatory function voluntarily, but the absence of a profit motive is central to credibility.

Government is also the logical entity to establish a basic battery of chemical tests. EPA's High Production Volume (HPV) program, a cooperative effort with the U.S. chemical industry, identifies a Screening Information Data Set (SIDS), and the European REACH proposal defines a set of data to be provided to regulatory authorities prior to the production of an industrial chemical.[59] Like the supervisory function, this standardization function emphasizes government as a credible and reliable source of information and guidance. Indeed, the more and better that government performs these functions, the more acceptable industry-generated information will be, adding further to the available chemical information.

One might usefully draw a distinction at this point between basic and applied research, or, in this context, between developing appropriate tests and test protocols, and performing the tests themselves. In the absence of outright fraud, which is fortunately a rarity, industry testing pursuant to public, recognized protocols and quality assurance procedures should enjoy a high level of reliability and credibility.

Interpretive and educational information, in particular, needs a governmental source. The characterization of information, or recommendations about how to respond to it, will be far more credible from a source with no economic stake in the outcome. For example, if the best practice for nonfriable asbestos is to encapsulate rather than to remove it, a government source is far more likely to be followed than information provided by the asbestos or real estate industries. When EPA does engage in interpretation or harmonization – for example, to give a recommended slope factor in the IRIS database[60] – one might justifiably believe that government is, in general, the more reliable interpreter. Proposals to create a Bureau of Environmental Statistics reflect this view. They seek an entity that will gather, analyze, and publish a consistent and comprehensive data set of measures and indicators of environmental quality.[61] These proposals emphasize the

---

[59]  U.S. Environmental Protection Agency, "Integrated Risk Information System," U.S. Environmental Protection Agency, http://www.epa.gov/iris/index.html.

[60]  H. Spencer Banzhaf, "Environmental Statistics," in *New Approaches on Energy and the Environment*, ed. Richard D. Morgenstern and Paul R. Portney (Washington, DC: Resources for the Future, 2004), 129.

[61]  Meier, sec. A.

independence of such an organization (even, or especially, from the political elements of government) on the model of the widely trusted Bureau of Labor Statistics.

Government, to sum up, does not have the only, or even the primary, role in generating chemical information. But it has a vital role to play in bridging structural gaps in the availability of information due to market and regulatory failure; in compiling, standardizing, and reporting otherwise dispersed or inaccessible information; and in lending credibility to information that would not otherwise be widely accepted as the basis for public policy.

## Doing the Work and Paying the Bills

### The Work

In calling for a significantly larger role for government in generating chemical information, this chapter raises two important questions of implementation: Who will do the actual work, and how will it be supported?

The "who" question is less obvious than it might seem. An agency like EPA has laboratories that produce high-quality chemical information, but the great majority of government-generated information will come from nongovernmental entities working under grants or contracts. Some of the work, especially the more basic, laboratory-based research, would presumably be undertaken by universities and university-affiliated researchers. Other kinds of work, such as collections of data or creation of laboratory standards, could be done equally well by consulting firms with scientific expertise.

Contract laboratories and consulting firms, however, tend to have industry as their main clients, and an industry-driven professional culture is as likely to be hostile to environmental concerns as industry itself. Although universities are more independent of the regulatory enterprise and possess strong internal norms of quality and objectivity, they are not immune from capture, as Professor Sheldon Krimsky discusses in Chapter 3 of this book and as recent revelations regarding drug testing illustrate.[62]

[62]  5 U.S.C. § 552.

And the government itself is not a monolithic entity. Political leadership changes, and some agencies (such as the departments of Energy and Defense) are themselves major polluters and so have an unavoidably conflicted commitment to environmental protection. Governmental neutrality cannot, therefore, simply be assumed in allocating information-generation responsibilities.

Nevertheless, government officials do not have the systematic financial bias that infuses industry-generated information. While industry employs and supports many professional, conscientious, and skilled scientists, the collective incentive system is inescapable. Moreover, government information is subject to openness requirements that simply do not exist for industry. The Freedom of Information Act,[63] the Federal Advisory Committee Act,[64] and even the Data Access Act[65] and Information Quality Act (also known as the Data Quality Act),[66] open the doors of government agencies, their laboratories, and their contractors.[67] The general requirements of administrative procedure – notice and comment, substantial evidence, judicial review – also offer opportunities to look closely at agency data. Industry data, by contrast, are immune from virtually all of these requirements, and industry routinely requires outside researchers to sign confidentiality agreements.[68] The "economic values of cost, secrecy, and ownership dominate until political values of access and freedom are violated."[69] Only government information is regularly subject to exposure and challenge, and that gives it a level of reliability and credibility that industry information lacks.

## The Funding

The federal government is far from a bottomless well of funding for environmental protection. Financing from the general tax fund is the default source of resources for environmental protection, and chemical information is indeed a public good that benefits the general public in important

---

[63]  5 U.S.C. app. 1.
[64]  Pub. L. No. 105–277, 112 Stat. 2681 (1998) (also known as the Shelby Amendment).
[65]  Pub. L. No. 106–554, § 515, 144 Stat. 2763 (2001).
[66]  McGarity, "Our Science," 910–13; Wagner, "The 'Bad Science' Fiction," 68–9, 98–9.
[67]  Meier, sec. A; Wagner, "The 'Bad Science' Fiction," 98–9.
[68]  E. Sam Overman and Anthony G. Cahill, "Information Policy: A Study of Values in the Policy Process, *Policy Studies Review* 9, no. 4 (1990): 803, 814.
[69]  Lyndon, 1836–41.

ways. However, it is exceptionally unlikely that the federal budget as currently structured and encumbered could support major new expenditures to generate chemical information.

A more plausible (though not, perhaps, in the present administration) financing source would be a directed tax, perhaps modeled on the Superfund financing scheme. As originally conceived, the cost of environmental cleanup was to be borne by entities with some nexus with the site (owners, generators, and such) when they could be found and were solvent, and otherwise by the government through a special fund – the Superfund – created by a dedicated tax on chemicals with some relationship to the problem. In other words, the Superfund policy looked first to industry and then to government for funding, just as this chapter recommends for chemical information generally. The relationship between the Superfund feedstock tax and the contaminated sites themselves was necessarily inexact, but it roughly met the goals of raising the needed public funds, internalizing environmental costs to generate industry, and vindicating a sense of fairness that the polluter (or polluting industry generally) was paying. Professor Mary Lyndon has suggested a "super study program,"[70] based on the Superfund, to address the chemical information data gap, and her proposal deserves renewed consideration.

## Conclusion

The United States has developed a system for environmental regulation that is based on a detailed analysis of the probability and severity of the toxic effects of chemicals. A wide gap exists between the amount of reliable information required by this regulatory system and the amount actually available. The reformer's task, therefore, is not only to establish the substantive policy and regulatory structures for environmental protection, but also to provide the information that the regulatory structures need to be effective.

From this perspective, while it is appropriate to look first to industry to provide needed chemical information, such reliance has serious and systemic limitations. Consequently, the principles that are the basis of this

[70] John S. Applegate et al., *The Regulation of Toxic Substances and Hazardous Wastes* (New York: Foundation Press, 2000), 67 (citing National Research Council, *Toxicity Testing*, 205–08

book rightly insist that public funding of research is essential to produce discoveries that benefit the public good.

This chapter has laid out a framework for determining the circumstances under which government is the better generator of chemical information. Government is, in general, better equipped or positioned to set a research agenda for chemicals; to undertake basic research; to establish protocols for testing and data collection; to require needed testing; to collect, analyze, and disseminate test results; and, of course, to incorporate chemical information into regulatory decisions. Industry, by contrast, is best suited to undertake the basic research on individual chemicals, under public protocols and procedures. Moreover, to the extent that appropriate incentives exist to ensure reliable, high-quality testing methods and other information techniques, industry can use its resources and familiarity with its products to take a leadership role in their development.

PART
IV

# RECOMMENDATIONS AND CONCLUSION

# Conclusion

## The Imperative of the Principles

Wendy Wagner, J.D., and Rena Steinzor, J.D.

### Science for the Future

Over the next several years, our society will be forced to confront the implications of evidence that human activities are causing the earth's climate to change, as well as dire predictions that oil will run out in less than a century. Debates will continue over the toxicity of ubiquitous pollutants such as mercury, the damage caused by nutrient loading of surface water, the use of scarce potable water resources, and the disruption of ecological patterns such as sharp decreases in the worldwide population of amphibians. It is difficult to think of a time in U.S. history when we have needed science more.

Yet essential science does not always reach the policy makers who must confront these important and difficult problems. The preceding twelve chapters of this book document the multiple ways that science is withheld, compromised, and distorted in the legislative, judicial, and regulatory arenas, with affected parties working overtime to ensure that contradictory data do not defeat their causes. Not only do these activities impose artificial limits on the supply of reliable research, they prevent science from informing policies designed to protect public health and natural resources.

This conclusion considers a series of reforms that would ameliorate the worst abuses. Once again, these proposals are informed by the principles of independent, disinterested, and transparent science that should be accepted as fundamental and incontrovertible by all participants in the debates:

- *Independence*: Scientists must be able to conduct research without unjustified restrictions, including undue influence from research sponsors.
- *Transparency*: The data and results of research must be communicated honestly and expeditiously to the research community and broader public. Researchers and those using their research must be careful to represent the findings accurately, including the limitations of that research.
- A *Public Infrastructure for Science*: Government support of independent research is essential to produce discoveries that benefit the public good. In appropriate circumstances, peer review may serve an important role in assisting the government's decision making regarding the use and funding of science, but peer review must never be used to censor research.

The book's authors identify four general categories of worrisome violations of these fundamental, noncontroversial principles. The first category includes legally backed efforts by special interests to silence scientists and discredit their work. A number of scientists who embark on research that suggests that industrial activities or products are more harmful than originally supposed have been the victims of unfair attacks on the validity of their research and their professional integrity. Not only do these assaults fly in the face of an essential characteristic of scientific inquiry – honest, disinterested debate over methods and data – they cannot help but deter the best and the brightest from entering the disciplines where they are needed the most.

Second, shortfalls in public funding of research and the absence of standardized testing requirements combine to place the private sector at the helm of crucial research. When the stakes are high enough, private interests can commission research to suit their needs, inappropriately influencing study design and the publication of results. Legal instruments, such as nondisclosure clauses in contracts, make these arrangements enforceable. Despite widely publicized lamentation about the "kept university," academic administrators and lawyers too often are ill prepared to defend scientists enmeshed in such disputes.

Third, government officials and stakeholders sometimes manipulate scientific information to make it look like the decisive basis for the policies they support, when in truth the decisions necessarily hinge on obscured value choices. The resulting lack of accountability and transparency alienates the public from the policy-making process by making such debates so complex and technical that the average lay person cannot hope to keep up. This alienation is destructive when policies informed by science ultimately depend on public support and participation for their implementation.

The fourth and arguably most pernicious category includes the related approaches of scientific deconstruction and "corpuscularization." Deconstruction means taking apart a piece of research by questioning choices made about its methodologies, even though the vast majority of scientists accept these choices as suitable resolutions of nonessential research questions. For example, deconstructionists might challenge the choice to keep six amphibians under study in a ten-gallon tank, asking why neither the number four nor eight was chosen, or why a fifteen-gallon tank would not be more appropriate. These admittedly arbitrary judgments most often have nothing to do with the merits of the research, but succeed nevertheless in creating an aura of suspicion about it. Science is particularly susceptible to deconstruction because scientists themselves believe in subjecting research to vigorous scrutiny. But scientists undertake such scrutiny with the goal of evaluating the reliability of the methods and the fit between data and hypotheses. In sharp contrast, the legal system's adversarial approach to decision making tolerates attacks on all aspects of a study, including generally accepted features of research methodology, even if they are launched for the sole purpose of undercutting the support of an opponent's arguments.

Through a related technique, referred to as "corpuscularization," legal adversaries work to undermine an entire body of research that indicates possible environmental harm by disassembling it into its individual studies and critiquing each one in such tedious detail that its credibility is undermined. Opponents then demand that each discredited study be excluded from consideration because it is flawed, even if the study includes otherwise useful information. Successful corpuscularization prevents the use of important data in the traditional "weight of the evidence" approach that scientists utilize: Under this alternative, "weight of the evidence" framework, scientists take all of the available and relevant research as they find it, recognizing the inevitable weaknesses in individual studies, but still accepting aspects of the research that offer some insight into the larger inquiry. Corpuscularization thus produces a decision-making process that is mired in significantly greater scientific uncertainty than would exist under a "weight of the evidence" analysis. Legal tools such as the *Daubert* rule, which requires judges to screen "junk" science before it reaches a jury, and regulatory challenges under the Data Quality Act (also known as the Information Quality Act), have made this technique not just available but inviting to adversaries throughout the legal system.

## Launching the Rescue

If the past decade is any indication of the future, efforts to undermine valuable research and discredit researchers will continue to increase in number, vigor, and creativity. To halt or at least slow these incursions, the legislative, regulatory, and judicial systems must be reformed with the goal of protecting scientists' ability to undertake research without outside interference. Each of the three principles points the way toward several concrete changes that will assist in rescuing science from politics.

The following recommendations begin by emphasizing the crucial role that scientists must play in launching and supporting these rescue efforts, arguing that the scientific community's active involvement in crafting effective reforms is indispensable. We also propose the creation of a "safety zone" for research that would protect scientists from destructive and unwarranted attacks. We stress the importance of expanded public funding for science, suggest ways to raise additional money, and urge the adoption of legal protections for scientists who undertake such research. This conclusion then turns to a series of recommendations that would increase transparency and honesty when the legal system uses science, including more thorough conflict disclosures and expanded access to private data. We explain why regulatory agencies must distinguish between science and the inevitable, legally required policy choices they make in formulating regulation. We oppose application of universal, overly bureaucratic peer review. We conclude by urging participants in policy making to prevent the use of legal tools that help to accomplish deconstruction and corpuscularization.

## The Fundamental Role of Scientists

Over the past five years, scientific institutions have become more involved in challenging legal intrusions on science. Expanding and intensifying these efforts are the quid pro quo for real reform. For example, scientists in a wide variety of disciplines are taking note of how economically motivated participants in policy making have deconstructed research and tarnished reputations. Toxicologists and epidemiologists have watched with dismay as scientists concerned about asbestos, lead, and various pesticides came under attack. Universities and other scientific organizations have convened conferences to explore and educate scientists about the harassment that has occurred when the results of their research have adversely affected special interests.[1] The tobacco industry's effort to derail the building of scientific consensus regarding the health effects of smoking is now a widely cited cautionary tale, although it reaped some important casualties, as explained by Paul Fischer in Chapter 4. And, as described by Sheldon Krimsky in Chapter 3, biologists and other medical experts have heard testimony from colleagues about the implications of incurring the wrath of pharmaceutical company sponsors. They have also witnessed the humiliation suffered by scientists who appear complicit in the suppression of research in such areas as the effects of antidepressants on children.

Professional societies, scientific institutions, and informal groups of scientists are also becoming more directly involved in policy making that depends upon scientific information. The most notable example is the June 2005 joint statement by the premier scientific academies of Britain, Canada, France, Germany, Italy, Japan, Russia, and the United States urging their nations to take action on climate change.[2] In addition, as Donald Hornstein explains in Chapter 5, mainstream scientific organizations such as the National Academy of Sciences and the American Association for the Advancement of Sciences participated vigorously over the past few years on proposals to improve regulatory science, including opposing overbroad regulation requiring scientists to share all of their research-related information, even for ongoing studies, with interested parties. When the Office of Management and Budget (OMB) proposed uniform peer review procedures that took an unprecedented approach to peer review, opposition throughout the scientific community was substantial,

---

[1] "Conflicted Science: Corporate Influence on Scientific Research and Science-Based Policy," conference of the Center for Science in the Public Interest (July 11, 2003) (available at http://www.cspinet.org/integrity/cs_conference_abstract.pdf); "Pulse of Scientific Freedom: In the Age of the Life-Sciences Industry," conference at University of California, Berkeley, CA (Dec. 10, 2003) (available at http://journalism.berkeley.edu/events/details.php?ID=2).

[2] Joint science academies statement: Global Response to Climate Change, available at http://www.royalsoc.ac.uk/document.asp?latest=1&id=3222 (visited on June 7, 2005).

and OMB was eventually persuaded to make substantial changes as a result of the scientists' feedback. David Michaels and Sidney Shapiro describe these ill-fated proposals and the scientists' role in counteracting them in Chapters 10 and 11.

Collective efforts by scientists to stave off unwarranted intrusions to science are an important first step, but these efforts must be supplemented with more proactive roles for scientists in informing public policy. Rather than positioning the scientific community as just another interest group forced to lobby for changes in regulatory proposals, policy makers must give scientists a more formal role in reviewing and revising legal rules that directly or indirectly utilize or affect scientific research. Many of the most problematic legal tools – the Data Access Act, the Data Quality Act, public records statutes, and the liberal use of subpoena power with respect to independent experts not otherwise involved in litigation – were all established and expanded without consulting with the scientific community in advance. Increasingly vocal opposition by scientific organizations has accomplished a few significant revisions to these tools. To avoid further damage, policy makers must consult the scientific community much earlier in the decision-making process.

In the future, laws and rules that would directly affect scientific freedom, quality, or transparency should be vetted through a panel of highly respected scientists before they are proposed. While the panel of scientists would not have "veto" power, their review of legal innovations at the front end of their development would identify potential problems and allow the establishment of less intrusive approaches that might not be obvious to nonscientists.

## Creating a Safety Zone

Scientists who conduct research that has potentially adverse implications for regulated industries should be protected in a "safety zone" that effectively immunizes them from the host of legal tools used to harass them and dismember their work. These safety zones would have the goal of placing scientists and their research "off limits" for those intent on mounting unsubstantiated or meritless attacks. The best way to accomplish this essential outcome is to increase the burden on those seeking to subpoena data from independent researchers, foreclose accusations of scientific misconduct except in the most egregious cases, and prohibit complaints that request correction of data when the requesters have other opportunities to explain their positions to decision makers.

"Raising the burden" on these challenges to independent research means more than simply asking for more evidence while allowing the attack to run its course. To deter the harassment of scientists who produce inconvenient findings, the law should impose stiff sanctions on meritless or unsubstantiated attacks.[3] Scientists should have the right to go to court to seek damages for harassment, including not only compensation for their time and expenses, but also punitive damages when the delays caused by the attack have undermined the progress of their research. To ensure that such challenges are not defeated by the high costs of litigation, the law should include the availability of attorneys' fees and costs for the prevailing party.[4]

In addition, scientific organizations like the American Association for the Advancement of Science or the National Academy of Sciences could provide an invaluable public service by establishing a balanced committee of scientists to investigate complaints and defend innocent researchers, much as the American Association of University Professors investigates complaints of infringements on academic freedom.[5] These panels could conduct full examinations of the legitimacy of "junk science" allegations and issue a public report that would be available to the decision-making body. More vigorous defense of harassed researchers will raise the costs to interest groups of exaggerating flaws in good research.

These recommendations will provoke controversy. Some will argue that they attempt to change fundamental characteristics of the legal system that are designed to ensure fairness for all of its participants. Among other things, they will charge that subpoenas and similar legal tools may be the only way to "discover" adverse information in order to prevent questionable research from causing grave and unjustified economic damage. Others will contend that these proposals are hypocritical: While this book expresses

---

[3] Few sanctions are in place to deter abuse of any of these procedures. Scientific Misconduct Regulations, 42 C.F.R. § 50 (2003).

[4] Frederick R. Anderson, "Science Advocacy and Scientific Due Process," *Issues in Science and Technology* 16, no. 4 (2000): 71, 74; Robert R. Kuehn, "Suppression of Environmental Science," *American Journal of Law and Medicine* 30, nos. 2, 3 (2004): 333.

[5] American Association of University Professors, "Committee on Academic Freedom and Tenure," American Association of University Professors, http://www.aaup.org/Coma/index.htm.

great admiration for the scientific tradition of engaging in robust debate regarding the merits of research, we now seek to forestall such debate within the legal system, where it counts the most. There are several responses to these concerns.

First and foremost, all science is not equal in terms of its significance for public policy. Scientists doing research that has important policy ramifications, especially when economic stakes are high, deserve extraordinary protection lest such fields of inquiry become a "no-man's land" for the best minds among us.

Second, the proposals are not designed to chill debate, but rather to prohibit extraordinarily destructive and highly personal attacks on individuals who can defend themselves only through significant sacrifice. Far from depriving potentially injured parties of a fair opportunity to counter the merits of research, these proposals are carefully aimed at eliminating additional, duplicative alternatives that cause far more damage than good. Scientists themselves have created ample opportunities for vetting the accuracy of research. More intractable scientific controversies can even be reviewed by high-level scientists under the auspices of the National Academy of Sciences or agency-specific scientific advisory boards, giving those wishing to challenge data or conclusions additional opportunity to make sophisticated arguments to their peers.[6]

Lastly, if other reforms presented in greater detail later in this conclusion are adopted, the use of science by the legislative, judicial, and regulatory systems will become considerably more transparent, with underlying data disclosed as a matter of course by those hoping to influence decision making. If Congress, agencies, and the courts implement these standards effectively, participants in such debates should have no lingering concerns that their only recourse is against individual scientists.

## Reform of the Regulatory System

Reforms directed at the protection of scientists are only the first step. The authors contributing to this book converge on several ambitious recommendations that require greater government support for regulatory research;

---

[6]  See, for example, National Academy of Sciences, National Research Council, *Climate Change Science: An Analysis of Some Key Questions* (Washington, DC: National Academy Press; 2001); National Academy of Sciences, National Research Council, *Toxic Effects of Methyl Mercury* (Washington, DC: National Academy Press, 2000).

more effective oversight of private research that informs regulation; greater transparency when science is used to make policy; balanced peer review; and penalties for deconstruction and corpuscularization.

### Greater Government Support of Research

Despite the growing economic and political pressure on regulatory science, the government has failed to ensure that this important research is supported by the public sector. Instead, federal funding in this arena is in decline. As Katherine Squibb, Sheldon Krimsky, and John Applegate discuss in their respective chapters, these shortfalls forestall the production of objective science and fail to address yawning gaps in information regarding multiple, significant threats to public health and the environment.

Greater government support of research is among the most important reforms needed to prevent science from being captured by special interests. Such support would solve several problems at once: It will avoid the suppression and bias that plague private research while simultaneously producing much needed knowledge on scientific questions that are fundamental to environmental and public health regulation. Conversely, without a strong federal presence, EPA and other regulatory agencies will remain dependent on the private sector for much of the science that informs regulation.

The most critical area for government investment is greater support of research that advances our understanding of how chemicals and activities affect health and the environment, such as mechanistic research. This type of research serves as the foundation for regulation. Because it entails considerable scientific discretion, it should be performed by disinterested government or federally funded academic scientists who are not influenced by sponsors or financial incentives. Moreover, this type of research often informs a number of overlapping regulatory programs and is not tied specifically to one regulated party's product or activity.

Since mechanistic research is dedicated to better understanding the extent of harm caused by industrial products and pollutants, however, it is only fair that industry help finance it. As John Applegate suggests in the final chapter of this book, it is appropriate to require those who produce potentially risky products or engage in polluting activities to pay a fee or tax to support basic environmental and health research.[7] Of course, the

---

[7]  See also Mary L. Lyndon, "Information Economics and Chemical Toxicity: Designing Laws to Produce and Use Data," *Michigan Law Review* 87, no. 7 (1989): 1795, 1799.

structure and level of funding provided by such a system remain to be negotiated.

Proposals to increase government support for regulatory research and to fund a portion of this work through a fee or tax on industry will undoubtedly encounter fervent political opposition. The fact that urgent calls for increased government support for environmental and health research from prominent scientists has not led to changes in funding reinforces the possibility that the scientific community alone cannot accomplish reform in this important area. Such resistance arises in part from the perception that scientists who lobby for increased funding of environmental and health sciences are self-serving.

Regulated parties may also lack enthusiasm for increased funding of regulatory science because the research could lead to increased liability and regulatory requirements if it suggests that harms are worse than supposed. In relation to the status quo, pervasive uncertainties are likely far more tolerable than what increased research might reveal. Recent discoveries, like the adverse effects of the popular herbicide Atrazine at relatively low doses explained by Katherine Squibb in Chapter 2, are likely to lead to only more resistance from the regulated community to greater government support of regulatory science.

## Greater Legal Protections for Federally Funded Research

A greater role for public science also demands more effective protections to keep publicly funded research from unfair, special interest attacks. The current regulatory system allows participants to abuse, with impunity, a variety of judicial and administrative mechanisms in order to delay regulation and harass and discredit public scientists. The Data Quality Act (also known as the Information Quality Act), the Data Access Act, third-party subpoenas, scientific misconduct charges, and state public records statutes have all been used strategically to intimidate researchers and delay or halt their research.[8] In fact, most of these legal tools arguably invite abuse, because even if the underlying petition is ultimately determined to

---

[8] The scientific community's leadership in urging major revisions to the guidelines for data sharing under the Data Access Act (see Chapter 5) and for various features of a centralized peer review guideline developed by the White House Office of Management and Budget (see Chapters 10 and 11) reveals the importance of the scientific perspective.

be unfounded, such challenges are effective in wearing down researchers and delaying their research. Few sanctions are in place to deter abuse of any of these procedures.

In some cases, the best recourse may simply be to repeal these tools altogether. McGarity makes a compelling case that repeal of the Data Quality Act is warranted. In other cases, the courts or administrators who preside over challenges to public science must be aware of the incentives and potential for abuse and become more suspicious of misconduct charges, subpoenas, and open records challenges when a special interest is bringing the claim and stands to profit from the delay and other interference that the request might cause. Safety zones that protect disinterested scientists from harassment, as discussed earlier, may also be necessary to ensure that researchers do not find their research activities halted or diverted as a result of these attacks.

At the very least, hefty sanctions should be levied for abuse of these processes, similar to the sanctions levied for violations of the ethical rules now imposed on other professions. As discussed earlier, individual scientists should be entitled to recover both compensatory and punitive damages for harassment. Complainants should also be required to pay for the agency costs associated with responding to challenges ultimately judged not to be meritorious. In the process of developing and implementing regulations for the Data Access Act, the scientific community convinced OMB to include a provision requiring the requester to reimburse nongovernmental scientists and other researchers for out-of-pocket costs incurred in responding to data requests.[9] Similarly, the Freedom of Information Act requires requesters to pay search fees and copying costs. This internalization of processing costs could provide a further disincentive for wasteful requests.

## More Aggressive Government Oversight of Private Research

Even with greater government financing and corresponding protection of public science, private sector research will remain an important source of information for regulation. Those in the private sector possess basic information about their products and processes and can conduct tests at an

---

[9] Uniform Administrative Requirements for Grants and Other Agreements with Institutions of Higher Education, Hospitals, and Other Non-Profit Organizations, OMB Circular A-110 (Nov. 19, 1993) (further amended Sept. 30, 1999).

early stage in production more cheaply than their public sector counter-
parts. As McGarity, Squibb, and Krimsky observe, however, affected interests who conduct these tests sometimes impose contractual nondisclosure
provisions on hired researchers that are antithetical to good science practices. More vigilant government oversight would ensure that private sector
research is shared promptly with regulators and is not subject to sponsor control that intrudes on scientific independence. Several additional
reforms are needed to make such oversight effective.

*Preserving Disinterestedness through Conflict Disclosure.* Most agencies fail to
require conflict disclosures from researchers funded by private sponsors
when their research is submitted for regulatory purposes. This laissez faire
approach to research can be corrected, in part, by requiring researchers to
provide conflict disclosures similar to those used by the best international
biomedical journals.[10] Specifically, scientists providing research or analyses to regulatory agencies and other decision-making bodies should be
required to sign a conflict form specifying the extent of financial and sponsor influence on the research.[11] In these forms, researchers should disclose
financial and other conflicts of interest that might bias their work, as well as
contractual provisions limiting their rights to publish their findings without
the influence or consent of the sponsor. When scientists conduct research
under the promise that sponsors will have the opportunity to review and

[10] For a description of the medical journals' requirements, see Frank Davidoff et al.,
"Sponsorship, Authorship and Accountability," *Journal of the American Medical Association* 286, no. 10 (2001): 1232–3; International Committee of Medical Journal Editors,
"Uniform Requirements for Manuscripts Submitted to Biomedical Journals," International Committee of Medical Journal Editors, http://www.icmje.org/index.html#top. The
academic community has endorsed this commitment to independent research, as have
several policy nonprofit organizations. Johns Hopkins School of Public Health, Office
of Research Administration, "Intellectual Property Policy" (Oct. 27, 1992) (available at
http://www.jhsph.edu/ora/IPG/nspolicy.htm#C.%20Publication); University of California
Office of the President, "Guidelines on University–Industry Relations" (May 17, 1989) (available at http://www.ucop.edu/ott/unindrel.html). The Center for Science in the Public Interest
also advocates the voluntary disclosure of funding sources. Center for Science in the Public
Interest, "About the Integrity in Science Project," Center for Science in the Public Interest,
http://www.cspinet.org/integrity/about.html. An industry organization, the American Chemistry Council, concedes that such disclosures are a positive step, while disputing that there
are bias and suppression problems with most industry-sponsored research; see Carol J. Henry,
"Questions about Disclosures," *Science* 304, no. 5676 (2004): 1447–9.

[11] For further discussion of the reasons that disclosure is an important and effective remedy, see
David M. Michaels and Wendy E. Wagner, "Disclosure in Regulatory Science," *Science* 302,
no. 5653 (2003): 2073.

even censor potential publications in advance, that fact should be disclosed as well.

These mandatory disclosures will benefit the public, policy makers, and the media by making it easier for them to assess the objectivity of individual research projects. Requiring standardized disclosures would also assist scientific colleagues in evaluating studies when they serve on advisory boards or are otherwise involved in reviewing regulatory science. Finally, mandatory conflict disclosures would reward sponsors who relinquish control over the design and reporting of their sponsored research, distinguishing them from sponsors who insist on controlling the design, methods, and reporting of research results.

*Greater Access to Private Data.* The Data Access Act requires publicly funded researchers to make their underlying data available under the Freedom of Information Act: There is no equivalent requirement that applies to privately sponsored research. This double standard erects unwarranted barriers to the public's evaluation of private research. These barriers should be eliminated so that the science supporting regulation is accessible to other experts and the public at large, regardless of whether it is publicly or privately produced. The first and most obvious reform, then, follows McGarity's and Krimsky's recommendation that the Data Access Act apply to all research supporting regulation, not just research that is publicly funded. As mentioned earlier, the Data Access Act exempts privately funded research from these public access provisions.

Second, to limit the opportunities for actors to conceal adverse information through nondisclosure contracts, by sealing litigation records, or by claiming various legal privileges, Congress or public health agencies should require mandatory disclosures of health and safety information used to formulate public policy. Already, four separate statutory provisions require actors to report adverse effects under relatively narrow circumstances.[12] By providing broader and more specific requirements for reporting under these same provisions, EPA could minimize opportunities for actors to dodge or delay adverse information reporting, while simultaneously enlarging the

---

[12] Clean Water Act, 33 U.S.C. § 1321(b)(4), (5) (2000); Comprehensive Environmental Response, Compensation, and Liability Act, 42 U.S.C. § 9603(a) (2000); Federal Insecticide, Fungicide, and Rodenticide Act, 7 U.S.C. § 136d(a)(2) (2000); Toxic Substances Control Act, 15 U.S.C. § 2607(c), (e) (2000).

circle of actors covered by reporting requirements. For example, requiring any party who works with the manufacturer and is aware of adverse effects (including scientists hired under nondisclosure contracts) to report such information would increase the probability that adverse information will be disclosed, especially if these provisions are backed by civil and criminal penalties.

To ensure that all private research that has a bearing on regulation is shared with regulators in a timely way, a registry of safety-related studies, along the general lines outlined by Sheldon Krimsky, is also necessary. As Krimsky notes, this registry would include, at a minimum, every study that is initiated to test safety or efficacy; the findings of that study, whether preliminary or final; and an explanation of the protocol used to conduct the research. Krimsky's proposal would apply to pharmaceutical research but could and should be extended to studies on pesticides, chemical products, and wastes. Despite disagreements on the precise requirements, there is widespread consensus on the need for such a public registry of private regulatory research.

### Preserving Scientific Honesty and Transparency

Greater public funding for research and more effective oversight of private research will go a considerable distance toward the correction of the problems discussed in this book. The remaining problems arise when science is used to formulate regulatory policy. Their solutions depend on persuading participants to rethink the ways they use science and reforming key aspects of the rule-making process.

The overriding problems with scientific honesty and transparency are produced by understandable but counterproductive efforts of agency staff and affected parties to obscure controversial value choices by making them appear scientifically ordained. As Holly Doremus explains in Chapter 7, both natural resources and public health agencies face a number of overlapping reasons to present science as the main determinant for policy decisions when in reality science can provide only partial guidance.

In the short term, the most effective antidote to the transparency problem is for policy makers to develop a more sophisticated understanding of the thin but essential lines that divide scientific analysis and policy, especially with respect to difficult decisions involved in taking action in spite of pervasive scientific uncertainty. Scientists, for their part, must resist strong temptations to blur and cross those lines, achieving influence at the expense of credibility. Regulators must also resist the strong, even overpowering, temptation to insulate their decisions from attack by pretending that, in effect, the science "made me do it." Finally, the judiciary has a role to play in reversing agency decisions that are misleading about where science ends and policy making begins. Some courts have already interpreted administrative law to require agencies to be clear about the justifications for their regulatory choices. This approach to judicial review could be advanced more generally. There are countervailing dangers with such an approach, however, since courts are likely to vary markedly in the criteria they apply in determining whether agency explanations are sufficiently clear. Indeed, some courts might use this basis for reversal as an excuse to hold up regulatory projects with which they do not agree. Therefore, the role of the courts needs to be reserved for the worst examples of agencies overstating the role of science in supporting policy outcomes.

In the international trade arena, a comprehensive reform of the prevailing standards for resolving trade disputes should also be considered. As Vern Walker discusses in Chapter 8, international courts resolving trade disputes sometimes interpret trade agreements as requiring countries to compensate foreign, aggrieved corporations or else abandon their own stringent health and environmental regulations unless they can demonstrate that their requirements are mandated by science. But in virtually all these cases, nations formulating such regulations have combined their understanding of the underlying science with strong policy choices. Failure to recognize those justifications for regulatory decisions is offensive to the country and damaging to science. Therefore, the text of trade agreements should be amended to recognize that science alone does not determine the stringency of domestic health and environmental regulations. In resolving these trade disputes, courts should adopt explicit rules that recognize the limitations of science in health and environmental protection, deferring to domestic policies and value choices where necessary.

### Judicious Peer Review
Policy makers must also reconsider their at-times naïve expectation that additional peer review can only be a positive development. David Michaels warns that requirements ostensibly designed to ensure adequate peer review of regulatory research are vulnerable to strategic deployment and

politicization. Indeed, one of the most important downsides of regulatory peer review is its use in situations where it is likely to do more harm than good. As the scientific community indicated in comments on the 2003 OMB proposal for peer review, indiscriminate peer review requirements can introduce bias and error into regulatory science. Given the politicization that can infiltrate peer review processes, the burden of demonstrating the need for additional layers of peer review should fall squarely on those advocating them.

Sidney Shapiro adds to Michaels' concerns by identifying important loopholes in the legal rules that are imposed on government peer review. The law gives agencies the opportunity to conduct peer review behind closed doors if they hire their reviewers as "consultants," undercutting transparency and public accountability. The law has also failed to require agencies to disclose when they have waived the requirement that a reviewer is free of conflicts of interest, giving agency officials the opportunity to create stacked or imbalanced panels. Finally, the law does not require agencies to document whether and how they have ensured that a peer review panel is adequately representative of the larger, disinterested scientific community.

### Weighing All Evidence

A final and more extensive set of reforms is needed to encourage decision makers to take advantage of all available evidence using a "weight of the evidence" approach, in contrast to the corpuscularization and censoring of individual studies that has become increasingly prevalent in both the courts and the agencies. As Carl Cranor discusses in Chapter 6, several recent judicial rulings excluding expert testimony are fundamentally at odds with approaches that scientists themselves take to similar evidence. Lacking clear Supreme Court guidance on these issues, the lower courts' counterproductive approach to incorporating science into civil adjudications is likely to grow only more dysfunctional in the future. Viable solutions to these problems include a congressional amendment to the Federal Rules of Evidence to clarify the courts' role in screening expert testimony and more vigorous training of federal judges so they will better understand scientific practices, including methods of scientific inference.

The corpuscularization of science is less evident in the agencies, presumably because agencies enjoy more freedom in weighing all evidence without concerns about juror confusion or the diversion of scarce judicial resources. Nevertheless, recent efforts to use tools like the Data Quality Act to exclude or even censor research from public data bases and decision-making processes has become a worrisome development. Particularly given the limited research available to inform regulation, the prospect that some of it might be singled out and excluded because of a flaw or weakness not only violates principles of good scientific practice but further reduces the scant research that is available to inform regulatory decisions.

## Epilogue

It is no small irony that just as public health and environmental decision makers need reliable science the most, the legal system continues to tolerate the suppression, deconstruction, and underproduction of valuable research that informs regulation. There are important reasons why regulatory proceedings must be designed to afford affected parties an opportunity to present their views. Yet as the issues involved in such proceedings become more complex and the financial stakes increase, these opportunities are being used strategically to slow decision making. Scientists have become targets of attack because impugning their reputations and discrediting their research allows adversaries to argue that their findings should be ignored.

The principles of good scientific practice help to highlight just how counterproductive these assaults have become and provide a benchmark for distinguishing legitimate advocacy from illegitimate distortion. No one would argue that science should be dependent on special interests; no one would suggest that scientists should suffer attacks on their professional reputations simply because their research is threatening as an economic matter; and no one would urge that scientific research that advances the public interest should be suppressed. Yet this book's chapters reveal how the legal system permits, and often encourages, the violation of these principles, with resultant harm to science and policy.

Obviously, articulating the principles and documenting how they have been violated does not solve these deep-seated problems, and the reforms summarized here may be incomplete or unsatisfactory. Yet if the book has accomplished nothing more than to initiate a debate about reforming the regulatory process to follow these principles, then it has accomplished something. Whatever reforms are adopted ultimately, scientists and policy makers can no longer afford to turn a blind eye to the increasing economic and political pressures on science. This book offers an overview of some of the causes and consequences of this troubling and destructive trend. We hope that others will soon follow in this effort to find solutions.

# Index